A Matter

Of

Opinion

The Incomplete Works

By

Roger Hicks

Mage Publishing
ISBN: 978 09527109 5 0

Mage Publishing
www.magepublishing.co.uk

Published in Great Britain & France by Mage Publishing
2006
Copyright © Roger Hicks

ISBN: 978 09527109 5 0

"A Matter Of Opinion" by Roger Hicks can be ordered through most major book shops by quoting the above ISBN number or by direct mail order from the publishers at the recommended retail price of £11.99 plus £1 p&p.

Foreword by
Frances Schultz

Los Angeles, May 1981: Roger was visiting a newly married friend, who went to bed quite early. Roger had also set his watch an hour early, so he had to fill the very long evenings. After four evenings of television and pizza he decided in desperation go to a Mensa Party. His 'excuse' for belonging to Mensa is that he joined when he was sixteen.

The party was not well attended. I was there to lend moral support to a friend who was searching for a man more intelligent than she. She brought her mother along too. Then there was a Texan architect who had received his degrees from Yale, and a black man whose sole interest in life was motor cars.

After doing the rounds, I noticed an interesting looking man with rather wild Auburn hair and a gold/red beard. He was dressed in a black Tibetan shirt and jeans. He kept going back to the wine box, and so I went over and stood beside it. Naturally we fell to talking.

This was Roger. He was a writer and he had worked as a photographer's assistant in an advertising studio in London. He had a degree in Law from Birmingham University. He was writing instructional material for International Computers Ltd. He was interesting.

As a teacher he managed to persuade a class of fourteen year olds that Shakespeare was wonderful because there were dirty jokes, and if you recited a sonnet while staring deeply into your girlfriend's eyes poetry has practical applications in the real world.

He has done lots of different things: he designed self-instructional audio visuals;drove a truck for South West

4

Electricity Board; packed groceries; worked a switch-board; stood life-guard for the U.S. Government in Bermuda. He was even articled to a firm of accountants.

What he enjoyed most was writing and photography and fortunately Colour Library Books in England had begun to produce a series of photography books using the pictures from the library. They asked Roger to write the manuscripts. As the work he did for ICL was off-site, contract work which didn't take up all his time, he could write the books for CLI.

The conversation was going very well and when my friend decided we had to leave immediately I was not very happy. I dug out a scrap of paper, wrote my name and number, said "If you want a guide to L.A. call me, but not before 9 a.m." On the way home my friend expressed the opinion that I was being very rash by giving my number to a strange man. I said "Well, he's only in the United States for three weeks, and how involved can you get in three weeks?"

Yes. well. Twenty-five years later I guess the answer is pretty involved. We spent much of the next three weeks together, then I went to England for three weeks in August. He proposed. He came to California in December to collect me and we married the following June. Our latest calculation is that we must be on about our seventh date.

December 1981 was a turning point. Roger had the confidence to give up the ICL job and go freelance. The Colour Library books were still going strong and he had been commissioned to write a biography of His Holiness, the Dalai Lama. In January 1982 we went home to Bristol and in February we flew out to India to work on Great Ocean. This was when Roger started encouraging me to take pictures. He put a camera in my hands and told me to just burn film.

The biography led to a working relationship with the Tibetan Government in Exile and Roger was commissioned to do a propaganda book for them. Several more trips to India resulted. One time Roger was asked to do some black and white prints for an exhibition in Delhi. When it came time to produce the prints he said "I don't have time to do this, you will have to learn to print." So I did.

About this time I noticed that it was often a struggle to find enough black and white images for the books Roger was doing, so I started to specialise. This led to our working more and more as a team.

Suddenly around 1986 photography books just weren't being commissioned. Roger wrote a few books on cars, but there wasn't much work around. We started talking about trying to make it across the Atlantic. After all our books were selling well over there.

In 1987 we made the move to California. To our surprise, we couldn't sell books directly to U.S. publishers. We were generally commissioned by English Packagers, who then sold the packaged book on to American Publishers. While in California we did three cookbooks and a book on the American Civil War. All four books were packaged in England and sold to the U.S.

Although the book publishing stayed in England, Roger started writing a regular column for Shutterbug Magazine in the U.S. The regular column, combined with the generosity of my long-suffering parents who shared their house with us for five years, gave us a lot of flexibility. We travelled lots, one year spending more than six months out of the country.

We really had intended to stay in the U.S. and buy our own place, but after a few months we realised that neither of us wanted to stay. My parents were very happy to have us there because we shared expenses, cooking and housework. It also gave my father a great deal of pleasure to watch Roger produce books and magazine articles because that was always his dream.

"Why don't you write an article about it?" That's what my father Artie said, all through my childhood in the 1950s. Any complaint; any argument; any strongly held opinion; anything out of the ordinary; his answer was almost always the same. Write an article. But I don't think he ever did it himself.

Fast forward to 1990. Artie is standing at the end of the dining room table where Roger is putting together a book to deliver to a publisher. Artie shakes his head: "I always thought I wanted to be a writer, but I don't think I'd want to work as hard as you do."

Fast forward another decade and a half. Roger now has his own weekly column in Amateur Photographer. Although Artie is long dead, I am sure that somewhere he is still shaking his head with wonderment. Roger is doing exactly what Artie said he always wanted to: writing an article about it. Every week.

So where does the inspiration come from? All kinds of places. Sometimes I'll say something. Roger looks thoughtful and disappears. A while later he calls out "Can you come and listen to what I've written?" As Robert Heinlein said, "Never trust a writer. He will take what you say, file off the serial numbers, and claim it for his own." Roger grinds off the serial numbers, melts it down, recasts it, fits new bearings and makes it his own. [Then I give to Frances to clean off the oil, dust and swarf -- R.]

Other inspirations come from reading. Roger reads somewhere between three to five times faster than most people, and retains most of what he reads. Sometimes a fan (or an irate reader) will give him an idea. Then there is the internet, the radio, travelling and just day to day experience. And of course there are photographs: a single picture can fire up his train of thought, which will in due course cause Holiday Rail Chaos as he derails others' trains and in some cases tears up the track and sets fire to the station.

Introduction...

The first hint of what was to become A Matter of Opinion
(and the first piece in this book) was in the issue of
September 22, 2001: it was a 'Backchat' column called
'Equipment Matters'. Then there was nothing until the issue
of January 5th, 2002: 'The Zone System: an idea whose time
has passed.' Garry Coward-Williams and I both expected a
lot of hate mail from that one, but to our surprise, letters
echoing my sentiments were much more common than death
threats from Zonies. The general tenor was, "Thank God! It
isn't just me who thinks that!"

In 2002 and 2003 another nine articles in the same vein
appeared: about how so many photographers are misers, the
worthlessness of grey cards and empty 'testing'; the false
exclusivity of large format; and more. Some appear here.
They were quite a lot longer than the Matters of Opinion
columns, which mostly run to 750-800 words, at 1000-1500
words

Encouraged by my success in what he called 'rattling the
cages' of some of our more stick-in-the-mud readers, and
positive reaction from some of the others, Garry offered me a
more frequent column from the issue of February 21st 2004,
which appeared just in time for Focus. For the first time, this
was entitled 'A Matter of Opinion'. It has appeared in every
issue since.

Initially, the idea was that I would do maybe half the
Matter of Opinion columns, mostly because Garry wasn't
sure that I could produce one every week. Some readers may
agree with him. But I never fail to be surprised at what
catches people's interest and imagination, and what doesn't.
A piece that one person regards as piffle, sets another
thinking.

That is what the column is for. I've challenged quite a lot
of my own assumptions since I've been writing it, and
changed my mind over a number of things. In particular I no

longer think that digital cameras are the exclusive province of His Satanic Majesty, sent to try honest God-fearing silver halide users, though I do believe that film is inherently superior in so many ways that I still shoot a great deal more with my 'real' cameras (mainly Leicas, of course, but also Alpa, Gandolfi, Linhof and indeed Nikon) than I do with my admittedly excellent Nikon D70.

So if you don't agree with me, reflect on this. Even I don't always agree with everything I say. But if my column makes you (or me) think, "Hang on a minute. Maybe I'm wrong about that... " then it had done part of its job. Another part -- more important by far -- is to get you (and me) out taking more pictures; and better pictures; and pictures that we enjoy shooting and showing to people. And if it makes you smile as well; in that case, it's a real success.

This is 'The Incomplete Works' for four reasons. The most important is that we couldn't get everything in. Almost as important is the fact that many early articles were illustrated, and we couldn't easily reproduce the pictures here; at least, not alongside the articles. The photographs that are included are to show that I really do take pictures as well as writing, but few if any of them originally accompanied AP articles. Third, going through half a decade's APs, Frances and I may have missed some of the early Backchats. Indeed, many of our APs from 2001, 2002 and 2003 are missing, the result of moving house twice in the period. Fourth, there are various technical articles and reviews that don't really fit, including the first pieces I ever did for AP, a technical series on black and white that began in the issue of August 4th 2001. There is a full list in the back of this book of all my AP columns to the end of April 2006, under their original titles, with a dagger against the ones that aren't reproduced here.

The pieces are in chronological order, because that seemed to make more sense than grouping them under headings. Besides, it makes it easier to dip into. I have no illusions about this: the present book is the sort that many people like to read in the smallest room.

I haven't added a running commentary to the ones that are included in full, much as I was tempted, because I always find it irritating to read someone else's commentary on their own work. This means that there are inconsistencies and changes in circumstances, most especially my acquisition of a Leica MP and 75/2 Summicron since starting the column: the Bessa-R2 mentioned in many early columns is an excellent camera (and Frances now uses it all the time, alongside her Bessa-T) but the MP is even nicer. Then there's the Nikon D70...

Some of the titles are the ones Garry chose; others are my original titles; a few pieces may have been renamed for this book. There are also small differences at times between the book and AP, where the columns were sometimes edited for length and (very occasionally) for style; in the latter case, I've put my style back because obviously I prefer it. Also, I've tried to clean up any errors in the course of compiling the book.

All in all, out of 100 Matters of Opinion and 18 other columns that have appeared in AP up to the end of February 2006, there are 90 pieces in all: 80 Matters of Opinion and 10 others. The ones that have been chopped out are mostly technical; or perhaps supernumerary contributions to the digital-film debate; or (usually topical) stuff of limited interest, though I have left in a number of topical columns on matters that have since been resolved, such as Ilford's financial troubles, as being of historical interest.

Roger Hicks
Moncontour
2006

Acknowledgements...

Garry Coward-Williams is of course the man most responsible for this colums -- I only write it, but he pays for it -- and he is a prince among men. I believe also that he has gathered around him the best AP team in my lifetime, and quite possibly in the history of the magazine; it is hard to make comparisons between now and 100 and more years ago.

On the inside, in Fortess King's Reach, I am happy and proud to know Damien Demolder; Angela Nicholson; Chris Gatcum; and of course Christine Lay, Garry's PA, who makes things happen. On the outside, I've known both Ivor Matanle and Geoffrey Crawley for years, and I can't imagine better (or more august) colleagues.

As for those at AP that I haven't mentioned by name, all that constrains me is a fear of the Oscar syndrome: tearfully thanking everyone in one's entire life, including the postman and the cat. Thanks are due to them too.

Finally, I must thank my wife, Frances Schultz, to whom I owe more than I can say: it would be pointless to enumerate all that she does for me (and is to me) because it would occupy another book and would be even more like an Oscar acceptance speech. Besides, she already knows.

Kit Matters

"It's not the camera, it's the photographer that matters. A good photographer can take good pictures with a Box Brownie..."

I've been reading that rubbish for over a third of a century now. It made me angry in the 1960s, and it makes me angry now, because it contains just enough truth to stop it being a flat lie, along with enough misinformation to be very dangerous indeed.

Yes, a good photographer can take a good picture with a Box Brownie. In good light. If he or she doesn't need a wide angle or tele lens, or a fast shutter speed to stop movement. And if he or she doesn't care whether the picture is sharp or not. But a better camera makes it far easier to take a wider range of better pictures under a much greater range of circumstances. Anyone who says otherwise is either a fool or a liar.

The truth is that there is a 'quality threshold' in cameras and lenses. Up to that level, for a given level of technical expertise on the part of the photographer, better equipment will make better pictures -- in particular, sharper. Beyond that level, yes, it's down to the photographer; but the threshold still exists.

It's not a very high threshold, but there are still some cruel deceptions practised. For example, I recently bought a really ratty Nikkormat FT3 with a 50/1.8 Nikkor for L40. That is well above the quality threshold, and a photographer who couldn't get good pictures with it would have only himself or herself to blame. But I have also judged enough photo competitions to know that there are lots of cheap, nasty and slow zooms out there, that really do take the edge off people's pictures. They're not very sharp to begin with, and because they're so slow, they invite too-long shutter speeds and camera shake. They also lack contrast, so the pictures look flat and muddy, and they may even distort straight lines near the edge of the picture.

What really gets me, though, is that many of those who say 'equipment doesn't matter' are the ones who have equipment that most people can only dream of. In the late '60s, I had a Pentax SV and three lenses, only one of which (the 50/1.8 Super Takumar) was sharp and contrasty. When someone with the latest Nikon and Leica lenses wrote 'equipment doesn't matter,' my blood used to boil, because I knew that if I had access to their kit, my pictures would be better.

And I was right. Sure, they'd still have been compositionally lousy, and the negatives would mostly have been under-exposed and over-developed, because I was a bad photographer. But at least they would have been sharp. When you know that no matter what you do, your pictures still aren't going to be all that good, it is disheartening.

There's another reason for buying first-class kit, too: pride of ownership. You have to live up to a good camera. When I had that Pentax and those lousy lenses, I always had an excuse. When I started using better lenses (the camera was fine), I lost that excuse: if I couldn't take good pictures, it was my fault.

Today, I have the kind of equipment that most people can only dream about: Alpa, Gandolfi, Leica, Voigtlander and more. I know that I can take good pictures with a second-hand camera and lens that cost forty quid together -- but only because second-hand kit can be incredible value for money, and because I now know enough to look beyond what's fashionable and expensive, to what delivers the results. You won't catch me saying that equipment doesn't matter -- because it does.

The Zone System

Ansel Adams was a great photographer despite, not because of, the Zone System. Among those who are attracted to this pernicious doctrine, I have met far more who have been hindered than ever I saw who were helped. For every competent Zonie there are ten who produce dull, over-engineered pictures, and a hundred who are simply out of their depth. Even the best Zonies often aspire to be no more than third-rate imitators of the Master, endlessly rehashing the same faux-wilderness shots as AA was shooting as early as the 1930s, before he actually formulated the Zone System.

This is not to say that Ansel Adams lacked genius, nor that the Zone System is unworthy of a glance; but the only real thing of use that survives is the naming of the Zones themselves, and even that is far less useful today, with the utterly unmemorable 11-Zone system that has replaced the original 9 Zones.

Those who are familiar with the Zone System will already be reaching for their quill-pens and releasing the safety-catches on their revolvers, but for those who are not familiar with it, it is a simplified guide to sensitometry, designed principally for the use of American photography students who might well have lacked the intellect to deal with the real thing, and who almost certainly lacked the will. Like photography students today, the majority of them just wanted to be photographers: they didn't want to be in a classroom studying theory.

The Zone System is simultaneously crude, and over-complicated. It is crude because it does not use the basic tool of the sensitometrist, the densitometer; this for no better reason than densitometers were expensive and unreliable when the System was invented, which is a bit like refusing to use exposure meters today because they were not available to Julia Margaret Cameron or Roger Fenton. It is over-complicated for two reasons. First, the 'work-arounds' that are required to get by without a densitometer are time-consuming and fiddly, and second, photography is simply not as complicated or precise as many Zonies believe: they are looking for a certainty that doesn't exist, and never has existed.

The late Ansel Adams, who was a college lecturer as well as a photographer, designed the System rather over 50 years ago, and it has been updated on a somewhat piecemeal basis ever since. The Three Gospels of the Blessed Ansel, each a substantial volume, are The Camera, The Negative and The Print. Exegetes have since added many more volumes, several of which are quasi-religious tracts that tell the acolyte how to perform the rituals needed to bring him into a state of photographic grace; and they are rituals, too, because they do not explain in any meaningful way why they are done.

The useful part of the Zone System is this. There were originally nine Zones, symmetrical about a mid-tone, Zone V (the use of Roman numbers is a part of the ritual). Zone V is defined as an 18 per cent grey in the print: a Munsell mid-tone. Zones IV and VI are respectively one stop darker and one stop lighter than Zone V, and are described (logically enough) as the dark mid tones and the light mid tones. Zones III and VII are another stop lighter and darker respectively, and are described as the darkest areas with detail and texture, and the lightest areas with detail and texture. Zone II is the darkest tone distinguishable from the deepest black of which the paper is capable, which is Zone I. At the other end of the scale, Zone VIII is the lightest tone distinguishable from a pure, paper-base white, which is Zone IX. The nine Zones are summarized in the panel for convenience -- with Arabic numerals for still greater convenience.

As you can see, these nine Zones represent a handy, readily comprehensible way of talking about the tones in a print. nfortunately, it is the last part of the Zone System that can be escribed as handy or readily comprehensible -- and when, as a result of improved materials, later versions grew to 10 and 11 Zones, even this table became less useful.

Zone 1   The maximum black of which the paper is capable
Zone 2   The first tone distinguishable from Zone 1 Zone 3 Darkest tone with texture: 1 stop lighter than Zone 2, one stop darker than Zone 4 Zone 4   Dark mid tones: 1 stop lighter than Zone 3, one stop darker than Zone 5 Zone 5 The mid tone: 1 stop lighter than Zone 4, one stop darker than Zone 6 Zone 6   Light mid tones: 1 stop lighter than Zone 5, one stop darker than Zone 7 Zone 7   Lightest tone with texture: 1 stop lighter than Zone 6, one stop darker than Zone 8 Zone 8   Lightest tone distinguishable from paper-base white Zone 9   Pure, paper-base white

The rest of the Zone System is principally concerned with metering; with establishing a personal exposure index or EI; and with establishing a series of personal development times, centred around 'N' for normal, that will allow every exposure to be printed on grade 2 paper. For unusually contrasty subjects, you use shortened or 'N-' development: N-1, N-2 and so forth, even unto N-6. For unusually flat subjects, you use longer or 'N+' development: this is unlikely to exceed N+3.

If you are really serious, a 'full house' Zonie, you determine your personal exposure indices and development times by shooting countless pictures of grey cards, and developing them for different times until, by experiment, you hit upon just the right speeds and development times for you. If you change films or developers, or if the manufacturers reformulate either, you have to repeat all these tests all over again. A willingness to put themselves through this drudgery argues, without any further objections (of which there are several) that Zonies are rather sad cases with nothing better to do.

By definition, to get the full benefit of the Zone System, such as it is, you have to develop every image individually;

16

unless, of course, you can group together (say) several N+1 in one batch, and several N-3 in another. This makes a nonsense of those who claim to use the Zone System for roll-film and 35mm. They are treating the Zone System as a talisman or mantra; they clearly don't understand it. At most, they are doing the same that any rational photographer would do, with or without the Zone System: adjusting the film speed and development time until they get an effect that they like. This is nothing very profound: the film and developer manufacturers' spec. sheets suggest that you do exactly the same thing.

Then again, the value of these multifarious development times is deeply disputable. There are at least three good arguments against such an approach.

The first is that a misty day should look misty, with a limited contrast range, while a sunny day should look bright and contrasty. There is a limit to how far you can (or more accurately, should) over-develop the first to increase the contrast, or under-develop the latter to reduce the contrast. Sooner or later -- generally sooner rather than later -- the results start to look profoundly unnatural.

The second is that often, you can achieve all you need by dodging and burning. As long as the information is there on the negative, you can hold back some areas and burn in others, which greatly reduces the need for N- development, and most of the time eliminates it altogether.

The third is that unless you choose for your own personal reasons to limit yourself not only to graded paper, but also to grade 2 paper, there is absolutely no need for this sort of manic pseudo-precision. If you have a negative that is a little more contrasty than usual, switch to a softer grade. If it is a little more contrasty, switch to a harder grade. You need to be quite a long way out before you need to go harder than grade 4 or softer than grade 0, and you really don't lose significant print quality by doing so. If you are competent enough to be able to make a start on the Zone System -- in other words, if you are reasonably in control of exposure, development and printing -- you should be more than competent enough to hold your range of paper grades to around 1-2-3, never mind 0 and 4.

In fact, this is the biggest single argument against the Zone System. If you know enough about photography in general, and sensitometry in particular, to be able to make sense of the Zone System, you don't need it, and if you don't know enough about photography in general and sensitometry in particular, you are trying to run before you can walk. You will only confuse yourself.

There's more that can be criticised: water-bath development, for example, a complete irrelevance with modern films. Variable-contrast paper developers for fixed-grade papers, which are fine if you don't mind shifts in image tone. A whole arcane language of 'placing' a given value on a given Zone (i.e. you meter it) while allowing others to 'fall' on other Zones (i.e. you don't meter them). The totally redundant word 'previsualization', which a moment's thought shows cannot differ from 'visualization'. But there is no point in attacking all of it: I have already demonstrated that this particular emperor is distinctly short of clothes.

I can already hear the responses: "When you are as good a photographer as Ansel Adams, you'll have the right to criticise him." Sorry, that's drivel. No, I'm not as good as AA, not by a long way, though I have to say that from looking at original AA prints instead of the reproductions in books, he wasn't always that good either: some of his prints were unquestionably over-enlarged. But there are plenty of other photographers who have produced prints of at least equal loveliness to AA's -- his countryman Edward Weston springs to mind -- and far from all of them are Zonies. In fact, I'd suggest that there are many, many more who aren't, than who are.

The people who really drive me crazy are the ones who say, "Even if you don't think you are using the Zone System, you are, because all black and white photography is founded on it." This is a bit like saying that the whole of automobile design is based on the workshop manual for a 1936 Ford, or that the whole of modern physics is based on a GCSE text book: it is getting things exactly backwards. Both the workshop manual and the school text book are distillations and simplifications of a vast body of work and knowledge that the reader is expected neither to have at his fingertips, nor necessarily to be interested in amassing. The Zone System is a simplification of a vast body of work which began with Hurter and Driffield in the 1890s and continues (albeit at a slower pace) to this day, but because so few people bother to read anything that is any deeper or more complex, they imagine that it is the last word. It isn't. Not by a long chalk.

Why Are Photographers Misers?

Most photographers are hopelessly mean about everything except cameras and lenses: they'll do anything, even if it compromises the quality of their pictures, to save relatively tiny sums of money on everything else. Time and again, for example, people ask if they can't use washing-up liquid instead of wetting solution. Why? Sure, a litre of Ilford Ilfotol costs eight or ten pounds, but it will last literally years in the average amateur darkroom, so where's the harm in the expenditure? If you can't afford that, you can't afford photography, full stop.

What's really weird is that these same people who would, as the old Cornish saying puts it, skin a turd for a ha'penny, are often the ones who spend the most on shiny new equipment. I remember looking at some truly awful pictures once, taken (I knew) with a great deal of very expensive Hasselblad equipment. They were so abysmal because they had been shot on grievously outdated film, then processed by the cheapest mail-order lab that ever put a leaflet in the local free-sheet. Why on earth did he bother to buy a Hasselblad? It certainly wasn't to get better pictures! By 'saving' a couple of pounds on film he had wasted thousands on his Hasselblad outfit. He'd have got better pictures with a Lubitel and some decent film.

Another place people waste money is by 'saving' it on paper. I'll pass over outdated paper -- grey and foggy, or, if you use benzotriazole to cure that, taking a week to develop -- and go straight to Bob Carlos Clark's observation (to Frances Schultz) that you should go on printing the same image until you make a print that isn't as good as the one immediately preceding it: then, you know you've made the best print possible. But how long does it take most photographers to come to this realization? Years!

Of course paper is expensive, but what are you spending money for, if not to get the best print possible? Even if you make your work prints as 12x16 inch, you are spending maybe L1.50 a sheet on the paper. If it takes five sheets to get the results you want, you have spent L7.50. This is the price of three pints of beer, or a couple of cinema tickets, or a medium-size pizza. Make your work prints on 10x8 inch, and scale up for the last one or two, and you're looking at a fiver. Isn't a good print worth that kind of money? And is a bad print worth anything at all?

Much the same arguments apply to film, and to developer, but let's switch our attention elsewhere entirely: to hardware other than cameras and lenses. How many people are still struggling on with the same developing tanks they used when they took up photography, with the reels so old and rough that loading them is a penance? A new spiral doesn't cost a fortune -- and it can make life an awful lot easier. For that matter, if you process much film, a Jobo CPE-2 is a lot quicker and more consistent than small, manual spirals, and costs a good deal less than a new camera, even new; used (and there are plenty around) they go for absurdly small sums.

And when did you last look at your safelights? Nova's new Five Star LED lights -- the ones you can 'daisy chain' and set up like Christmas lights -- are a lot more expensive than the old red plastic domes, but if you can read a newspaper by the light of your safelight, that has to be worth a few bob. The list goes on: decent graduates, a stop-clock instead of relying on your wrist-watch, a grain focuser...

Outside the darkroom, what's your tripod like? A good tripod is hellish expensive, but it lasts a lifetime, and it will do a lot more for most people's photography than any new camera or lens. And do you even own any lights? Again, they look expensive, but they can do an incredible amount for your photography.

Then there's 'saving' money by buying junk. Often, top-quality kit seems disproportionately more expensive than the cheapest available, but you are normally paying for increased precision, much greater durability, and the use of superior materials: brass instead of pot metal, that kind of thing. For instance, at £79.95 (VAT paid) a Q-Top quick-release plate is five or even ten times the price of a cheapo -- but it's fifty or a hundred times as good. It will last far longer; it locates the camera far more accurately; and besides, what is it going to cost you when your expensive camera falls off a cheap and nasty head?

Plenty of people, too, save money by avoiding labour-saving devices. I've already mentioned the Jobo CPE-2, but the vast majority of my prints are processed in Nova deep tanks. Yet again, these are expensive, but the amount of time they save is staggering: they are ready for use at a moment's notice, and set-up and clear-up are reduced to removing and replacing the tank lids, and wiping up the odd drip. They also save substantially on chemistry bills, and allow you to work in a tiny darkroom: all our prints for nearly a decade, during which time we wrote several books and countless magazine articles, were processed in a Nova darkroom tent just 1.1 metres (42 inches) square. For most people today, time is money, and time wasted by a refusal to spend money is even worse than money wasted by soending unwisely. After all, you can always earn more money, but how do you earn more time?

Perhaps the best way of all of wasting money by saving it, though, is to buy 'bargains'. We all do it. For example, I have a 300/4 Pentacon that cost me £30. A bargain! But I've never actually used it, so actually, it wasn't a bargain at all: it was a complete and utter waste of money. I've also got a 135/3.5 Takumar (£10), a Pentax SV body (£35), a monster Benbo tripod, the biggest they ever made (£80), and more. Add up a few 'bargains' like this, where you spend a few quid that you feel you can readily afford, and you soon get to the sort of sum that would have bought you something ten times as useful, but that you wouldn't consider buying because you 'can't afford it'. Well, one of the reasons you couldn't afford it is because you've already wasted the money elsewhere!

I can guess what you are saying, if you have read this far. "It's all right for him, but photography is expensive enough already, and I can't afford to buy anything else." Sorry, I don't accept that. It's a question of priorities; of being honest with yourself; and of asking yourself just what you are really buying with your photography budget. What I want to buy is better pictures, and I have a pretty clear idea of where my expenditure will do the most good -- which is why I am still using cameras that are thirty and more years old, but always use first-rate film and paper. And I'll finish with an example of priorities.

A good few years ago, I was at my local camera club. Another member was much taken with my Nikon outfit. "Of course," he said, "I could never afford that." Then, at the end of the evening, he drove off in his 18-month-old Ford, bought new, and I drove off in my 16-year-old Rover, bought (very) second-hand. Take what you want, and pay for it, saieth the Lord.

Testing, Testing…

One of the most popular activities among many photographers is 'testing' new black and white films and developers. It is also one of the most useless. Most people don't shoot enough of a new film to do a meaningful test, and they don't shoot enough of any film to have a meaningful basis for comparison.

What, after all, is the point of 'testing' a new film or developer? There is the hope that it will give you something better than your current film(s), and the hope that it will give you something new and different.

But if you don't actually have a standard film or films, because you are always trying a roll or two of this, a roll or two of that, then you don't have a basis for comparison. The vast majority of photographers never get the best (or anything like it) out of any film, because they don't even try.

If you read the manufacturers' instruction leaflets, you'll see that they actively encourage you to vary their film speeds and development recommendations to suit your own personal preferences and techniques. They are not kidding. With a spot meter, I find that I can almost invariably use the box ISO speed, sometimes a little higher if I am using a speed-increasing developer such as Ilford DD-X, often a little lower if I am using a fine-grain developer such as Ilford Perceptol.

If I rely on the camera meter, I normally knock off at least a third of a stop as compared with my spot-meter speed, sometimes more, depending on my assessment of the scene and what I am metering. Likewise, I normally tend towards the higher end of most development recommendations: it gives results that I, personally, like better.

But in order to do this meaningfully, you need to shoot quite a lot of film. You have to see how it behaves in a wide variety of situations, and you have to print a lot of it. This is an important point too: different films print different ways, and if you keep switching films and developers, you are fashioning a rod for your own back in the darkroom.

My wife Frances Schultz and I get through several hundred rolls of film a year, so we can make comparisons with dozens of other prints of more-or-less similar subjects. But most people don't have this sort of basis for comparison. Many quite keen photographers shoot as little as four or five rolls a month, call it 60 a year, and if you try (say) three new films across the year, and two new developers, then as many as one-half of your shots are taken using an unfamiliar film/dev combo.

If you don't shoot that many films for testing, the results are valueless; or at least, if they have any value, it is sheer luck. For instance, I recently tested Fuji's new Acros for Shutterbug magazine in the United States. I found it very, very finicky. Exposure needs to be spot on (and like everyone else, I have found it rather slower than its nominal ISO 100); it responds very differently to different developers; and development times and temperatures are extremely critical. I reckon it would take me at least half a dozen rolls, and maybe ten or a dozen, before I could get results that fully realize the potential of this film. Anyone who shot only a roll or two would, unless they happened to hit the right combination of exposure and development by sheer luck, most probably dismiss it out of hand.

Of course, you can get lucky. That's how I came back to HP5 Plus. I was in Switzerland, not expecting to be doing any shooting on 120, and I was lent an Alpa and given a brick of HP5 Plus. Having nothing else, I shot it, and having no other recommendations to go on, I developed it for the recommended time in Paterson FX39. It was gorgeous, and I've since found that it's almost 'bulletproof' and can be processed in virtually anything. But the initial success was pure luck: it wasn't real testing.

Because of what I do for a living, I am quite often asked to test films and developers, and quite honestly, it is not my favourite part of the job. A meaningful test involves all kinds of drudgery, comparing resolution and speed and plotting characteristic curves, and I'd rather be taking pictures. There are two side benefits -- I get paid (poorly) for doing it, and occasionally I find something I really like -- but because I do it properly I know how difficult it is, and I know that very few photographers are even equipped to do it properly. How many, after all, even own a densitometer?

Another thing I know full well about testing is that an awful lot of testers have their own agenda, usually based around the Zone System, and that unless you accept their world-picture, the results of their tests may be of limited usefulness. To return to Acros, for example, one internet site recommended double-strength PMK (Pyro-Metol-Kodalk) developer and an EI of 32 for Acros cut film (imported from Japan), before going on to laud its ultra-fine-grain qualities; the latter, in my view, being totally irrelevant to large format photography.

If I am so against testing, what do I recommend? Basically, that you stick with the materials you know and like, but that if you see something in the magazines that looks as though it would give a real benefit for your sort of photography, try it. For example, when Ilford Delta 3200 came out, I couldn't wait to try it: I was already shooting a lot of Kodak TMZ P3200, and now I had a choice. But with Acros, quite honestly, I don't think I'd have bothered if I hadn't been paid for the test. I don't shoot much ISO 100 black and white in 35mm (which is where the ultra fine grain is most useful), and when I do shoot, I'm perfectly happy with Delta 100. If I shot a lot of ISO 100, on the other hand, and I wanted finer grain than I could get with Delta 100, I'd have fallen on Acros with glad cries.

What I'm arguing against, really, is 'testing' for the sake of it, and against 'testing' that isn't really testing at all, but just playing about with new films and developers. If you enjoy doing either, then the very best of luck to you; but it is unlikely to do anything to improve the quality of your photography, and most of the time, you shouldn't dignify it with the name of 'testing' anyway.

Technical Details

(Or, What you don't know, won't hurt you!)

A perennial joke in amateur-oriented publications -- and one that occasionally excites interest in the letters columns of AP -- is exposure information. You know the kind of thing: '1/30 at f/5.6' or '1/250 at f/11'. Almost as big a joke is the equipment information: what camera and lens were used. Then there's the question of what film was used.

These are jokes for three reasons. First, they are simply made up in many (perhaps most) cases. Second, they are almost completely worthless, and they displace information that could be a lot more useful. Third, they provide an illusion of information and stop people thinking for themselves.

A few people may still write down the exposure data for every picture they take, but you have to ask why any sane person would do so. Even when it comes to unusual effects such as slightly blurred foliage or 'cotton candy' waterfalls, too much depends on specific details. How windy was it on the day the foliage was blurred? How fast was the water flowing?

Far more useful would be information on how a shot was metered, and what modifications were made to the meter reading before the exposure was made. A spot meter reading for negative film will often be (and should often be) quite different from an incident light reading for slide film. With the spot meter and negative film, you should read the darkest area in which you want texture and detail, and give 2 to 3 stops less: the exact amount should be constant, established from experience. With the incident meter and slide film, you might decide to use the indicated exposure; or up to a stop less to 'pop' the colours; or maybe a stop more for a dreamy, desaturated look. This is useful information: simply saying that you used 1/30 at f/5.6 isn't.

When it comes to equipment, format matters a lot, because it's a good deal easier to get a stunning, grain-free black and white print with roll-film than with 35mm. Some lenses, too, are better than others, though you are unlikely to see the difference in reproduction, and besides, if you use Canon and I use Voigtlander, why do you care what lens I use? The important question is how you would do it with your kit. Then again, I used to know a prominent American photographer who used both Pentax and Mamiya 6x7cm cameras and always attributed all his best shots to Mamiya because they gave him free kit and Pentax didn't.

Even when the photographer trying to be honest, equipment information often made up, or at best, based on imperfect recollection. In 35mm over the last 20 years my wife and I have used Nikons, Nikkormats, Contaxes, Leicas and Voigtlanders. Inevitably, there has been a great deal of overlap, and after a few years or even a few months we may be quite unable to remember which system we were using, let alone which lens.

We therefore take a best guess at the system we might have used, then look at the image for internal evidence (especially perspective) about what focal length we used. But you'd usually do better to make your own guess rather than take our word for it: you'll be thinking, instead of just nodding sagely and believing blindly.

What about film? This is the least useless piece of information, but even then, an enormous amount depends on how it was metered and exposed and (with black and white) how it was developed and printed.

When it comes to development, some films are all but bullet-proof. Ilford's HP5 Plus, for example, has memorably been described as the AK-47 of films: you can bake it, freeze it, drop it in the mud, and it will still work perfectly. Other films may require countless iterations for exposure, developer choice and development regime (time, temperature, dilution and agitation) before you can get results that are even acceptable.

Even if someone else gives you their precise development regime, it's a safe bet that it won't be identical to what's best for you. Why, after all, do you suppose that film and developer manufacturers tell you to vary development times to suit your personal requirements? If one single time were best for all, then that would be the only time recommended by both the film and developer manufacturers and all gurus -- and that'll be the day!

Next, at the printing stage, some papers suit some films better than others. Ilford's Multigrade Warmtone is superb and forgiving -- but put it through the wrong developer and it won't be very warm, and it won't have good tonality. How often do you see detailed information on the paper and paper developer used to make a print? Or the burning and dodging that was used?

This is of course before it appears in the magazine. Many's the time that I've had a good but unremarkable print turn out far better than it deserved in print, and even more often, I've had superb prints reproduce appallingly. This is purely down to origination and printing: the latter can vary from minute to minute on the press. In a book or magazine, you have to rely on what the text says, rather than on what the image looks like.

Not only are technical details useless, therefore: they are positively dangerous in that as well as suppressing original thought, they foster discontent with the materials and equipment the reader is using; and an example is a good way to finish.

Some of the best original black and white prints I've ever seen were made by a retired Russian submarine commander called Rustam: I met him in Moscow about 10 years ago. He shot with an old Mamiya Press, and printed on paper that was so old he had to dose the developer with benzotriazole to control the fog. But because he had dedicated himself to getting the best possible results with the equipment and materials he had, instead of worrying about how something else might be better, his prints were stunning: rich, with a superb tonal range and plenty of 'sparkle'. When I'm as good as he is, I'll start worrying more about equipment and materials.

Large Format Lunacy

Large format (LF) black and white photography can deliver some of the most stunning results that are possible in any photographic medium. But if you have ever thought of trying LF but been discouraged because it all sounds too difficult and too expensive, I don't blame you. I do however blame all those LF users who have built up such a worthless mystique around their often limited technical prowess and the supposed exclusivity of the equipment they use. The truth is that LF photography is very nearly idiot-proof; and it needs to be, because so many LF users are idiots. That it need not be expensive may be more of a surprise, but hear me out...

Let's begin with film. As long as you like the tonality, things like grain and sharpness just don't matter: you aren't going to see them at all in a contact print, and the film needs to be truly lousy before you will see them in a 3x blow-up, which is 12x15 inches off 4x5 inch. In fact, there aren't any films that won't stand a 3x enlargement today. But all too many LF users agonize over acutance and grain. The only explanation for this can be idiocy.

It takes a little practice to load sheet film into a holder, but it's nothing you can't master with a sheet of scrap film and a bit of practice. Begin with your eyes open; then close them as you gain more experience; and finally try working with the light out. This should not be unduly demanding for a photographer of normal dexterity.

Exposure ain't too critical, as long as there is plenty of it. A stop or two, or even three, of over-exposure won't show, except perhaps to give you better tonality. Willful over-exposure reduces sharpness and increases grain. This matters with 35mm, but with a contact print or a modest blow-up, you are never going to see the difference. In any case, many people prefer the tonality they get with generous exposure.

The joke here is that so many LF users get really excited about exposure readings and use spot meters, establishing personal exposure indices to the nearest third of a stop. The great thing about a spot meter is that it stops you under-exposing, because it reads the darkest area where you want texture and detail. But if you don't have a spot meter, take a reading however you can (or just guess) and then err on the side of over-exposure.

Development? Once again, the more precious members of the LF brigade get really carried away. Sure, if you like highly toxic developers with a short shelf life, use 'em. But why bother? Why not use something nice and easy and off-the-shelf? Some will give you better tonality than others, to be sure -- so if you need guidance, ask around among those whose prints you admire. Find out who uses what developer, and then pick the easiest. Only an idiot would choose to do things the hard way, when there's an easier way.

You don't need much developer, either. Another favourite belief among idiots is that you need huge volumes of developer to develop a sheet of 10x8 inch film. In fact, all you need to develop the film is about a teaspoonful. All the rest of the volume you use is just to make sure that the film is wetted quickly and evenly.

If you don't believe me, consider this. Think of using a traditional two bath developer with a 35mm film. You pour in the first bath, which contains the developing agent. If you used this bath alone, the film would typically take a quarter of an hour or more to develop. But after a few minutes -- five at the outside -- you pour out the first bath and pour in the second, which contains the alkali that activates the first bath.

If you are using a small, stainless steel tank, at most about 25ml of the first bath will stay behind. Some of that will have been absorbed by the emulsion; the rest will simply wet the tank. The _only_ developing agent, remember, is what is left behind in the tank: the second bath contains none. A 36-exposure roll of 35mm film is close to 90 square inches, and even a Zone System devotee can work out the area of a sheet of 10x8 inch. Now, tell me again how much developing agent you need for a sheet of 10x8 inch film.

As for how you develop LF, I have yet to find anything easier than a Paterson Orbital processor. Trays are good, and even cheaper. They are slower, and use more chemistry, and you have to work in the dark, but even so, this is not difficult. Enlarging is much the same regardless of what format you're using, and there are enough 4x5 inch enlargers about on the used market that you are not looking at much more money than a good used 6x9cm enlarger. Indeed, in the last few months I've heard of several 4x5 inch and 5x7 inch enlargers being given away to anyone who would come and collect them. But LF idiots tend to have wonderfully fixed ideas when it comes to enlargers, generally revolving around cold cathode light sources. It's true that cold cathodes give the closest tonality to a contact print, but if that worries you, why not make a contact print?

Many cold cathodes, especially older ones, are of limited or zero use with variable contrast (VC) papers, and you will lose far more by being locked into graded paper than you will gain by trying to emulate the tonality of a contact print. Admittedly there are a few cold cathode heads made especially for VC, and very good they are; but then again, most LF users wouldn't be seen dead using VC papers anyway. They seem to derive a feeling of moral superiority from using graded paper, even though it's been at least a decade and probably closer to 20 years since VC caught up and in many cases overtook graded.

By now, I hope I'll have convinced you that LF isn't difficult. I may have slightly more difficulty in persuading you that it isn't expensive. It is, I freely admit, quite easy to spend between L5,000 and L10,000 on all-new cameras, lenses, tripods, spot meters and the like, before you start on the darkroom. But I'd suggest that you can get a good, old, 4x5 inch or even 5x7 inch camera with lens and dark-slides, and a good second-hand tripod, and all you need to process the films, for about one-tenth of that, maybe less. You won't need an enlarger, because you'll be making contact prints.

It's true that £500 to £1000 is a lot of money, but in the context of even a mid-range 35mm outfit, it's not so much. Also, you've got it for the rest of time. Large format cameras don't wear out, or go out of date: you won't be tempted by the latest multi-mode model because there aren't any multi-mode models. If you buy a new camera, you'll have something you can leave to your children or grandchildren. If I could afford about £2000, I'd buy a new 5x7 inch Gandolfi Precision: it's probably the most beautiful LF camera on sale today as well as one of the most usable.

And if you do decide to sell your £500 outfit, either to trade up to something like the Gandolfi or because you've decided that LF is not for you, it will still be worth £500 when you do. See how much you are offered for your second-hand, £500 digital camera... If you don't think I'm telling the truth about what you can pay for an LF camera, go to a few camera fairs, or ask some of the better dealers who handle LF gear. You'll be surprised.

OK: even if the cameras aren't expensive, what about film? How can I tell you that film isn't expensive, at 20 quid-odd for 25 sheets of 5x4 inch or 30 quid-odd for 5x7 inch?

Quite easily. It takes a while to set up an LF camera, so you don't bother until you're reasonably sure you've seen something you want to photograph. Even then, there will be times when you'll set the camera up, look at the ground glass, and decide not to bother. Fine. No problem. Just don't shoot. You don't have to.

The net result of slowing down like this is that half a dozen sheets of film -- a quarter of a box -- can represent a fairly busy day's shooting. On some days, you'll shoot only a couple of sheets. Do the sums, and ask yourself how the costs compare with two or three rolls of 35mm, 36 exposure. This is cheap entertainment!

Partly for financial reasons, and partly because I actually like writing books and magazine articles, I can't actually imagine ever retiring. But if I could, I'd go for 5x7 inch, precisely because it is cheap and easy and enjoyable. I'd make contact prints; I wouldn't ever need to worry about buying a new camera or lenses; my only expense would be materials, and not too many of them. And I think I could get to be a better photographer than I've ever been.

Note: If you do use a Paterson Orbital, then roughen the base so the film won't stick to it. I used a Dremel tool, 'kissing' the base hundreds of times so it was pitted all over. Another photographer of my acquaintance put hundreds (or thousands) of spots of glue on the base. Also, DON'T rely on the mechanical agitator, which can lead to uneven development. Agitate manually, as randomly as possible. This is contrary to my earlier advice to use the mechanical base -- uneven development only shows up in areas of reasonably even tone and it was a while before I saw it.

Moral Superiority

For the last year or so, a friend of mine, an excellent photographer, has taken to using a single fully-manual camera; a single prime lens; and a single black and white film. He doesn't use a meter: he just guesses the exposure, erring (when he is not sure) on the side of generosity. He takes a lot of very good pictures.

The most interesting thing, though, is that this approach - simplicity, taken to its limits - is often perceived as somehow morally superior to relying on technology. Certainly, he and I both take it this way: those who have to rely upon autofocus, auto-exposure and DX coding seem to us to lack moral fibre. The question is, why?

Like so many questions, it is easier to ask than to answer. At first sight, there is a good deal to be said for the exact opposite viewpoint: artistic talent should stand best when it is least tramelled by technical constraints. Why, after all, should the artist be limited by technical considerations?

But as soon as you start to think about the great artists of the past, in any media, you realize that the vast majority of them - arguably, all of the greatest among them - were and are extremely skilled technically. They understood or understand both the limits and (more importantly still) the potential of their equipment and materials.

A great artist can do more with a piece of charcoal and a sheet of paper than an indifferent Sunday painter can do with the entire Windsor and Newton catalogue; or think how Picasso created the head of a bull by setting a pair of bicycle handlebars over a bicycle saddle.

And then you say, so? If I buy a bicycle and take it to bits, that won't make me another Picasso. But if I buy a Canon Eos 3 or a Nikon F5, it will make it a great deal easier to make good pictures.

And this, I suspect, is the nub of the argument. An all-singing, all-dancing, fully-automated camera won't make it easier to take good pictures. It will just make it harder to take bad ones.

If I go out with my Alpa 12 WA, I can make every mistake in the book. I can forget to pull the darkslide, and make no exposure at all. I can forget to wind on, and thereby make a double exposure. I can forget to focus, or I can focus badly. I can mis-set the shutter speed or the aperture; for that matter, I can forget to cock the shutter. In other words, there are lots of ways that I can make really bad pictures, or indeed, fail to make pictures at all.

But if I get it right, the lenses will give me results that cannot be bettered, especially by anything that zooms, and the roll-film formats will give me sharpness and tonality that 35mm cannot begin to equal. The point of focus will be exactly where I want it, which is far from invariably the case with autofocus, and the exposure (determined with a spot reading of the darkest area in which I want texture and detail) will be exactly what I want; again, a far cry from what auto-exposure can deliver. This is the first thing that simplicity is about: being in control, and getting it right.

The second thing is that simplicity is about simplicity itself. With a single camera, a single lens and a single film, I don't have to rely on a crowded gadget bag and a lot of batteries. The Alpa doesn't have batteries; and if the batteries in my Voigtlander R2 die, I can still guess the exposure, because the only thing that is battery-dependent is the meter.

This still leaves moral superiority. Here, I think, the key point is this. Someone who knows what he or she is doing, and how it works, is reasonably entitled to feel superior to someone who has to rely on a combination of luck and idiot-proofing. Not to someone who chooses to rely on automation, but to someone who has no choice.

To some extent, we all rely on others: I'm glad I don't have to coat my own sensitive material, for example. But I can. And I can use a fully manual camera; I can even guess the exposure with a fair degree of accuracy. It may not be moral, but it's certainly hard not to feel some form of superiority.

Overstatement & Alchemy

"Ilford's FP4 Plus is the finest medium-speed film ever made; Delta 100 is a cruel deception, designed solely to save money for the manufacturers by reducing the silver content. Agfa's paper is the only stuff worth using; Kodak's is unfit to wrap wet fish. Anyone who uses any developer except Kodak D-76 is an idiot..."

Statements like these can be heard wherever photographers gather, and indeed can sometimes be found (albeit in watered-down form, to avoid libel suits) in the correspondence pages of most photo magazines. And they are all codswallop. Photographers have a terrible inclination to overstate their case.

It's true that we all have favourites. For example, I use almost exclusively Ilford black and white films. But if (God forbid) there were an earthquake in Mobberley tomorrow, and the Ilford factory disappeared into the bowels of the earth, I wouldn't have to give up photography. For my 'standard' 35mm film I'd switch to Paterson Acupan 200, and for speed, I'd go back to Kodak TMZ P3200. In 120 I might go to Fortepan or Bergger; in large format, Bergger or Maco. There's always a choice.

If we're honest, in any case, a lot of our choices come down to accident, or to a lucky chance. Until late 1998, I hadn't shot Ilford HP5 for years: in fact, I had stopped using plain old HP5 long before HP5 Plus was introduced. Then, a manufacturer lent me a camera and gave me a handful of HP5 Plus to test it with. Well, the camera turned out to be stunning -- it was the Alpa 12 WA -- and so did the film. Today, HP5 Plus one of my standard films. I love the tonality, and you can develop it in almost anything. But if it hadn't been for that chance encounter, I doubt I'd have tried it again.

Even without happy accidents, a great deal depends on how much effort we are prepared to put into mastering a particular film. One of the reasons I love HP5 Plus is because it's dead easy, but I know that any film can be made to yield good results with the right developer and the right development regime. The reason I've never had a decent negative yet from Kodak TMX 100 is that I've only ever shot three or four rolls of it, and I've probably never used the optimum developers. In other words, I've never made a real effort to get the best from it. Why should I, when there are Ilford films I like better? But I know lots of photographers who get excellent results from it, far better than anything they have ever had from Ilford. And films that I have found to be very tricky indeed, requiring considerable effort to get even a printable negative, have revealed themselves in the hands of others to be absolutely superb.

Perhaps the bottom line is nothing to do with accidents or effort, after all. Rather, it is pure alchemy, or perhaps shamanism. Many alchemical operations had to be performed at a particular time of day, or during a particular phase of the moon; and a shaman who cannot see visions before he starts work might as well go back to bed for the day. An alchemist or shaman, faced with developing a film, might well be less concerned with time and temperature than with abstaining from sex before mixing the developer, or with whether Tuesday was an auspicious day for Kodak yellow.

And who is to say they are wrong? We have all met photographers who can coax the most extraordinary results from the most unpromising equipment and materials; and most of us have had the depressing experience of using the finest films and developers, and following the instructions scrupulously, only to be faced with results that are, to be charitable, indifferent. Perhaps it is a question of mental or spiritual preparation after all; perhaps we should all pay as much attention to incantations and belief-systems as to science, at least when it comes to black and white photography. It would make more sense than the assertions that some photographers make about what works, and what doesn't.

Taking 35 mm Seriously

Years ago, whole magazines were devoted to 35mm photography. Journals with a wider remit, including AP, ran specialist articles on 35mm equipment, materials and techniques. Today, with 35mm dominant (despite challenges from digital), people tend to forget that techniques which work well with larger formats (or at least, cause no harm) can be detrimental when applied to 35mm.

The most obvious considerations are sharpness and grain. With modern films, at normal enlargement sizes, variations in these are irrelevant with large format (4x5 inch and above) and of limited relevance with roll film. With 35mm, they warrant serious attention.

Sharpness probably matters more than grain, but both are influenced by the same considerations: film speed, exposure, developer choice and development regime. For maximum sharpness, you need a slow film, though in all fairness, Ilford Delta 100 is sharper than Ilford Pan F, despite being twice as fast. You need to keep exposure a minimum. This is very important: a film that delivers 100 line pairs per millimetre (lp/mm) with minimal exposure may well drop to 80 lp/mm with a stop extra and 70 lp/mm or less with two stops extra. You need a suitable developer, though developers that deliver maximum sharpness do not deliver finest grain, and vice versa. During development, you need as little agitation as is consistent with even development.

You can compromise on any of these, but the cumulative differences will matter most with 35mm. An 8x10 inch (20x25cm) enlargement, borderless, is effectively 8x off 35mm, but rather under 4x off 6x7cm or 6x9cm. My own rule of thumb, based on more than a third of a century of experience, is that up to about 5x you can use pretty much any modern film and developer, but beyond that, differences start to show.

The other thing that limits sharpness is camera shake. With a 35mm rangefinder camera such as my Voigtlander Bessa R2 and a 35mm or 50mm lens, I can get acceptable sharpness as often as not at 1/30 second. Going to 1/60 will usually give me more sharpness, but 1/15 will be unacceptable more often than not. I specify rangefinder cameras because (like most people) I find that I can hold them steadier than reflexes: about one shutter speed step, on average.

But with a 4x5 inch camera and a 135mm or 150mm lens (the equivalent of 40mm to 45mm on 35mm) I can get acceptable sharpness more often than not at 1/10 second, with 1/5 second offering much the same chances of sharpness as 1/15 on 35mm. Why? Partly inertia -- the big camera can't wobble as fast -- and partly because the big negative isn't enlarged as much.

This is one reason why the press-men of yore used to be able to get good pictures in poor light with woefully slow lenses, even without flash: a popular lens was the Xenar 135/4.7. Admittedly Kodak Royal-X Pan at ASA 1250 was another reason, but (as compared with 35mm Kodak Tri-X, ASA 400) this offered only 1-2/3 stops increase in film speed to compensate for the 2-1/2 stops that the Xenar lacks next to an f/2 lens on 35mm, or the three and a half stops it yields to an f/1.5.

The format you choose will also make a difference to the extent to which you should stop your lenses down. This is because of diffraction limits to resolution. By f/32, the diffraction limit to resolution is around 40 to 50 line pairs per millimetre, depending on the contrast criterion you choose.

This doesn't matter with large format, which is enlarged very little, but it's right on the edge for roll-film: this is why so few MF lenses stop down further. With 35mm, stopping down too much is a recipe for disaster. At f/16, diffraction limited resolution is well under 100 lp/mm at zero contrast; at f/22 it is under 70 lp/mm. At worth-while contrast levels, these figures drop still lower. For optimum sharpness, if depth of field allows it, you should shoot at f/5.6 or f/8.

Unless you are making very small prints, you are likely to see a detectable loss of sharpness by f/16 and a serious loss of sharpness at f/22.

Does all this matter? Yes. Far too many 'serious' writers on black and white photography have forgotten what it is like to use 35mm: they have cast in their lot with big cameras and the Zone System. But as I hope you will understand by now, 35mm is different. Still.

A Bit Of Everything...

It's a simple enough question: what do you shoot? But it's very hard to answer. At least, most people seem to find it so. It's one of the first questions I ask when people seek my advice on matters photographic. Partly, it's so they don't waste their time asking me about subjects about which I know very little: sports photography, for example, or macrophotography of insects. And partly it's because different subjects demand different types of camera, materials and technique.

The usual answer is, "Oh, a bit of everything, really. I'm just an amateur, you see."

Well, so am I. I've been a professional, and I've come out the other side. From time to time I go back to professional photography, which I define as shooting things that somebody else wants me to shoot, rather than shooting things I want to shoot for myself. But being an amateur is much more fun.

So what do I shoot as an amateur? Travel; architecture; landscape; still life; a bit of portraiture; some reportage. This sounds rather like "A bit of everything, really," especially travel, which can be almost anything. But what is missing is as important as what's there. No sports and action, for example. No nudes. No flowers. No interiors.

Sure, I've tried sports and action, and nudes, and flowers, and interiors, and ballerinas, and all kinds of other things. I was once offered a lucrative three-week shoot in Saudi Arabia, photographing interiors, on the strength of some of my published work; but I turned it down, because it was too much like hard work, and besides, I have no great sympathy with the Wahhabi version of Islam and my wife is even less enamoured of it (we always work together).

What's important is that there are some things that I shoot habitually, and others that I don't. Professionally, I'm pretty good at how-to shots, and step-by-steps, and food photography, but frankly, a lot of my professional work has been much the same as my amateur work: travel and reportage.

Next question: why do I shoot some things, and not others? All kinds of reasons. Let's take nudes, for example. Some photographers seem to be able to separate the way the feel about the model, and the way they take pictures. I can't. Either I fancy the model, or I don't. If I fancy her, I may or may not be able to take good pictures, but my mind is on other things. And if I don't fancy her, I can't really take good pictures. When I was an assistant, I wasn't allowed to book models, because as my gaffer said, "You only ever book the ones you fancy, not the ones that look right for the shoot." Guilty as charged.

Or take flowers. They just don't interest me very much. I've seen great pictures of flowers; I've taken a few that aren't too bad. But as far as I am concerned, a flower belongs in a garden, in three dimensions, with its scent and the breeze and the surrounding greenery and everything else. I just don't feel any impulse to photograph them. Maybe that's the same argument why I don't shoot nudes!

Natural history? Nah. Again, I can appreciate the pictures, but from a biological point of view I'm much more interested in intellectual analyses of evolution, behaviour, ecosystems and the like than I am in looking at the animals. I'm particularly fond of tigers, and I've taken one or two good pictures (at Mysore zoo, a treasure trove for tiger lovers, though many are kept in cages that are far too small), but birdwatching leaves me cold. I can't muster the enthusiasm for sitting in a hide for three days to see a Prize Tit or Pointless Albatross or whatever. I find it much more pleasant to sit in my back yard with a glass in my hand and watch the antics of the sparrows.

I could multiply examples, but you are probably getting bored already. I hope, though, that I may have prompted you to think about what you don't photograph, and why, for the light it throws upon what you do photograph, and why.

There's one more thing: distinguishing between the photographs that you like to admire, and the photographs you like to take. As you might guess, I can be well taken with a photograph of a nude (as long as I fancy the model), but less expectedly, I also like American pseudo-wilderness pictures. I've been to Yosemite, Ansel Adams's old stamping ground, several times (I used to live in California) and once again I've taken a few pictures that I like; but there was always something lacking, apart from talent, and it took a few years to realize what it was.

The clue is in 'pseudo-wilderness'. I've never seen true wilderness - just about all the landscapes in Europe, and most in the United States, are substantially man-made - and I don't really care for imitation wildernesses with roads and marked trails. What I do like, though, is what I call the 'hand of man', the way that man leaves his traces on the landscape but nature slowly reclaims or integrates them. Old buildings, weathered wayside crosses, grass-grown paths, terraced fields: that's the kind of stuff I really like to photograph.

Does all this matter? Yes. Unless you know what you like to photograph, it can be hard to put your camera in front of it - and it can be all too easy to be persuaded to shoot something that doesn't really interest you, whether for a competition or just because you admire someone else's pictures of the same sort of thing. By all means try "a bit of everything," especially if you want to be APOY; but you may well find that if you concentrate a bit harder on the things that really interest you, and cut down on the rest, it is actually easier when you want to photograph "a bit of everything."

Instruction Book Syndrome

It would be nice to believe that there is no such thing as a stupid question, only stupid answers, but it is increasingly hard to cling to this comforting, egalitarian myth. I do not believe that people on average are growing more stupid, but I really do believe that they are being trained to ask stupid questions.

What prompts this observation is that over the last few months I have seen more and more people asking for instruction books to help them do tasks that must surely be self-evident. The question is normally phrased in terms of "I need an instruction book for a camera I have just inherited/been given/bought [for some reason they normally say 'won'] on eBay."

I don't care how little you know about photography: it is not hard to work out the controls on any conventional, basic, manual camera. The wind-on lever? Hardly incomprehensible. The rewind? Likewise. The shutter release? Undemanding. The focusing ring: how much difficulty can that present? The shutter speed setting, whether it's a dial or a ring around a leaf shutter? Where is the difficulty? If there's a rangefinder, look through the eyepiece and twiddle the focusing ring. You'll soon see what happens.

Of course there can be unexpected problems. Seasoned photographers are regularly fooled by such tricks as the wind-on on a Werra (concentric with the lens) or the rewind clutch on a Zorkii-4K (concentric with the shutter release), and it's a fair question, if the camera needs a battery and doesn't come with a dead one so you can ask for "one of these, please", to ask what sort of battery it takes.

But these difficulties are not on a par with such questions as "Will my camera continue to work if I take the battery out?" If you are too stupid to try this for yourself, will you understand the answer if someone tries to tell you? Or "Has it got a meter?" Are there any little needles that look as if they might move over scales? Or anything that looks like an LED that might light up? Has it got a battery compartment or a selenium cell? If not, well, it probably hasn't got a meter unless it's REALLY old and has an extinction meter.

As I say, I don't think people are growing more stupid, but I do think they are being trained to ask stupid questions, especially by the instruction books for the vast majority of modern cameras, with digital cameras the worst offenders.

Most begin with the sort of injunctions that only a cretin or a very, very young child would need: advice on a par with "Do not stick your fingers in the electric wall socket when attempting to recharge the battery" or "Do not attempt to change film underwater" or "Do not beat people to death with this camera." Get past the first five or ten pages of this sort of drivel, which is presumably there to satisfy American lawyers, and you are into the meat of the thing.

This is where you learn that there are 84 metering modes, 38 of which are indistinguishable from one another; 27 different autofocus programs, at least 19 of which are worthless; and the names of the 32 buttons, knobs, switches, dials and levers that are supposed to control the camera. They don't, however, mention that if you press the wrong pair of buttons at the same time you will have a camera that only takes pictures on alternate Tuesdays during Lent, unless you have inadvertently pressed a third button which further restricts it to leap years but auto-brackets when it does.

Yes; OK; fine. Maybe you like that sort of camera. The very best of luck to you if you do. But not all cameras are like that. They don't have to be. And interestingly enough, an awful lot of the best cameras ever made are not like that. An Alpa or a Gandolfi doesn't have any metering modes at all. Or autofocus. Or indeed anything else much, including instruction books. Anyone of average intelligence, who has ever seen a camera and knows more or less what they do (focus light onto film or a sensor, and open and close a shutter) should be able to work out just about everything from first principles.

Admittedly, crazed instruction-book writers (and readers) are not the only problem. The other is that for far too many people, the internet forum has replaced the evening down the pub with friends, the trip to the camera club, the enjoyable half-hour at the club-like camera shop, even the trip to take pictures. People don't see each others' cameras any more: only their own, and even then, then they can't figure out how to use them. O tempora, o mores.

A Personal Style

A personal style, we are regularly assured by the pundits, is something we should all strive to develop. At its most extreme, this advice is couched in terms which preclude looking at others' photographs, lest we be contaminated by their preconceptions.

Rubbish. Personal style is not something you can develop in the same way that you beat an egg, or plan a shooting trip to Cornwall, or buy a new camera. It is something that sneaks up on you while you are doing something else -- and looking at others' work is absolutely essential in developing it.

To begin with, there is technique. Unless you see others' pictures, you never really know what technical quality can be. Time and again I have seen beginners' pictures that were awful: gruesome colour casts, or dirt and hairs all over the negative, or hideous oversharpening in Photoshop, or black and white prints that had clearly been snatched out of the developer because they were going too dark, too fast, when any competent photographer would have thrown them away and remade the print.

You cannot fully judge technique from magazines, either. The reproduction medium is inherently inferior to the best that can be done at home, either in the digital darkroom or the traditional wet darkroom, but master printers have a very great deal of experience and are skilled at making silk purses out of sows' ears. Comparing magazine repro with the production of originals is a bit like comparing canned food and fresh. Canned pineapple tastes very good, and so does fresh; but they don't taste much like one another. You need to see original prints.

Then there is the old idea of apprenticeship. The craft or misterie of art has a far longer and more honourable history than art as self expression, which is pretty much a late 19th century invention. Until then, it was often very difficult to have a new idea accepted, let alone praised. The classic example of this was Ruskin, a thoroughly nasty little man, who accused Whistler of being a coxcomb who flung a pot of paint in the face of the public. Whistler should have let his painting (The Falling Rocket) speak for itself, but instead, he sued like a fool. Although he won damages, he was crucified by the costs, which were awarded against him.

Since then, and partly as a result of that lamentable example, people have all too often confused originality -- yes, the much-vaunted 'personal style' -- with quality. The argument is a classic omitted middle: because much great art is shocking when it is first seen, anything that is shocking when first seen must necessarily be great art. The fallacy does not need elaboration.

Above all, though, there is a simple truth. If you have any talent at all, you cannot continue indefinitely to work in the style of your exemplars. Let us say, for the sake of argument, that you regard Roger Fenton's still lifes or Julia Margaret Cameron's portraits as among the greatest of all photographs in all history.

You therefore do your very best to emulate their style. Of course you can't, because you are working well over 100 years later, with completely different equipment and materials. As you try to equal their genius, you come up with your own ways of doing things, your own preferences, your own favoured models. Part of what you do is forced upon you by necessity, and part is reactive: no, you think, this is actually a better way of doing things, and besides, I am me, I am not Roger Fenton or Julia Margaret Cameron. Thus does a personal style sneak up upon you.

Or maybe it doesn't. Some people continue their entire photographic careers as poor shadows of their mentors: to borrow Bob Shell's memorable phrase, "Very minor Whites." Adamites are particularly prone to this: the number of abysmal imitators of the Blessed Ansel of Carmel is legion. But what would hapen to these sad creatures, so devoid of imagination and originality, if they did not have their heroes to look up to? Would they blossom, developing that Holy Grail of a personal style? Almost certainly not. Everything they have is borrowed, and if they did not have what was borrowed, they would have nothing at all.

So don't strive for a personal style. It is a chimaera, a mirage, a will-o'-the-wisp which will elude you as long as you seek it. Instead, take pictures. And more pictures. And more pictures. Choose the best. Develop your strengths. Never be afraid to borrow, or indeed steal, ideas from others: as the old saying goes, "Talent borrows, but genius steals." In the meantime, forget about a personal style.

Real Engineering...

For many years I was uncomfortable working with my hands. My father joined the navy as an E.R.A. (Engine Room Artificer) and could make almost anything -- he made me a working toy steam reciprocating engine, for example -- but I have never been very good at wood, metal and things mechanical, so I avoided them. And you didn't get metalwork classes at the sort of school I went to.

Increasingly, though, I like working with my hands; and, of course, this means that I am getting better at it. The reason for my change of heart is a reaction to computers and allied electronic devices.

For example, my main imaging computer suddenly decided that it didn't have a card reader installed; didn't know what a card reader was; and didn't believe that card readers existed or should exist. It behaved, in short, like a three-year old who, after eating cabbage quite happily since first discovering solid food, suddenly decides that he HATES it and will NEVER eat it EVER AGAIN. The usual rigmarole of uninstallation and re-installation followed: half an hour gone. This was followed by a conflict between Adobe Photoshop and the anti-virus software on my internet computer: this time, two hours wasted.

And so I stripped, cleaned and reassembled a pair of Taylor, Taylor Hobson 6x30 Binoculars, Prismatic, Mark 2, manufactured in 1942. The mist and haze that flattened the contrast are gone, and they are about as bright and clear as you can reasonably expect from a pair of uncoated glasses made half-way through World War Two.

Then I decided to sell an electronic film SLR I didn't use, and hadn't used for years. First I had to buy a battery, of course: almost a tenner. When I fitted it, the autofocus didn't work. OK: work the manual focus a bit, loosen that up; the autofocus followed suit. But what were all these modes? Which buttons and dials did what? Why did some appear to do nothing? And why couldn't I see the shutter speed and aperture in the viewfinder, except during the instant the shutter fired? Oh, well: that was money wasted on the battery, because the camera was only half-functional.

Right: more 'real' work needed to take my mind off this. The two steel trunks that normally live in the back of my Land Rover now accept three 6mm U-bolts each so I can bolt them on the roof rack if I need extra storage space. On a long shooting trip the Land Rover sometimes fills up so much (often with unusual local drinks) that I need this option. I'd been meaning to do it for months but it was the stimulus of working with electronics that finally led me to get around to it.

The day after, much to my surprise, all the camera functions had come back. Why? I can hazard several guesses, but ultimately, I don't know and I can't find out by direct means (opening it up and looking inside). Increasingly, I give the same answer to all such questions about inexplicable glitches: "It's a computer."

Certainly, I'm not the only one who thinks this way. A phrase I have encountered more and more often in the last few months is 'post-digital photography'. This comes from people who tried digital; found it wanting; and turned to silver halide. To my surprise, these are not just older photographers who are going back to silver halide, but also young ones who were brought up on digital and are coming to silver halide for the first time. Often, too, they are choosing simple, 'classic' cameras with a minimum of controls, manual-everything, and quite possibly no meter: often, in fact, rangefinders, whether modern Bessas or old Leicas. The rich ones even buy new Leicas, which is greatly to be encouraged.

Now, believe it or not, I am not knocking digital photography. I believe that both digital and silver halide can and should exist side by side. I'd be as unhappy using my Leica MP for things that my Nikon D70 can do better as I would be using my D70 to do things that the MP can do better. I frequently scan my Leica slides with my truly superb Konica Minolta Dimage Scan Elite 5400II, which has only one fault that I have discovered, a ridiculously long name. But ultimately, I need things I can understand and fix -- or at least, where I can see what the problem is and make a judgement about getting it fixed -- as a counterbalance to electronics where, if something goes wrong, my only option is the Microsoft fix. You all know that one. Turn it off; wait a minute or two; start it again and see if the problem goes away. Give me real engineering any day.

Customer Support

He would probably have fixed the problem under guarantee, said Eddie, but he'd have asked me to pay carriage. After all, the Gandolfi Universal 12x15 inch camera and its case together weigh about 60 lb (27 kg). Besides, it is the best part of 100 years old, which is rather outside the usual guarantee period.

Eddie Hill, proprietor of Gandolfi, was only half joking. Given that the camera that I had just purchased was made at least 85 years ago and had apparently not been back to the factory since, a repair under guarantee would have been remarkable even by Gandolfi's demanding standards. But I think he'd have done it, at least if he was convinced that someone else hadn't bodged it in the intervening period. Here's the story.

One of the locking tabs for the rear standard was missing. It didn't take me very long to make up a new one, using the other as a pattern. I telephoned Eddie to check the thread size that I needed (2 BA) and then cut, filed, drilled and tapped a suitable bit of brass from an old drawer-lock.

When I tried to fit it, my heart sank: a tiny piece of wood beside the focusing track cracked outwards. Then I looked closer: it had already been repaired once, in the same place, for the same fault. I looked closer still. The problem became clear. Louis Gandolfi, who made the camera some time between 1907 and 1920, had cut the original a fraction too big.

Rather than file down his original, I made up a second locking tab, keeping Louis's as a spare. The back now locks, and the camera now focuses, without problems. But that fault had been there since the camera was new, almost a century ago. That was why I jokingly asked Eddie about a repair under guarantee, albeit after I had done the job. And it is why his reply was only half joking.

There are at least four morals to derive from this story. The first is Horace's reminder: indignor quandoque bonus dormitat Homerus. Horace was upset when great Homer began to doze off: in other words, when he lost concentration or fell short of perfection. I felt that Louis had let me down the same way.

The second is what after-sales service means. With Gandolfi, it means standing by any product they have made, for the rest of time. They won't necessarily repair it under guarantee, but they will always repair it, rebuild it, restore it or update it. New lens panel? Replacement front? Replacement back? New bellows? No problem. And with the exception of the glued-in bellows, the new parts would be completely interchangeable with the old: it could be restored to original condition, with the original parts, in minutes. Museum piece, or usable camera? Take your pick: whichever you want. Somehow I can't see anyone performing a similar resurrection on a digital camera in 90 years time.

This brings me to the third moral. Film is wonderful stuff. All right, I can't get 12x15 inch plates (yet, though I'm working on it). I can however 'fudge' film into it. I've already contacted Ilford about both 12x15 inch and 10x12 inch (the holders also accept 8x10 and whole-plate). This is a camera I am going to use, and enjoy using. I'm even enjoying cleaning it up and putting it back into working order: cleaning, polishing (with beeswax and turpentine polish) and the rest of the work. It is literally a pleasure to own. Unlike my CF card that suddenly decided it wasn't formatted after shooting 52 pictures...

The fourth moral is that I don't really own this camera. I am its custodian. It was built long before I was born, and it will still be serviceable long after I have died. Right now, as well as the locking tabs I fabricated, it needs new septums in the plate-holders, because the old zinc ones are rotting to pieces. There are also a few pinholes in one of the wooden sheaths to the plate-holders, so tiny I could probably fix them with a couple of dabs of black paint alone. I can do all this, and so could anyone else with even the crudest of mechanical skills: it does not require an electronic test rig and a degree in engineering. It is comprehensible; it is reliable; it is fixable.

I find this continuity comforting. Yes, progress is wonderful. But it isn't the be-all and end-all. There is still a lot of pleasure to be gained from the past, and the trick lies in knowing when to look forwards, and when to look back. Sure, there is no way that the Gandolfi can replace my Nikon D70. But -- and this is equally important -- there is no way that the D70 can replace the Gandolfi, either.

Gresham's Law...

We live, we are constantly told, in the 'information society'. Wealth no longer resides in manufacturing or bricks and mortar, but in the possession of information.

Unfortunately, this is nonsense. Information is free; more free than it has ever been, thanks to the internet. If it were not so, those who scrabble a living by peddling information -- authors of non-fiction books and news reporters, for example -- would be a lot better paid than they are.

Of course, there are exceptions: the star writers and reporters whose names and faces we see all the time. But this is merely further illustration of my central argument. The money is in entertainment, not information. Unless the information is entertainingly presented, no-one will pay for it: it becomes a commodity, like sugar or tin or cocoa.

This is why it is so difficult to earn any money from presenting information on the internet: there too much that is free. Of course, a lot of it is nonsense. For instance, there's at least one web-site that confuses incandescent quartz-iodine/tungsten-halogen lighting, which is essentially a clever modification of the familiar domestic light-bulb, with metal halide lamps, which are essentially modified mercury-vapour discharge lamps. This may not matter much to you, but if you are trying to find out about different types of lighting, it's an irresponsible, stupid statement by someone who doesn't know what he is talking about.

It's an example, though, of Gresham's Law. Sir Thomas Gresham (1519-1579) advised Queen Elizabeth that bad money cannot circulate alongside good; H.D. McLeod accorded this the status of a law in 1857 and appended Gresham's name to it, though the same sentiment had been expressed by earlier writers including Copernicus. McLeod's version was that the worst form of currency in circulation regulates the value of the whole currency and drives all other forms of currency out of circulation.

This is not quite what has happened on the internet, because plenty of good information is still available, but increasingly it does mean that unless the good information is free (as it is, for example, on Michelin's excellent route-finder site, www.viamichelin.com), it is not consulted. And who, apart from an advertiser (like Michelin) or an academic or someone else who is already drawing a salary, can afford to do research and put up good information for nothing?

The result is that the proportion of good, reliable information on the internet declines steadily, because no-one can afford to fund it. Worse still, the internet infects other media: why should someone buy a book, or a magazine, when they can get the same information for nothing on the internet?

The answer, of course, is that they can't get the same information. The internet is useful only if you already know enough to be able to separate the wheat from the chaff. If you are an extremely critical reader with no prior knowledge of the subject, you may be able to deduce the truth from reading enormous amounts of internet information, but the problem is that the biases are not known; the only reliable constants are high levels of ignorance, stupidity and hearsay.

Entertainment is a lot more complex, because it doesn't necessarily deal with facts. Of course it may use facts if it chooses, though it can also choose to be be cavalier with those facts. American 'historical' movies are notorious for this, but you need to be pretty stupid or ill-educated to base your entire knowledge of history on movies.

Now, a cynic might argue that the worst form of entertainment in circulation does indeed drive out all other forms of entertainment, and 'reality' or 'celebrity' television might seem to bear this out. But entertainment is an endless series of niches, and a genius such as Terry Pratchett can sell in very respectable quantities alongside 'airport novels' (the Victorians used to call them 'railway novels' for much the same reasons) and AP can sell alongside kiss-and-tell magazines and supermarket tabloids.

Is AP entertainment? I'd say it was. To be sure, we have to get our facts right, but being able to rely on the factual correctness of most of what we say (we all make mistakes) is surely part of the entertainment value. Also, because magazines cost money to produce and still more money to circulate, they cannot be created by obsessives in funny-smelling anoraks in quite the same way that web-sites can.

Indeed, the very opposite of Gresham's Law might be said to operate in magazine publishing. Since AP was founded there have been scores of competitors. Some were very good; some were very bad; a few (a very few) have been as good as AP, but not as well managed. Most are long gone, and we are still here. In the long term, the good has driven out the bad. I find that curiously comforting.

Had A Nice Holiday ?

Had a nice holiday? That's what people always ask me when I come back from a shooting trip. For years I tried to explain that no, it wasn't a holiday; I was working; I was often getting up a lot earlier, and working a lot harder, than I usually do at home; and without such trips, I wouldn't actually be able to earn a living.

But they never really believed me, even if I had painstakingly explained before I left that it was work, not holiday. Nowadays I just smile and nod and say yes, though I do have to bite my tongue a bit when they say "Back to work now then, eh?"

Don't get me wrong. I'm not complaining. I get paid to do the things that most people pay to do, and I do them in my working day, not in a few hours per week or a few days per year of week-ends and holiday time. I earn a living by travelling, and taking pictures, and even cooking: look at my web-site and you'll see that I've done several cook-books. For that matter, I earn a living by writing. I've belonged to enough writers' groups to know that this is quite a privilege too.

Even so, I do feel the urge to set the record straight from time to time. My late father-in-law summed it up quite well. He once said to his baby daughter, my wife (who would have been in her 40s at the time), "You know, I always wanted to do the things you do, writing and taking photographs, but now I've seen how hard you have to work, I'm not so sure."

Do not imagine that the life of a professional photographer (or writer) is all a bed of roses. Or actually, maybe it is. Allow for the thorns, the blackfly, the rainstorms, the long leafless spells in the winter, the generous servings of fertilizer, the vicious prunings... Yeah, OK, it is a bed of roses, but not as popularly portrayed.

But enough of such matters; you don't read AP to be depressed. If you have any sense, though, you do use it as a yardstick against which you can measure your dreams.

First, how good a photographer are you? I never cease to be amazed by how good our readers are. Many are far better photographers than I. But then I reflect that some of the reader portfolios reflect weeks, months, years or even decades of work. If I pull out my very best work, yes, I'm probably as good as all but the best of our readers. Here's one of the differences between a professional and an amateur, and one where the amateur has the advantage.

Second, how focused are you? The readers' portfolios are a tremendous guide here, too, and I have recently resolved to try to narrow my attention more. I know what I'm best at -- or at least, I think I do, and I certainly know what I enjoy most -- and I think I should concentrate a lot more on these subjects, rather than trying to spread myself too thin. On the other hand, my editors expect more than the same old subjects again and again. In that sense I'm like an amateur driven by entering competitions: I'm more or less obliged to spread myself too thin. But a sensible amateur, the sort who shoots what he likes rather than being a slave to competitions, again has the advantage over the professional.

Quality and commitment are far more important than the equipment you use, or whether you use silver halide or digital. And both of them are, to a large extent, a mixture of dedication and hard work. My own belief is that anything between one-tenth and one-half of our readers could, if they wanted and if they dared, turn professional. But they might not like it. It takes your life over. Not everyone is willing to make that commitment, and even fewer of their spouses are prepared to see them make it. I have seen more than one photographer's marriage break up when the spouse wouldn't accept the importance of the photography.

I'm not saying it's better for everyone to be an amateur than to be a professional. If I believed that, I'd still be a schoolteacher or an accountant or maybe something else entirely. But equally, I know more amateurs than professionals who can afford new Leicas, and I always remember the old story of the man who got a job backstage at Le Crazy Horse (the same story used to be told of the Follies Bergere). The first month was heaven; the second was hell; and after that, it was just a job.

The Automatitic Marshmallow Toaster

Imagine, if you will, an automated marshmallow toaster. For those who have never toasted a marshmallow over an open fire, this may take some explaining. A rather dull, mushy sweetmeat turns, as it is toasted, into a magnificent delicacy: crisp and golden on the outside, gooey and liquefied in the middle. Blindingly sweet, right on the edge of burning your mouth, the perfect toasted marshmallow well demonstrates the razor-thin margin between pleasure and pain.

The scope for error in preparing these morsels is considerable. You must keep them at exactly the right distance from the fire, and rotate them at exactly the right speed. You can burn them, especially on one side; you can fail to get then warm enough, so that they droop and melt without ever cooking properly; and even when they are spot on, you have to be extremely careful because they go from effectively raw to overcooked in a matter of seconds. When they are perfect, there is a tiny window of opportunity for eating them. Too soon, and you will burn your mouth. Too late, and they will probably fall off the skewer.

An automated marshmallow toaster would overcome all these difficulties, supplying perfect, succulent toasted marshmallows at the touch of a button; after the required cooking time, obviously. After cooking, it would sound a bell or buzzer to tell you the marshmallow had cooled far enough to eat: this would be adjustable for individual preferences. You would then have a few seconds' grace in which to pop it into your mouth and enjoy it.

And this, of course, is missing the whole point. Skewering the marshmallow; juggling it over the fire; judging the perfect moment; mocking your fellow gourmets (and being mocked by them) when things go wrong; all of this is part of the pleasure of eating toasted marshmallows.

Oscar Finn O'Flaherty Wilde described a cigarette as the perfect type of a perfect pleasure: "It is exquisite, and it leaves one unsatisfied. What more can one want?" All I can say is, the poor man must never have toasted and eaten a marshmallow: after that, a cigarette is indeed like cold rice pudding.

The parallels with photography are exact. We do not seek the quickest and most efficient route to a perfect picture, not least because anything that is arrived at by the quickest and most efficient route is unlikely to partake of perfection. It may be good; it may even be excellent; but it is unlikely to share that transcendence which is the nature of perfection.

This is not to say that we should always make life difficult for ourselves, living on bread and water, flagellating our bared shoulders with knotted cords and utilizing the Zone System. No: I am advocating the exact opposite, namely, hedonism. We should always do what gives us the most pleasure, subject, of course, to not hurting others.

If we prefer using ancient film cameras to using modern digital cameras, then we should use ancient film cameras. If we prefer the darkroom to the computer, we should choose the darkroom. And if we prefer to spend three hours in Photoshop processing and printing out a couple of dozen snaps that we could have dropped off in the mini-lab at lunch time and picked up after work, then we should spend the time on the computer, especially if we can use it as an excuse for not cutting the grass or doing the dishes. Suffering may purify the soul, but it doesn't necessarily make a better photographer.

Now, I don't like automation. I don't like autofocus, and I don't like auto-exposure. I do like, very much, that feeling of joy that comes when I get it right, and the credit doesn't have to be shared around too much: sure, with Leica for the mechanical perfection of the MP and the optical genius of the 75/2 Summicron, and with Ilford for the exquisite tonality of HP5 Plus and Multigrade Warmtone. But there is no faceless software team telling my camera where to focus, what exposure to give and indeed (with some of the older cameras) when to take a picture.

In other words, when I do something, I want to do as much of it as I can do well; as much as I have time for; and as much as I enjoy. I have finally mastered the art of lighting a fire with a single match (I was never a boy scout -- at my school it was a choice between the Cadet Force and the Boy Scouts, with the latter regarded as wimps), so I split my oak logs and cut shavings; I build my fire; I light it; and I toast my marshmallows. And I take my pictures under the guidance of a similar philosophy.

Memories...

Our memories are not always what they should be, and they grow ever less reliable as we grow older. Still less do photographs necessarily correspond to our memories; so which should we trust more?

The obvious answer is that we should trust the camera, as it is far more objective than our memories. Sometimes this may be true, but even then, things aren't always as clear cut as they seem.

Recently, for example, I was in Romania. I had just finished photographing a (rather dull) Saxon castle in showery weather. When I made my way back to the Land Rover, there were two young girls sheltering from the rain under a tree beside the car. 'Take me photie, mister' is not hard to convey in any language, so I exposed eight or ten frames: they were classic young friends, maybe ten years old, clearly half inseparable, half deadly rivals.

I thought nothing more of it until I came to sort and mount the slides a few weeks later. I remembered one of the girls as a blonde and the other as a brunette, but when I came to look at the pictures, I realized that the difference in colouring was minimal: one could best be described as light mouse, while the other was dark mouse. But the one with the light mouse hair was wearing a white dress, and the one with the dark mouse hair, a dark dress. Thus was my memory deceived.

Or was it? I am not convinced that my memory was necessarily inferior to the 'objective' record of the camera. Rather, I suspect that the fault lies in my photographic ability: I should have been able to take pictures that corresponded more closely to my memory, and less closely to the photographic reality.

In the studio, I could. There are all sorts of tricks I could use. High key and very flat lighting for the 'blonde'; even a touch of soft focus, perhaps, with the Dreamagon on my

Nikon D70, and maybe a hair light from the back. For the 'brunette', harder and more directional lighting, to throw her hair into shadow, and more contrast between her and the background.

The real test of my skill -- which I failed -- was to make then look the way I saw them, using what was at hand: overcast, rather blue lighting and the super-sharp 75/2 Summicron on my Leica MP loaded with Kodak Ektachrome EBX. It may seem odd to say that one of the finest cameras in the world, and one of the finest lenses, limited me; but in a sense they did. I might have done better to switch to my old Canon 50/1.2 from the 1960s, which I happened to have with me by accident, than to stick with the Summicron.

What I am saying, therefore, is that the objectivity of photography is grossly overrated. It's not objective. If nothing else, the photographer decides where to point the camera, and when to press the button. In this particular case I could have changed lenses and film: Fuji Astia, which I also had with me, would have changed the mood again, or indeed, I could have used black and white. Had I been so minded, I could have modified the lighting with flags and diffusers, even in the open. In the studio, as I have already said, I could have used still more tricks. And that's before we start to talk about make-up; my wife Frances Schultz is a talented make-up artist, a skill she acquired while taking her undergraduate degree in theatre at the University of Southern California.

Where, in this trail of possibilities, does the camera start to lie? When I choose the camera and lens? When I choose the film? When I decide where and when to shoot the picture? When we go into the studio? When we start to use make-up? When I get the blonde to lighten her hair, and the brunette to dye hers black (not in this situation, obviously, but the argument holds good)? When I print the image? When I choose what to say in the caption?

Here's a suggestion. The camera starts to lie as soon as it diverges from what I had intended or expected to portray; or indeed, from what I remembered. It is memory, not the camera, that should be believed.

This turns the whole saying that "The camera cannot lie" on its head. The camera always lies. This is a commonplace. It has to lie, as it can never tell the truth, the whole truth and nothing but the truth. The question becomes one of how we want it to lie. A sufficiently skilled photographer knows the answer to this, and it is slightly chilling. Properly used, the camera tells the lie, the whole lie and nothing but the lie.

Shoot The Terrorists !

An elderly friend was very senior in the Intelligence services from the 1930s to the 1950s. Many years ago, he pointed out to me a blindingly simple fact. Extensive round-the-clock surveillance is next to impossible: you can't get the manpower.

If you have someone or somewhere under 24-hour surveillance, you need three 8-hour shifts of analysts. You also need the surveillance crew, the 'plumbers' who install the equipment, the technicians who maintain it, and the couriers and administrative staff who make sure that it ends up in the right place instead of the Iranian or American Embassies or the front page of a tabloid newspaper. And they all have to have holidays and week-ends.

So: 24-hour surveillance is likely to need at least half a dozen full-time operatives per person or place, and quite possibly more. Take 200 suspected terrorists and 1000 selected video camera locations (the latter a very modest estimate) and you need maybe 10,000 front-line staff to take care of them.

A more recent Intelligence contact told me in 2003 that a great deal has been taken over by computers: human surveillance staff can now get away with skimming through edited highlights. He is probably right, but a front-line intelligence officer (on leave from Iraq when I last saw him in the United States in 2005) says that the role of electronics is easy to overstate. As the last was working full time on intelligence, and the other guy appeared merely to fancy himself a bit, I'll place more reliance on my American chum.

All this is prompted, of course, by the recent news that the July 7th bombers in London were captured on videotape a week before the bombings, doing what was described (with rather poor taste, I thought) as a 'dry run'. As one of the commentators portentously said, this demonstrated that they had carefully planned their attacks several months in advance. Well, yes. How many of us, sitting around of an evening at a loose end, have said, "'Ere, John [or Iqbal, as the case might be], you doin' anything tomorrow? 'Ow about a bit of suicide bombing? You know: passes the time, like." Not many, I suggest.

Now, I do not mean to play down the enormity of what our own home-grown terrorists, or those imported from overseas, have either planned or accomplished. Nor do I mean to diminish the skills and, well, intelligence, of the Intelligence services. Military Intelligence is famously regarded as an oxymoron, but I know and have known enough people in this line of business to appreciate that there are some ferociously bright chaps involved in it: people whom even I, not noted for my deference in such matters, regard as very clever indeed.

What I do question, however, is the value of the ubiquitous CCTV camera. I do not deny that it is possible that CCTV records may be of some use in re-creating the story once an atrocity has been committed, but I seriously doubt that such records can play any preventative role whatsoever, for the simple manpower reasons given above.

So here's another idea. Let's have a campaign to encourage street photography; let's make it an offence to stop someone taking pictures unless they are being actively offensive or a nuisance. Let's extend it into anywhere the public has free access, such as shopping malls. If they can train their CCTV cameras on us, why can't we train our cameras on them? There's a lot of free manpower out there.

Now let's go further still. Let's have a nationally organized and nationally funded street photography competition, with ten prizes every month of a thousand pounds, and ten annual prizes of ten thousand, paid for out of lottery money. That's rather under a quarter of a million a year in prize money. At a rough guess, the organizational costs might quadruple that: under a million a year. In government anti-terrorist terms, pocket change.

The advantages for national security are obvious. Instead of trudging about, eyes fixed on the floor, terrified of being accused of paedophilia or terrorism, a lot of photographers will be looking around them, trying to earn a thousand quid. This knowledge alone has to put a little more pressure on terrorists.

There's another advantage as well. Britain will become a magnet for street photographers. Move over Cartier-Bresson, Brassai, Doisneau: who knows what talent we have in our midst?

But of course, our political lords and masters will never go for it. For a start, it puts power and responsibility in the hands of the people, not control freak politicians. Second, it's cheap and it might work, unlike the vast majority of government initiatives. And third, it's fun; and that would frighten them most of all.

Tolerance

Tolerance. Say this word to most people and they immediately start thinking about things like religious, racial and sexual tolerance. Mercifully, more still seem to be in favour than not, though the percentage that prefers intolerance seems to be rising steadily.

Then there are engineering tolerances. Religious and racial intolerance brings us wars and riots; sexual intolerance brings us gay-bashing. Incomprehension of engineering tolerances takes away things like transport and running water. Oh: and photography, in case you think I was getting off-topic.

Nothing is made perfectly. Let's take cameras as an example. With a wooden camera, +/- 1mm (near enough 1/25 inch) on many dimensions would be entirely accurate enough. Indeed, with wood, I'd be deeply suspicious of anyone who said he was working to 0.1mm (1/250 inch, or 'four thou" for old-fashioned engineers). Wood absorbs and loses too much moisture with changes in humidity, never mind thermal expansion, to make such precision meaningful.

With a precision all-metal camera, +/- 0.1mm would be taken for granted, and with the very highest precision cameras such as the Swiss Alpa it would not be unrealistic to claim +/- 0.01mm or better: 1/2,500 inch, or a bit under half a thou'. But the different kinds of camera well illustrate the different kinds of precision that can be expected.

In fact, the plus-or-minus (+/-) sign tells you a lot as well, because it talks about repeatability as well as accuracy. At +/- 0.01mm, sometimes the dimension will be as much as 0.01mm oversize; sometimes it will be as much as 0.01mm undersize; and quite often it will be even closer to spot on. If it goes outside +/- 0.01mm, it is rejected.

Now, photography is wonderfully tolerant. Not only do we put up with truly awful pictures alongside the really good ones: we can also stand an extraordinary degree of sloppiness in such things as film speeds, metering and processing. ISO standards tolerate +/- 1/3 stop on nominal film speeds, and that's in a specified developer: change developers, and true ISO film speeds (with ISO standard shadow detail and contrast) can go up by 2/3 stop or more in something like Ilford DD-X or Paterson FX-50, or drop by a stop or more in a fine-grain developer. In other words, Ilford HP5 Plus, nominal ISO 400, could be anything from ISO 200 (or less) to ISO 650 (or more).

Not only that. You could use a spot meter; or an incident light meter; or a through-lens camera meter; and still get acceptable exposure. The recommended exposures from the three styles of metering could easily vary by a stop, but all three are likely to be inside the range that most people would regard as good or even excellent.

At the processing stage, the same again is true. Even with slide processing, Kodak E6 or compatible, it's amazing what you can get away with. A friend of mine once had an elderly Jobo CPE-2 give up the ghost in the middle of developing a batch of slides: it was old and ratty and second-hand when he bought it, and it had suffered further at his hands. The motor simply died. So he sloshed the chemicals around by hand -- and the slides were perfectly acceptable.

With black and white, the window of acceptability -- variations in time, temperature and agitation -- is even bigger. The degree of precision that so many devotees of black and white seek is unattainable, and even the modest degree of precision that is attainable is rendered worthless by their failure to understand what film speeds and metering techniques actually mean. They are saved by the tolerance in the system.

Another thing that many people forget is that engineering and technical tolerances can be asymmetrical or even one-sided. Film speeds, for example, are based on the minimum exposure required to give a good print. After allowing for a designed-in 'safety factor' (itself a variety of tolerance), 1/2 stop underexposure will give worse results than 2 stops overexposure. Likewise, although you can only trim a few seconds off the usual E6 bleach-fix bath of 6 minutes, it will do no harm to give an extra minute or two, or even three.

Whatever you do, it is worth trying to find out what the real tolerances are. Not so you can get sloppy, but for peace of mind, so you know when you have to be really, really careful and where it won't matter too much if you get it wrong. You should still strive to work as perfectly as possible at all times, but it's always worth knowing how badly things are likely to turn out if you get it wrong; and indeed, how wrong you can afford to get it. This is as true in photography as in the rest of your life.

They Can Smell Fear, You Know..!

Dogs, they say, can smell fear. Increasingly, I suspect that computers can do the same thing. Certainly, I get a lot more grief from computers than I do from dogs, though saying that will probably ensure that I get bitten tomorrow.

The thing is, I'm not convinced that dogs actually will attack if you are afraid, as long as you don't run away. I'm not even sure that dogs modify their behaviour all that much: what the frightened person sees as aggression, the dog-lover (or dog-tolerater, which is more how I would classify myself) sees as normal inquisitiveness, friendliness or indeed common-or-garden stupidity (several of my friends have labradors).

Computers are another matter. I have seen countless computer aficionados tap casually at a few keys while carrying on a normal conversation, in the sort of situation where I would be sweating like a chief stoker and concentrating very hard indeed on pressing exactly the right button in case the wretched thing locked up on me, losing all the work I had just done and presenting one of those infuriating error messages which require access to the computer that has just locked up -- a classic example of a locked box, with the key inside the box. They really can smell fear.

This is not lack of familiarity. I used to work with computers in the days of mainframes; the first word processor I ever used, in about 1979, was a terminal on an ICL Dual 2903, about three million quids' worth of kit, and my first personal computer was an 8-bit MS-DOS machine which cost £1600 of my own money in the early 80s: the equivalent of maybe twice as much in today's money. I must have had over a dozen computers since: I still own five that work, for a given value of 'work'.

But I don't like them, and they don't like me. I certainly take no pleasure in using them, any more than I take pleasure in using an egg-slicer. In fact, the analogy is exact. Egg-slicers, those little things with the cheese-wire harp-strings that I used to try to get a tune out of when I was a small boy, do cut eggs quicker and more neatly than I can do it with a knife, but they are not always very reliable (sometimes they crumble the egg rather than slicing it) and they have a life of about 18 months to three years before the wires break and you need to get a new one. Just like computers, really. The main difference, and I have to admit that it is a pretty significant difference, is the price: egg-slicers are a lot cheaper. Also, until an egg-slicer breaks, it works. Quite unlike Windows, at that point.

Obviously, my difficulties with computers have significant implications for digital photography. Is there anything, therefore, that I do about my relationship with the beastly things?

Increasingly, I think there is. First, I don't have to do everything on my own. I bought my last two computers (2004 and 2005) from a local dealer in the nearest town. I may have paid slightly more than I would have if I had bought it from a mail-order discounter, but the level of service I receive is a bargain at the price. Any problems, I take it in and he fixes it.

Second, I don't have to define myself in terms of my relationship with computers. I can't sing, either, but that doesn't stop me singing when there's no-one around.

Third, computers and silver halide photography are not mutually exclusive. I don't have to give up one to use the other, any more than I have to give up my Wuesthof kitchen knives to use an egg slicer -- or indeed, eating eggs in order to eat cucumber.

Fourth, I don't have to enjoy using them. The result is what I enjoy, not the process -- exactly as I enjoy neatly sliced eggs. If someone else enjoys slicing eggs or using computers, the very best of luck to them, but I can't help wondering how dull and boring the rest of their life is if that's a high point.

Finally, I don't have to have the latest and the 'best'. This was written on a 15-year-old 386 using Wordstar under DOS. If a computer and software do what I want, I don't have to update them. This was brought home to me very forcefully a few years ago when a computer nerd was telling me that I 'needed' this, that and the other thing. I asked him why. "Oh, all the latest games need it," he said. "Ah," I replied, "there is the difference between us. You use your computer to play games. All I do with mine is earn a living."

Morphic Resonance

It is strange, but true, that beer tastes different according to the shape of the glass from which you drink it. The Belgians carry this to extremes, with every brewer making different glasses for every brew; but even in England, many pubs still offer the choice of a sleeve or a chamber pot, assuming you don't care for good honest pewter. Then again, champagne doesn't taste right out of pewter: you need silver or glass.

The analogy with photography is precise. For example, M-series Leicas are inextricably associated in many people's minds with gritty, slice-of-life black and white images: so much so that recently, I was much amused when someone asked if Leicas were actually suitable for colour photography, because they had never seen any colour pictures taken with Leicas. I'd be surprised if they really hadn't seen any; they just hadn't realized it.

Likewise, most people think of Ansel Adams wannabees when they see big wooden cameras, but it doesn't have to be that way: Jock Sturges, a sort of cinema-verite David Hamilton, uses 8x10 inch. For that matter -- showing off my own prejudices -- I suppose that some people have taken 'real' pictures with camera phones: not just bleak records of the moment, whether London bombings or party animals, but pictures that people admire despite their content, instead of because of it.

Then there are long lenses. If we see someone with a 300/2.8 or longer, and he doesn't lead us to suspect that he's a wildlife photographer by wearing camouflage clothing, gumboots and a hat with feathers stuck in it, the immediate reaction is "Paparazzi." Though I suppose that really diligent and resourceful paparazzi might indeed dress that way and get good pictures as a result.

The interesting question is where these prejudices come from -- and how much they vary with age. We must acquire them from a multitude of sources. Photo magazines and magazines that use photography, obviously: I can't be the only AP reader who, on seeing a feature about Picture Post, is profoundly grateful and thinks, 'Truly, there were giants in those days.' Books equally obviously feed our expectations. So do exhibitions, if we live close enough to somewhere we can see exhibitions reasonably often. And films, for that matter: who that has seen the movie can forget David Hemmings in 'Blow Up', or for that matter (once they have got over a glimpse of young Brooke Shields in the nude) Louis Malle's 'Pretty Baby?

But these are, to a large extent, openly photographic. An awful lot of our appreciation - and I use the word 'awful' with some feeling - comes from the general media; or, to use the disparaging but depressingly accurate assessment of the modern world, the 'meejah', the self-serving, self-praising coterie parodied in Private Eye as Phil Space and Polly Filla. An older phrase was 'the gutter press', though nowadays even broadsheets and once-broadsheets (now 'mid-size') are happy to fill their pages with 'celebrities' and similar rubbish; 'celebrity', of course, being defined as 'someone who is famous for being famous'. And they all love to tell us what to think.

It's true, of course, that some cameras are better for some purposes than others. I'd rather have a Linhof or a Gandolfi, or even a Sinar, for studio pack-shots, rather than an M-series Leica. And I'd rather have an M-series Leica for street photography than any other camera ever built, though Voigtlander Bessas come a very good second and I'm still waiting on a Zeiss Ikon.

Terry Pratchett -- a writer I quote a lot because I think he is our modern Dickens, only (being modern) more readable -- has a theory of 'morphic resonance'. Put a hell-hound into a terrier body, and it inevitably has to start behaving more like a terrier; and a witch who borrows the mind of an owl, and flies with it, must be careful lest she starts turning too much into an owl. The same thing, surely, must apply with cameras. Put a Leica in our hands and we are Cartier-Bresson or Sebastiao Salgado; hand us a brace of 1960s Nikon Fs and we are Tim Page in Vietnam or David Hemmings in Blow Up. Give us a Deardorff and we are Ansel Adams or Edward Weston. Actually, better still, give us a Gandolfi, a vastly better designed and better-made camera, which may explain why Gandolfis are still in production and Deardorffs aren't, though that's another story.

But where are our modern role models? And can we actually emulate them? Even if you can afford a pro-type digital SLR, where do you buy the flak jacket? Most importantly of all, why has the photographer as hero fallen from view, to be replaced in the public perception with a pervert wielding a mobile phone?

Where Do We Go From Here ?

The vast majority of enthusiastic amateur and indeed professional photographers have always followed more or less the same path. They take a few snaps with simple cameras, as everyone does in most of the rich world, and then, for one reason or another, they become more interested in photography. It may be a few personal successes; it may be that they admire the work of a friend or relative, who encourages them to buy a better camera. Whatever it is, they start to get more serious.

Unless they are very rich and very enthusiastic, they seldom buy a brand-new Leica MP, Alpa or Gandolfi, though nowadays they may well stretch to a digital SLR such as the Nikon D50. While this is an incomparably better camera than the fixed-lens rangefinder that they would probably have bought in the 1950s, Nikon themselves would be the first to say that there are better cameras in the world, many of them made by Nikon.

So let's say that our hypothetical new photographer gets really hooked and replaces his D50 with a top-of-the-line Nikon digital SLR. Great. But where does he go from there?

Well, you could say that he doesn't need to go anywhere: his Nikon will do all that most photographers ever need, so all he has to do is concentrate on becoming a better photographer. And for many photographers, this could be the simple truth.

Except, of course, that the finest camera in the world, no matter how you define it, isn't necessarily the best camera for shooting absolutely everything. Our new enthusiast might start to notice the work of Sebastiao Salgado and decide that he needs a small, light rangefinder camera with top-flight interchangeable lenses. If he wants to stick with digital, at least until the long-awaited Leica Digital-M comes to fruition, he has a choice of precisely one camera, the Epson. If he's willing to switch to silver halide, there's Leica, Voigtlander, Rollei and Zeiss Ikon on the new market, and a whole lot more second-hand.

Or he might fall under the spell of Ansel Adams, and decide that he wants a large-format camera. Well, it's true that there are some first-class large-format scanning backs around, but they are hardly convenient, and the prices defy belief. Once again, silver halide starts to look like the only option.

For that matter, he might simply decide that he wants a bit more quality than current 35mm-style digital SLRs can muster, and decide to move up to a 22-megapixel (or higher) Hasselblad. Once again, though, he is going to have to find some serious money if he wants to do this: several times as much as the price of a rollfilm camera. There's not many as can afford this option.

The question therefore becomes, will digital become a gateway or a dead end? The latter would be all too easy, especially if the fundamentalists in the digital camp have their way, the ones who are the equivalent of American TV evangelists or the less appetizing variety of Waha'abite mullah. Because they, in their blinkered certainty, are happy with digital cameras, they genuinely cannot see that other people may prefer something else; they believe it to be their holy duty not only to educate the infidel, but to stone him if he strays from their personal view of the path of righteousness, and of course to smash the false idols he constructs from silver halide.

A gateway is a much nicer idea, and to this end, I've actually become something of a booster for mid-range digital cameras. Digital is quick'n'easy (or it looks it); it's not very expensive; and it should immediately offer the opportunity of better results to the photographer who aspires to something beyond a snapshot.

Once you've got them hooked, of course, you start showing them other kinds of photography. Ernst Haas.

Margaret Bourke-White. Shinzo Maeda. Raghubir Singh. Yes, and Ansel Adams and Henri Cartier-Bresson and Julia Margaret Cameron and even (God help us all) David Hamilton.

They start wondering: how can they aspire to this sort of thing? You explain to them that yes, you can replicate an awful lot of it with digital. But some of it is in the process, in the camera. You use different cameras in different ways: the camera you choose influences the way you see.

From there, it's a short step to silver halide. Not necessarily as a replacement for digital, just as digital has not replaced silver halide for me, but as another tool to use alongside it. Train the photographer first - and that's easiest with digital - and worry about the technique second. Because if they're any good, sooner or later they will start worrying about technique. Then the gateway opens.

The Comfort Zone

Old wine is the best to drink, old horses are easiest to ride and old friends are the best friends. I forget which of the ancient Roman writers said this, but most of us would agree with him. The question is, how old does a camera have to be to fall into the same 'comfort zone'?

Although it is wonderful to take a new camera out of the box for the first time, it's also a bit nerve-wracking. Have you spent your money wisely? Are you confident you can actually use it? And there's always the worry about the first scratch or scuff. Until you have got over all this, you can't get into the comfort zone. So how do you speed the process?

The first thing to do is to think hard about what you really want. My advice has been the same for years. Don't buy anything unless you know (or believe on good grounds) that it will either improve your photography or shake you out of whatever photographic rut you may have fallen into.

What will a new camera do that your current one won't, after all? Trading a consumer-end Canon against a consumer-end Nikon is very unlikely to make much difference. Upgrading to a pro-grade Nikon or Canon may. Changing from a reflex to a rangefinder will certainly get you out of your rut, as will changing formats, though it may or may not improve your photography. Whatever the answer, when you unwrap that new camera, you need to have a pretty good idea why you spent all that money.

This is not the same as being able to afford it. I well remember my first new Leica lens, a 35/1.4 Summilux. I couldn't really afford it: I was badly stretched. But from the moment I bought it (and I'm still using it) I knew it was one of the best investments I had ever made in my own photography.

The next trick is to avoid babying your new camera. Don't spend so much time worrying about it that it distracts you from taking pictures. I find that the easiest way to do this is to take it out alongside an older camera that has already had the shine taken off it. Then I treat both cameras identically.

Of course, if you really are too worried, just don't use it. That's what I did with my last Leica IIIg, which I bought in the 1980s, mint and boxed. The first (and only) time I took it out shooting, I was so worried about marking it that after half a roll I went home and picked up an old Nikon F instead. This advice isn't much use for new cameras, except to say that if you really can't afford a camera that will get worn when you start using it, don't buy it.

Learning to use the thing is another matter. If you keep chopping and changing, you'll spend far more time learning how to use today's super-complicated cameras than you will taking pictures. How do you shorten the learning curve?

Well, how good are you with instruction books? For some, reading and re-reading the instruction book, and just playing with a new camera, is part of the pleasure. Not for me. I want to use something new, be it tool or toy, as soon as I get it. I still don't understand all the functions on my Nikon D70. The day before I wrote this I even had to consult the instruction book to remind myself how to set a custom white balance. If you're not a natural instruction book reader, the only way you are going to learn to use the camera is by taking pictures, referring to the book when you have to.

This means that you need to take a lot of pictures, or you'll still spend more time checking the book than taking photographs. I don't know how many hundred or (more likely) how many thousand pictures I've taken with the D70, but I do know that most of what I want to do with it, I can now do without the instruction book. But if you aren't going to take a lot of pictures, don't buy a complicated camera. It will take too long before using it becomes second nature.

Think hard about all this before you lay out your hard-earned money, and the comfort zone will be there before you know it. Fail to address these questions, or give yourself dishonest answers, and you'll never get there. Then you'll find yourself unwrapping another new camera, wondering if you've spent your money wisely, wasting time trying to figure out how to use it, and worrying about scratching up your latest acquisition.

Landscape Photography Is Boring !

Landscape photography is boring. David Hockney told the world this when he was interviewed by the BBC Home Service (all right, Radio 4) in November 2005 at the launch of his exhibition of water-colours at Somerset House. Painting, he said, is much more interesting.

His extraordinary generalization fairly took my breath away. It is probably as well to leave aside the quality of his own paintings (and indeed photographs). Some like his work; others don't. I find some of it quite pleasant, and some of it, yes, boring. Certainly I can think of half a dozen landscape photographers whose work I would rather have on my walls than most of his output. His dismissal of rather over 160 years of the work of many of the finest photographers in the world seemed to me rather odd.

Then it occurred to me: perhaps he wasn't talking about the result, the final pictures, but the process. It's not the pictures that he finds boring: it's the process of taking them. Unfortunately this is even more insupportable.

Landscapes are, after all, one of the most popular subjects for photography: arguably the most popular, bar none. People love to take pictures of mountains, lakes, woods, valleys: you name it, if it's a landscape, they'll shoot it. In doing so they give the lie to one or other interpretation of Hockney's assertion. Even if the pictures they take are boring, and let's be honest, we've all taken boring landscapes at times, the process isn't.

This is something I've been thinking about more and more. Why do we do anything? Not the things we have to do, like earning a living and keeping the house waterproof, but the things we don't have to do? After all, for most of us, this includes photography.

In fact, it probably includes photography for all of us. Even if you earn your living as a photographer, there is probably something else you could do. I could have stuck with the law, or schoolteaching, or even (God forbid!) accountancy. But I prefer photography. Why?

Well, it's easier than a proper job, isn't it? I mean, it's much easier to stay at a filthy village inn in rural China, and to get up well before dawn to walk for an hour and a half to see the sun rise by the Great Wall than it is to be at Bishop Road Secondary School by twenty to nine. On second thoughts, maybe that wasn't such a good example.

The simple truth is that all in all, we take photographs (or indeed paint water-colours) because we enjoy doing it. We may not enjoy every aspect of it, all the time, but if on balance the pleasure were not a good deal greater than the pain, we wouldn't do it.

What, then, do we enjoy? I can think of at least seven things.

First, we enjoy being creative. This seems to be something that is hard-wired into the human brain (or perhaps soul). As William Mortensen pointed out, we are all like small children saying "Look what I've done!"

Second, we enjoy (if we are lucky, and skilled enough) the results. If you look at the 'Diary' section of www.rogerandfrances.com, you'll see one of the pictures that my wife Frances Schultz took that morning at the Great Wall.

Third, there is an inherent pleasure in mastering any craft, and a justifiable pride in that mastery. Even if we haven't mastered it yet -- and it's disputable whether any of us ever masters it fully -- there's the pleasure of learning and getting better.

Fourth, we're actually doing something: getting off our backsides instead of staring at the goggle-box or reading the latest load of alarmist drivel in the newspaper. Or indeed listening to David Hockney on the wireless.

Fifth, photographing landscapes gives us a first-class excuse to seek out beautiful places, ideally at the most beautiful times of day.

Sixth, it's a welcome break from what most of us do, most of the time. We get out in the fresh air and take a bit of exercise. Not a bad idea.

Seventh, even if the final picture is indeed boring, it can still be an excellent souvenir of a time we were enjoying ourselves. We can be sitting and marking essays by 3b, or wondering whether the audit evidence of treating capital as income is sufficient to justify qualifying the accounts, when our eye falls upon the picture and we think, yes, this is why I do what I do.

I'm sorry, David. I don't find any of this boring.

Magret de Canard

When I began this piece, I had just finished Sunday dinner. Magret de canard with roast potatoes, roast courgettes and roast garlic. A 'magret' is the lean part of a fat animal, in this case, one large duck breast, scored, salted and grilled. Grill the upper (skin) side first, then the other side. It's something we eat quite often, perhaps three times a month, especially when duck is on sale.

It's always good, but this time it was even better than usual. Everything came out right. The duck was outstanding: crispy skin, juicy, tender meat. The potatoes were unusually good, too: crispy-crunchy on the outside, floury-soft on the inside. And the garlic, whole cloves roasted unpeeled alongside the potatoes and sliced courgettes, was classic: butter-soft inside its papery skin.

In between the various chores of preparing dinner, my wife Frances Schultz was printing black-and-white pictures as well. Over the course of the day she printed about ten of hers and a couple of mine. Two of hers were outstanding: the Chateau d'Eau at Mazeuil and the greenhouse at the 19th century chateau at Bressuire. Again, everything came out right.

Which reminded me, not for the first time, how close cookery is to photography. There are certain levels of competence. You know that if some of your friends invite you to dinner, you will eat well, while others you go to see more for the friendship than the food. Likewise you know that if some of your friends invite you to look at their latest pictures, it will be enjoyable, while others are at best clumsy acolytes in the great temple of the visual image: patience, grasshopper.

Now, there are two measures of how good you are at either cooking or photography. One is how often you do a good job. The other is how often you do a superb job.

I don't believe that anyone does a superb job all the time. Even such geniuses as Aleksandr Rodchenko and Edward Weston produced the occasional lemon. So did Roger Fenton, Julia Margaret Cameron and Margaret Bourke-White. The same must be true of cooks. I've never had the money to eat at a Michelin three-star restaurant, but I can't believe that the standard is absolutely consistent from day to day. It can't be. Some days have to be better than others.

But the more often you do a good job, the higher your standards rise when it comes to defining a superb job. Quite honestly, my wife and I are good enough cooks that our standards of excellence are very high indeed -- and I think the same is true of our photography. We don't always reach that standard of excellence, but at least we know it exists.

And, I believe, the skills required in both photography and cookery are very similar. There's craftsmanship, and experience, and luck, and, yes, art. If you are too much of an Artist, and disdain craft, your souffles will fall and your prints will lack tonality. If you are too much of a rule-follower, too afraid of Art, your food may well be edible but it will never be inspired.

A baker has to know when a cake is ready: you can't rely on time and temperature. It's smell and sound and colour and maybe even a sixth sense: you just know it's done. The same must apply to knowing what a picture needs: what to do, and (at least as important) when to stop. It's composition and sharpness and colour and tone and shape and yes, another unnamed sense -- a seventh sense, maybe.

Actually, there are a lot more senses than just seven. How about the sense that tells you that you are near something, even in pitch darkness? Or the sense that tells you that someone is looking at you? Don't tell me that these senses can't be counted because they aren't reliable. No sense is fully reliable. How often have you failed to see something, even though it is right in front of you? How often have you misheard something?

I'm not trying to come over all mystical and neo-mediaeval here: I have too high a regard for science, technology and medicine to do that. But what I am saying is that once we have mastered (at least sufficiently) the logical, mechanical, technical side of things, then it's time to follow your hunches and instincts and whims and 'what-ifs', because that's where success lies. Not everyday success, mere competence, but real success, artistry. Oh, yes; and have faith in luck, as well. The green-eyed goddess does not always smile upon you, and she notoriously never answers prayers; but if you don't believe in her, she may never help you at all.

Pastures of Plenty

Christmas is often the season of excess. We eat too much, drink too much, and surround ourselves with yet more material goods. We can very easily have too much of too many good things.

An interesting (but completely different) example of excess came up on my recent trip to China. According to my Guide Routard, Chinese emperors of the Qing dynasty (1644-1911) were entitled to one empress (huanghou); two secondary wives (shufei); four imperial concubines (guifei); six concubines of the fourth rank (fei); several more concubines of the fifth rank (ping); and an unlimited number of other concubines (guiren).

Not only was the last category unlimited; its ranks were regularly replenished with beautiful Manchu and Mongolian girls aged 13 to 15. Many were returned to their families at 18, with a small retirement gratuity, unless they had earned seniority by bearing children (especially sons). At least, this was the case under Emperor Kangxi (1662-1722). Before that, things were even more complicated: the Ming dynasty (1368 to 1644) had no fewer than 12 ranks of wives and concubines.

Most men must have wondered at least occasionally about being surrounded with such pastures of plenty; but how many have come to the conclusion that possibly, it might all be more trouble than it is worth? After all, constant distraction - and few men could fail to be distracted by a limitless supply of beautiful teenagers - is hardly conducive to a mature, intelligent and considered approach to anything. This may help explain why China has so often been so appallingly governed.

It is of course all too easy to overstretch the parallels between a harem and a camera collection, and indeed, there are those who would say that such a comparison is inherently shameful: a camera is a thing and a woman is a person. But the very nature of Chinese politics has generally been to treat people as things. After all, Mao himself said that China was not afraid to lose a million people in a war, presumably because he was reasonably confident that he would not be one of them.

A rather more cogent argument is that you don't actually get 'new and improved' people, just younger ones. Many men do indeed swap ageing wives for younger models, but this is rather different from my preferring my Leica MP to my Leica M4-P: no matter how much we may become attached to it, a camera is indeed just a thing, and when a better thing comes along, there is no reason not to switch to it - provided we can afford it and provided it is in fact demonstrably better.

The important point in both cases, the women and the cameras, is the question of distraction. No-one is perfect (though my wife comes close) and it must surely be tempting simply to switch to another wife or concubine when difficulties arise, whether the fault is theirs or yours. Of course, as Emperor, you are never wrong, so it's always their fault.

It must also be that you never really get to learn enough about one woman or one camera. You're like a spoiled child in a sweet-shop, unable to decide what you want. Again, you can't draw the parallels too close, but equally, they are not as far apart as you might think.

Much of the pleasure of travelling, as far as I am concerned, is that I travel with my wife. We share the good times, which more than doubles the pleasure, and when things go wrong, we have each other, which greatly reduces the pain. I don't think I deceive myself when I say that this sounds better in the long term than the company of a bevy of teenage beauties whom I hardly know. I accept, of course, that I may be making a virtue out of necessity.

Likewise, the pleasure of taking pictures is heavily tied up with using cameras and films that I know and like, and in which I have confidence. Give me my Leica MP, some Ilford

HP5 and some Kodak EBX, and I am happy. Give me a 'bridge' digicam and I might not bother to take any pictures at all. I might not even bother to travel at all: like my friend and mentor, the late Colin Glanfield, if I can't take my camera, I'm not sure I want to go.

What I'm saying, in a way, is no more than 'count your blessings'. But what I'd add to this is perhaps more important. Think hard about what your blessings are, and about whether the things you think you want would really be better than what you have. To quote another old saying, be careful what you pray for, for you will surely get it.

Jamming...

Those of a nervous disposition are heartily encouraged to read a recent paper, "Preventing Camera Recording by Designing a Capture-Resistant Environment" by Khai N. Truong, Shwetak N. Patel, Jay W. Summet and Gregory D. Abord of the College of Computing and GVU, Georgia Institute of Technology. It appears on pages 73 to 86 the Proceedings of the 7th International Conference in Ubiquitous Computing (UBICOMP -- I am not making this up) held in Tokyo on the 1st to the 14th of September 2005.

The basic premise is fascinating: that camera phones are now so ubiquitous that they present a significant security concern for organizations and individuals. I am indebted to the same paper for the statistic that 75 per cent of mobile telephones sold in Japan in the last quarter of 2004 incorporated cameras, and that the market in Japan was expected to reach saturation at 75-85 per cent in 2005.

Messrs. Truong, Patel, Summet and Abord (hereafter TPSA) suggest that as camera-phone users are unlikely to voluntarily adopt hardware/software solutions that stop them taking pictures wherever they wish, some mechanism is needed for 'jamming' camera phones. It is hard to summarise a 14-page learned paper in a few words, but basically, what they propose is a mechanism that detects the very high retroreflectivity of CMOS and CCD chips in camera phones and non-reflex digital cameras, then fires pulsed light at them so that they can't take pictures. By way of refinement, the pulsed light is designed to have the minimum possible impact on human eyes, which is (a) jolly sporting and (b) a good way of avoiding lawsuits.

Do not deduce from the last sentence that I wish to mock Messrs. TPSA. Few things could be further from the truth. I am fascinated by their ingenuity and rigour -- and also by their assumption that if you can in one way or another knock out camera phones, it makes a significant difference to clandestine photography as undertaken by anyone other than the rankest beginner.

Because, after all, clandestine photography is neither new nor difficult. One of the most notorious shots was Tom Howard's photograph of the judicial electrocution of Ruth Snyder at 11:06 pm on January 12th 1928, for which he used a camera strapped to his ankle. The picture ran in the next day's Daily News and they sold half a million extra copies.

Stop and think about this for a moment. First of all, there is the moral question of selling half a million extra papers by portraying someone's death, though in all fairness Rainey Bethea was the last person to be publicly executed in the United States, on August 14th 1936 in Owensboro, Kentucky. As the execution attracted a crowd of 20,000, perhaps we shouldn't be too hard on those 'barbaric' regimes who still hold public executions more than 50 years later. It's cheap; it's a crowd pleaser; and among many, it's a vote winner.

More to the immediate point, let us return to the logistics of shooting clandestine pictures in places where control is a lot tighter than (for example) a company boardroom, shopping mall or night-club. Tom took his picture more than three-quarters of a century ago, using a relatively large metal camera. Today I'd cheerfully bet on the ability of my Chadt to evade detection, because it's smaller than a matchbox and almost all plastic.

All right, the Chadt wasn't a commercial success, but I'd be astonished if this little Minox-format (8x11mm on 9.5mm) camera had not been stockpiled by Intelligence agencies prior to its demise. After all, to this day, the TLR Tessina (14x21mm on 35mm in special cassettes) enjoys considerable popularity among Intelligence services. For that matter, as an aside, a friend of mine in British Intelligence once stole some American classified documents during the closing days of World War Two; photographed them with a Rollei TLR; and then returned them to the safe, stamped 'Seen and Approved'. That's another story.

In other words, clandestine photography depends on two things. One is the skill and daring of the operative. The other is a knowledge of the technology available.

So here, in the spirit of Jonathan Swift, is a Modest Proposal. Those who profit from it by selling their pictures to the gutter press may, if they wish, slip me a plain brown envelope with a percentage of their ill-gotten gains: 25 per cent seems reasonable to me.

Any venue that wallows in a false sense of security generated by TPSA anti-camera-phone technology can easily be photographed either with a digital SLR (the mirror masks the sensor) or indeed just about any silver halide camera that is not equipped with the sort of flash that cannot be turned off. That's it. Thank you and goodbye.

Zoom, Zoom, Zoom !

Few would deny the unparalleled convenience of zoom lenses; but equally few, I suspect, have much idea of just what they sacrifice in return for that convenience.

Normally, I would begin an attack on zooms with the obvious technical arguments: lower resolution, lower sharpness, lower contrast. Then I'd move on to lower speed, extra weight and (if you want decent quality) higher cost. But lately, I've been thinking that there are even more pressing arguments: poor composition and poor lighting.

This may seem bizarre. How can composition or lighting be affected by whether you use a zoom or a prime lens? Surely, that's down to the skill of the photographer.

Well, yes - sort of. But put yourself in the real world. Not some other photographer, who may or may not be as experienced as you are, but yourself. Imagine you have a zoom on your camera. You see something you want to photograph; you zoom to the right focal length; you take the picture. Sorted.

Now imagine that you have a prime lens on your camera: as it might be, the 35mm that I regard as the 'standard' focal length on my Voigtlanders. It's too short for the picture you want to take, so you take a few steps towards the subject. As you do so, all sorts of spatial relationships change. Things that were in front of the subject are now to one side. You realize, perhaps, that by moving to the left or right, or squatting down for a lower viewpoint, or climbing onto a bollard for a higher one, you will get a better picture. Would you have done that if you had used the zoom? We all like to say "Of course I would," but who are we kidding? I know that a lot of the time, I wouldn't -- because I don't.

Moving about in the real world also engages you more. This may sound a bit mystical, but I think I can defend it. A camera with a zoom lens is like a TV: it magically delivers different pictures to you, from a single viewpoint. A camera with a prime lens effectively forces you to become a part of what is in front of you: you do not, whether literally or metaphorically, shoot out of the window of the tour bus.

How about lighting? This comes down to another well-known deficiency of zoom lenses: they are slow. A 'standard zoom' is considered fast if it maintains a constant f/2.8 aperture across the entire zoom range. Most deliver something like f/3.5 at one end of the range, and f/5.6 at the other. Compare this with my Voigtlander prime lenses: 28/1.9, 35/1.7 (shortly to be replaced with a 35/1.2), 50/1.5. Admittedly the 90mm is only an f/3.5, but I do have a 90/2 Leitz Summicron if I want the extra speed. And if I felt the need of a 75mm, I could buy an f/2.5 Voigtlander or (at several times the price, it's true) an f/1.4 Leica.

With a slow lens, you often have a simple choice: flash, or camera shake. 'Flash' generally means 'on camera flash', and we all know what that means. Where I'd have to use flash in order to avoid shooting with an f/2.8 zoom at 1/15 second, I can shoot my 50/1.5 Nokton wide open at 1/60.

Let's switch sides for a moment, though. What about the obvious disadvantage of prime lenses, that if one lens is the wrong focal length for a particular picture, you have to waste time changing to another?

If you want an answer to that one, watch an experienced photographer at work with a rangefinder camera. He (or she) just doesn't change lenses much. Instead, he (or she) contrives to be in the right place to frame the picture with the lens on the camera, whether it is 28mm, 35mm, 50mm or whatever. The concept of a 'favourite lens', or to be more accurate, a favourite focal length, is much more germane to the user of fixed focal lengths than to the zoom user.

There's also the truth that with a prime lens, it's a single action: focus, shoot. With an autofocus camera, you don't even have to focus. But with a zoom, although you don't have to change the focal length, you normally do, so it's zoom, focus, shoot. Which is quicker?

Actually, the whole concept of 'fast handling' is something I want to explore in another column, so I'll finish here with a quick recitation of the other defects of zooms as compared with prime lenses.

First, they do not have the resolution or sharpness. It is true that thanks to modern computer-aided design, today's very finest zoom lenses are capable of astonishingly good results. But, of course, exactly the same optimization programs can be run on prime lenses. The improvements in performance may not be as great as in zooms, but the very finest prime lenses are (unsurprisingly) still better than the very finest zooms.

Second, they do not have the contrast. Even the cleverest multi-coating cannot eliminate flare altogether, and simpler lenses are always contrastier than more complex ones.

Third, they are heavy, unless they are very slow indeed.

Fourth, and perhaps most tellingly, most people don't use the very finest zooms, partly because they are too big and heavy, but mostly because they can't afford them. And make no mistake: while today's modestly-priced zooms are infinitely superior to many of the best zooms of the past, they still can't hold a candle even to modestly priced prime lenses. As far as I'm concerned, it isn't even a contest.

As an illustration, please take a look at the photograph of the bicycles on page __ Try and shoot this hand-held with a zoom! I used a 35/1.7 Ultron on my Voigtlander Bessa-R, with Ilford HP5 Plus at a true ISO 650 in Ilford DD-X developer. With even an f/2.8 zoom, I'd have needed EI 2000 to shoot at the same shutter speed, and the highest true ISO you can get from a B+W film is 1250 (Ilford Delta 3200 in DD-X or similar). With an f/4.5 zoom I'd be out to EI 5000...

A Matter of Perspective

Perspective, say many people who should know better, is governed solely by viewpoint. It doesn't matter what focal length you use: all that matters is where you stand.

If you point out to them that this is arrant nonsense, citing the way in which ultra-wides 'stretch' perspective and long teles compress it -- a matter of common experience for all photographers -- they nod sagely and say, "Ah, but that's just apparent perspective."

What is the other sort? Is there some kind of perspective that isn't apparent?

Besides, to a very large extent, perspective is a convention, nothing more, nothing less. How else do you explain the fact that we have no problem with linear perspective on the horizontal plane -- we are perfectly happy to see railway lines converge to a point in a photograph -- but we don't see it the same way in the vertical plane: we don't like the way that buildings look as if they are falling over backwards. Photographers use 'perspective correction' lenses (actually, of course, perspective distortion lenses) and painters just ignore vertical perspective: they paint the sides of buildings parallel because that's the way they know they are.

Insofar as you can say anything very meaningful about linear perspective, it's a question of the angle subtended at the eye. Thus, for example, if you extend your arm and make a 'thumbs up' gesture, your thumb will subtend about the same angle as someone's head a couple of metres away.

We deduce perspective, depth and distance from the relationships between apparent sizes (angles subtended) and a host of other visual clues such as position (if A obscures B, we assume it is in front of B), atmospheric haze, and the feedback to our brains from the focusing and convergence of our eyes. Oh; and from the rate of convergence of lines that we know (or believe) to be parallel.

If, in a photograph, a reasonable number of these clues add up the same way they do in real life, then the perspective photograph seems natural and realistic. If they don't, we can immediately tell that a wide-angle or tele lens was used. We can accept quite a wide range as 'natural' before the perspective starts to look wrong, but equally, there is quite a small range that looks really three-dimensional.

You can often show this quite quickly and easily by choosing pretty much any picture in a book or magazine, provided it's a decent size -- half a page or more -- and examining it at a wide range of viewing distances, from as close as you can focus (with glasses, if you need them) to arm's length or beyond. Surprisingly often, it will appear uniquely three dimensional at just one distance. It will hold that three-dimensionality only over a shallow range, especially if you look away and then look back again after moving it.

Many photographers believe that a 50mm lens (on a 35mm camera) gives more natural perspective than any other, but because so much depends on print size and viewing distance, this is very disputable. Fortunately, the mathematics are quite simple.

Let's begin with the print. Let's assume a 20x30cm (8x12 inch) image, simply because that's the proportions of 35mm: it would be a bit over an 8x blow up. Pythagoras tells us that the diagonal of the print is 36cm or just over 14 inches.

Now let's assume a viewing distance of 50cm (19 inches). It's quite a big print, so this is a fair assumption. The angle subtended by the diagonal of the print is about 40 degrees. Calculate this by dividing 18 (half the diagonal) by 50 (the viewing distance) to get 0.36. A tangent, you will recall, is obtained by dividing the opposite side of a right-angled triangle into the length of the adjacent side: the angle corresponding to 0.36 is 19.8 degrees. Double this to get the full diagonal: 39.6 degrees, or near enough 40.

Shoot with a lens that covers this angle on the diagonal, and anything in the picture will subtend roughly the same angle, at the eye, as the subjects in the original scene -- which will be a pretty powerful perspective clue. On 35mm, the focal length required would be 60mm -- so the old 58mm 'long standard' would work very well. On 6x9cm, you'd need 140mm: a 135mm would work quite nicely. Calculate this by dividing half the negative diagonal (21.6mm for 35mm, 50.5mm for 6x9cm) by the tangent of the half-angle (tan 19.6 degrees = 0.356).

Now look at the print more closely: just 25cm away, 10 inches. Now, for the same definition of perspective - things in the print subtending the same angle as in real life - you'd need a lens that covers 71.5 degrees on the diagonal. With 35mm, that's near enough 30mm; with 6x9cm, 70mm. Halve the viewing distance, and you halve the necessary focal length, too.

You can calculate the rest yourself, and quite instructive it is. A stand-offish portrait, to be examined at a metre (39.4 inches) would look best with something like a 105mm lens on 35mm, or 150mm on roll-film: precisely the focal lengths so often recommended for portraiture. Or if you are doing big prints for in-your-face reportage -- prints a metre across, let's say, but still examined from only half a metre away -- and you need a lens that covers about 65 degrees. What a coincidence: that's a 35mm on 35mm.

As my dear old physics master used to say, Science Works!

World Wide Waffle

The World Wide Web is, without doubt, an incredible respository of information. The trouble is, an awful lot of it -- probably the vast majority -- is completely useless.

The problem isn't the manufacturers' sites. It's true that these contain errors, but they are usually insignificant: sorry, Kodak, but Tri-X wasn't introduced in 1954. Much more of a problem is a combination of the drivel put up by people who can barely read and write, and blind acceptance of that drivel by people who should know better.

Why, after all, do you read AP, or books on photography? Because there's a fair chance that the people who write them have a modest idea of what they are talking about. This is not the case on the web. You can't tell. Blithering idiots have the same right to publish as people who are world authorities on their subjects.

In scientific journals, there's something called 'peer review'. Basically, this means that you put your ideas up in front of other people in the same field. If the ideas are sound, your reputation grows. If you are a raving loony, it declines. All right, at AP we don't pretend to be a learned journal, but most of us have a pretty good idea of what we are talking about. If it's complete rubbish, we don't usually print it.

The trouble with the Web is that peer review is indeed carried out. The work of the terminally ignorant is reviewed (and often blindly copied) by others who are equally ignorant. Sometimes, this is downright dangerous: I certainly wouldn't treat pyrogallol with the insouciance that some people do, let alone assert that it's less dangerous than metol.

But inaccurate information on the web isn't the worst of it. What is really depressing is the vicious infighting that you see, with the most ignorant and least informed often fighting their corners hardest. Those who partially understand the Zone System are among the worst. Others latch onto concepts such as ISO speed, telling you that films 'really' have lower ISO speeds than the manufacturers say. Yet other discuss acutance in pseudo-learned fashion, talking about how to get more acutance from patently nonsensical film-developer combinations. You soon feel like screaming "Buy an acutance developer, stupid -- but first, find out what 'acutance' means."

Almost as bad are those who know a little and are therefore accounted 'experts' by a small circle of friends. They assume that they know it all, or at least, that they know more than anyone they are likely to encounter. Argue with them at your peril: I was once told, "You do not know how little you know." Actually I have a pretty good idea of how little I know, because I have met quite a number of people who know a lot more than I, and who have (as a result) achieved high regard and sometimes high office in the photographic industry. Needless to say, my critic was not among them.

Another basic problem with the Web is those who refuse to read conventional books and magazines; tho tu judg from there speling i dont think that sum of them coud reed books enyway. There may be no such thing as a stupid question, but there are certainly some remarkably stupid people asking sensible questions. There are also some questions that regardless of their originators' literacy and intelligence are somewhat puzzling. I mean, would you buy a 4x5 inch technical camera without learning how to pull out the front standard so that you could see the image on the ground-glass? A few seconds' advice from the person who sold you the camera, or a glance at a book on large format photography, might at least give you some idea how to start answering your own question.

And that, perhaps, is the most besetting problem: people who want to be told everything, but don't want to believe the instruction sheets, or to make simple tests for themselves. "What development time should I use for Ilford Delta 3200 at EI 3200 in Ilford DD-X?" The instruction sheets for either would tell them. But they don't want to do that. They don't trust the manufacturers, and they are too lazy or stupid to test the film for themselves. Instead, they ask someone else what they have done, completely ignoring the fact that this is almost certainly a less reliable good starting point than the manufacturer's guidelines.

The depressing thing is, they get answers. And they get them from people who think they know better than the manufacturers; who say, in fact, that the manufacturers deliberately lie about everything from the speed of films to the composition of developers. Where do you begin to correct their errors? Not on line, for a start. Try AP instead. Or a good book.

The Child's Rattle

Our tastes greatly alter. The lad does not care for the child's rattle, and the old man does not care for the young man's whore.

Dr. Johnson said that in 1766. He is as right today as he was then. But how does this work itself out among photographers? Certes, I am not the same photographer as I was in 1966 when my father bought me a two-year-old Pentax SV. Are there any generalizations that can be drawn from my own experiences, and from those of other photographers with whom I have grown older?

Perhaps, perhaps not. One is that reportage is a young man's game. Sticking your camera in someone's face gets harder as you get older. In my teens and twenties, I can remember running from angry tramps. Today, I think maybe they were right to complain. What right had I to steal a picture? Not to ask, to give them half a crown for a bottle of cider, to exchange a few words, but to treat them purely and simply as subjects -- objects, even -- to be photographed?

But the world has changed as well. Many of today's readers won't even know what half a crown is, for a start. For the record, it's 12-1/2 pence, one-eighth of a pound, or about 18 centimes in euros. Mere financial reform is however as nothing as compared to the change in the moral climate.

Maybe 25 years ago, I was taking pictures at Christmas Steps in Bristol: architectural shots and details mostly. Three girls drifted by. They were fourteen or fifteen years old. They asked me what I was doing. I told them. They said, "Photograph us instead!"

No problem. They were kids at a loose end; I was a photographer at a loose end. One of the pictures from that day amuses me still. There were three niches in the wall, the sort that normally house statues of saints. They were empty. The three girls squatted, one in each, as the Three Monkeys:

see no evil, hear no evil, speak no evil, hands over eyes, ears, mouth.

Today, they probably wouldn't ask me; they'd be too frightened. And I probably wouldn't have taken the pictures: I'd be too frightened. And if I had taken the pictures, there would have been some busybody rushing to the police at Bridewell to report a Suspicious Photographer.

Or to go back to the tramps, when I was a young photographer, there weren't many of them, and they resembled the tramps that Orwell described in 'Down and Out in London and Paris' in the 1930s. We didn't have 'street people' in those days: we had tramps in cracked boots and greasy raincoats tied with string. 'Street people' are a lot easier to get on with, and generally smell a good deal better, but tend to be less picturesque. Now, I give them a pound coin - it's worth less than half a crown, anyway - but I don't usually take their pictures. Which has changed most. Society? Or them? Or me?

Then there's equipment. By the time I took up photography, colour was well enough established that only the oldest of old fogies maintained that it wasn't 'real' photography. But through-lens metering was recent enough that plenty of photographers still maintained that it couldn't compete with a 'real' hand-held meter. Well, it isn't as good as an incident-light meter, or a spot meter, but it's a lot easier to use, and ease of use counts for a lot.

Today there's digital. I don't like it. Why not? Is it because I'm an old fogey? Or is it because I don't have the money to waste on cameras that deliver inferior quality to a 30-year-old Nikkormat and go out of date (and plummet in value) in 18 months?

Or is it just that digital is just the latest in a line of crazes that has existed ever since photography started? In the 1920s, there were lots of books and magazine articles on enlarging. In the 1930s, the novelties were flash bulbs and miniature cameras. In the 1950s, it was colour: monochrome, the pundits cried, would soon be dead. Then came through-lens metering and autofocus.

Every innovation, we were regularly assured, would sweep away the old order utterly. It never has. This, perhaps, is the most valuable lesson that an ever-lengthening perspective has taught me. For example, I would cheerfully bet that there are more people shooting 4x5 inch and above for pleasure today than ever before. It's just that there are even more people shooting 35mm. The 35mm users assume that larger formats are irrelevant, and the digital people assume that film is irrelevant. But the lad does not care for the child's rattle, and the old man does not care for the young man's whore.

Grey Days ? No Thanks !

How often have you read these assertions: "You can't get decent pictures when the sun is overhead" and "Overcast days are often better for photography than bright sunny ones"?

Do you believe them? I don't. Maybe you get better pictures on overcast days. I don't. Yes, I can shoot on overcast days, and I can get good pictures. But I'll enjoy myself more, and most of the time I'll get better pictures, on sunny days -- especially if there are big, puffy white clouds in a deep blue sky. As for not shooting around noon, I'd agree that it's often easier to get good pictures when the light is low and slanting; but I have also taken some of my best pictures (not many, but a few) when the sun is high in the sky.

I reckon I have a pretty fair base for comparison. In the last twenty years, I've lived in Bristol; in California; on the Kent coast (at Minnis Bay, reputedly the sunniest spot in the British Isles, though lots of places make that claim); and in France, south of the Loire, where I live now. I've also spent a lot of time, several months in total in some cases, in India, Malta, Greece, Portugal, Florida and Alabama, plus shorter periods in several other countries and states. Without exception, I'm happier (and I usually get better pictures) when it's sunny.

To a considerable extent, it's true, this is because of the kind of pictures I take. I don't normally shoot outdoor portraits or nudes, where overly bright sun can cause the subjects to screw up their eyes unattractively. And I don't shoot certain kinds of flora or fauna that are at their best when out of the sun. But equally, I'd suggest that there are a lot more photographers like me, who prefer sun and get better results in sunlight, than there are who do better on overcast days.

Now, it may be that I am unusually thin-skinned and lacking in self-confidence, but whenever I read a statement such as 'overcast days are the best for shooting', I start to feel uncomfortable. I know that I don't much like shooting on such days; I know that I get relatively few good pictures on such days; and I can usually see that the people who are making these assertions are backing up their claims with first-class pictures. I begin to wonder, therefore, if I'm doing something wrong; about whether I'd be a better photographer if I took their advice.

What I don't do -- and this is stupid -- is look at all the really superb pictures taken in bright sunlight. Plenty are published every week in AP, quite apart from the pictures in the hundreds of books that I own on photography. Clearly, overcast days aren't best for all kinds of photography. They are best for a few kinds of photography, and they are not too bad for several other kinds; but there are quite a lot of subjects for which sunlight is either indispensable, or highly desirable.

Actually, although I described myself a couple of paragraphs back as unusually thin-skinned and lacking in self confidence, it would be more accurate to say that I used to be like that. Nowadays, I increasingly believe that while I may not be right all the time, I am probably wrong less often than most.

I make this seemingly immodest assertion on simple grounds. I know what works for me, and I'll tell people how to do the things that work for me, if they want to hear. I also have a pretty good idea of the fundamental theory behind a lot of what I say, so there are rarely any glaring inconsistencies between the methods I advocate and the theory that underlies them. In other words, I do not rely (as surprisingly many people do) on the inherent latitude of pos/neg photography, then make up theories to suit what I do.

But unlike many photographers, I freely accept that there are other ways of doing things. Even things that conflict with fundamental theory can be made to work, such as exposure determination for landscapes via the use of grey cards: most people who do this re-rate the film so slow that it is almost invariably generously exposed, so witless metering doesn't matter. Nor is there any reason why you shouldn't expose black and white prints sequentially through two filters if you find it easier or more intuitive to do things that way, even though there will always be a single filter value and exposure time that would give identical results. Just don't tell me that your way is the only way of doing it, because if you do, you'll be wrong.

Tool Happy

This is bound to raise some sniggers, but there's no other way to phrase it; at least, not easily. The question is this. Why are men so obsessed with their tools?

Vulgar answers aside, you can't deny that it's true. Go into Halfords, or Homebase, or B+Q, or Wickes, or any garden centre. You'll see men caressing power screwdrivers, socket sets, orbital sanders, garden tractors. Often, rather than buying the one tool they actually need, they buy a boxed set: five drills instead of one, half a dozen spanners, a complete tool system. Even when they buy only what they need, they often buy far better than they need: Snap-On where Taiwanese cheapies would be good enough. Overkill is the name of the game.

I don't exempt myself. Admittedly, I do service my own vehicles, and in the last year or so, I've done more D-I-Y than in the rest of my life put together. And with a log fire in rural France, a chain-saw makes sense. But I have to admit that I have probably never used something like one-third of the tools I own. Usually, these are part of a set: I just don't have much use for sockets of 5mm and below, for example, let alone Torx drivers. But a few are things that I bought because I thought I was going to use them, and never have. Some are alarmingly expensive, like my Easy-Outs and tap and die set.

To be fair to myself (and others), there's a certain amount to be said for tools that are bought or kept 'just in case', especially if you don't have to get someone in to do the job for you, or waste half a day trying to find someone that sells the tool you need. I very seldom use my brake hose clamps, for example, but I'm certainly glad I've got them.

Women tend not to be like this. I'm not talking about the ones who come over all girlie and say that they don't understand mechanical things. Unless they are genuinely stupid, this is almost certainly a lie. At best, they mean that they can't be bothered to learn about mechanical things, which is a perfectly legitimate approach. Indeed, if you look at some of the appalling bodges that men hammer together, you might wish that more men were more honest about what they don't understand.

Most reasonably resourceful women will, however, start off by trying to effect a repair with the tools at hand, even if this means a thirty-year-old adjustable spanner with V-shaped jaws, a kitchen knife and a hammer with a loose head. If they see that this isn't going to work, or that they are likely to make the problem worse rather than better, they will either buy the right tool for the job, or get someone else to do it. A man, on the other hand, will look at the job; decide what tools he needs; and then either buy them as soon as possible or use their absence as an excuse for not doing the job at all.

You can see where all this is leading. Cameras. I know quite a lot of very good women photographers. I'm married to one. Very, very few of them are equipment freaks in the same way that most male photographers are.

This doesn't mean that they don't appreciate good kit. If anything, they often appreciate it more than men, and will make greater sacrifices in order to get it. If you see a woman photographer who is using anything more than a happy-snap camera, it is unlikely to be a flavour-of-the-month, heavily advertised multi-mode idiot box. No: this is where you see the Hasselblads, the Nikons, the high-end Canons. Not usually very new, either; or at least, not new for the sake of newness. Once they have a camera they like, women tend to stick with it. If they need another, they buy a second camera body, the same as the first.

Nor do they go for overly stuffed gadget bags. They don't have a full set of Cokin filters, with adapters for every single lens they own. Instead, they have two or three filters that they use all the time -- or no filters at all. And their tripods don't have the geared centre-posts and oversize quick-release plates: that makes them too heavy and too expensive. All a woman normally asks of a tripod is that it should stop her camera wobbling.

Of course, this is all a farrago of wild generalizations. There are plenty of exceptions to the general rules I have just stated. But equally, I suspect that if you have read this far, you will agree that there is a good deal of truth in what I have said. So perhaps it's time for men to let go of their tools and get in touch with their feminine side.

Quality ? Why ?

How much quality do you actually need? Are you fooling yourself? A lot of people pay a lot of money for 'professional' cameras, and then ask no more of them than they would ask of a point-and-shoot. They use them relatively little - a few dozen films a year - and shoot colour negative film, which they have printed at 10x15cm at the local mini-lab or by mail order.

When you buy a 'pro' camera, after all, you are not necessarily paying for extra image quality. You can put the same lenses on a bottom-of-the-line Canon as on top-of-the-line, and lenses are what determine image quality. Nor are you necessarily paying for more versatility: a plain old manual camera is as versatile as anything you can buy, though you may need a bit more skill and foresight than if you rely on one mode for this, another mode for that, and so forth.

What costs the money, as a rule, is durability: the ability to withstand heavy use, and occasional accidental abuse. Some point-and-shoot cameras reputedly have a design life of less than a hundred films: by the time they have had that much film through them, the owner will want something new. A top-quality professional camera might digest a hundred rolls in a month, or even in a week.

The simple truth is that top-quality cameras are hardly ever used hard enough to wear them out. There are exceptions, of course: I have seen Leicas used by beach photographers where the term 'precision instrument' was no longer applicable. A more typical example, though, is one of my old Nikon Fs. It was used for six years in an audio-visual studio, for copying slides. Three or four films a day was nothing unusual, and some days, it was a dozen. I know: I was the assistant who had to shoot them.

When the studio switched to F2s, I bought the F. I'm still using it. I don't expect it will ever wear out. I don't use it as often as I used to, but I must have put around a thousand rolls through it in the last 25 years or so. I think it will stand another few hundred.

So much for durability. What about quality? This was first brought home to me some 25 years ago, when I bought a 9cm collapsible Elmar for my M2 Leica. It was from a reputable dealer, and it looked fine. Then I put a test film through it, and it was completely unacceptable: 8x10 inch prints were just plain soft. I think someone must have had it apart, and not reassembled it properly.

Understandably, I contacted the dealer. "No," they said, "we tested it and it was fine. Before you send it back, let us send you our test pictures."

I was younger and even more foolish in those days, and more easily impressed by people who thought they knew more than I did. Maybe I was doing something wrong. Maybe there was something wrong with my camera, though I couldn't see how, seeing it worked with my other lenses. So I waited.

Their test pictures, when they arrived, were a joke: 4x6 inch (all right, 10x15cm, nowadays) machine colour prints on satin surfaced papers. They were quite miffed when I pointed out that I hadn't bought the thing to take happy-snaps. My pre-war uncoated 9cm f/4 was better than this. They gave me my money back, but you could tell that they thought I was being unreasonably picky.

Since then, I have seen the same sort of mentality time and again. My favourite - which I have now seen or heard of some half a dozen times, at least twice in Internet photo forums - is people who buy some super-de-luxe lens and then complain that they can't see any better quality than they had before. It soon turns out that they are shooting colour print and getting postcard-sized happy snaps made. No wonder they can't see the difference! Even a 3-megapixel digital camera can look as good as a Leica under those conditions.

One of these unfortunates - I think he actually was a new (and disappointed) Leica owner - said that he had asked his friend about this, a friend who knew a thing or two about photography, and the friend had reassured him that the pictures really were better, but the differences were so subtle that only top-flight professionals would be able to see them. Oh boy!

There are countless good reasons to buy top-flight cameras, if you can afford them, and if you are going to use them for anything like serious photography. But if you only shoot happy-snaps; well, maybe you'd be better off with a happy-snap camera.

The Great Leica Debate

Leica's MP seems to have touched raw nerves with all sorts of people, beginning with the usual class warfare and sour grapes: they're snob cameras, they're not worth the money, and so forth. This happens with every Leica when it comes out. If you can't afford one, tough. You may not realize how much we have in common.

Others have claimed that it's 'too retro' and want 'more progress'. Eh? When you get something as right as the original Leica M3, there's no room for anything but refinement of detail: you can't change the concept. Complaining that it's not innovative enough is like complaining that bicycles only have two wheels.

As for the black paint, it's got to be better than the 'black chrome' on my M4-P. This wore so quickly and so badly that a friend of mine, a Leica dealer, couldn't see why I didn't return it under guarantee. Besides, show me someone who doesn't appreciate worn black paint on a top-quality camera, and I'll show you a philistine.

Next, although I feel really sorry for anyone who is too clumsy, uncoordinated or palsied to load a Leica M-series through the base, I can't help feeling if you can't load a Leica it's either stupidity, refusal to learn, or what Lucille Barringer memorably called 'hardening of the categories': the belief that everyone ought to do things the same way. Like many long-term M-series users, I can load a Leica at a dead run, probably quicker and easier than I can load a conventional opening-back camera. And my wife, who has quite a bad 'benign essential tremor' (the medical term for 'shaky hands, but don't worry about it') finds an M4-P no harder to load than her Voigtlander Bessa-T.

The argument that really puzzles me, though, is that the MP is primarily a camera for collectors. It puzzles me because when I first heard about the MP I thought, "At last! A Leica for photographers again!" Handling it only reinforced this belief, especially with the MP/Leicavit style trigger base: once you're used to these (as I am with my Bessa-R2) they are hard to live without. This is the first new Leica I've wanted in decades.

The original (pre-ttl flash) M6 was OK, but had the same flare-prone rangefinder spot as my M4-P, bought new around 20 years ago: enough of a fault that I often use an M2 instead, just because it handles better in poor light. From what little I've seen, the MP addresses this problem: Leica in Germany has promised me a camera for a long-term test. The M6ttl and the M7 are a complete waste of time as far as I am concerned. When you have been using Leicas for decades, the last thing you need is a substantially identical camera where the shutter speed dial goes the wrong way.

What, then, do I have to say to those who object to the MP as an outmoded design with an over-inflated price tag? Well, it's not difficult to counter their arguments.

First of all, if you think it's outmoded, don't buy it. No-one is forcing you. Either a Leica suits the way you work, or it doesn't. There are good photographers in both camps, so don't try to say that no-one but poseurs use Leicas. It's certainly not outmoded from where I'm standing, and there are plenty who will agree with me.

Second, most of the people who are so violently anti-Leica are also anti-rangefinder. They believe in battery-dependent reflexes with autofocus, auto-exposure and the electric thumb. Which is better: apples, oranges or chipmunks?

Third, what do you mean by 'over-priced'? If you just mean that you can't afford one, you can shut up right now. Are Rolls-Royces overpriced? I don't know. On the one occasion I considered buying a second-hand one, I looked at the price of spares and decided that even if I could raise the money to buy it, it would cost too much to run, so I'm not the person to ask about whether they are good value or not. But a friend of mine used to buy a new one every two years, so presumably he reckoned they were good value.

If you mean that it's not worth the price to you, it's the same answer as if you think it's outmoded. Don't buy it. It is worth it to me. As soon as I can find the money.

Fourth and finally, it's always tempting to believe it when someone debunks a legend -- and plenty of people have plenty of reasons to want to debunk the Leica legend. The cameras aren't perfect, because nothing made by man ever is, and it's true that Leica can be arrogant, stupid and insensitive. I'm still rankling from when I bought my first ever new Leica lens, a 35/1.4 Summilux, over 20 years ago. The focusing mount jammed, and Leica said it would take three weeks to fix. After a few choice obscenities, it was replaced by return of post. More recently, a friend of mine queried the delay on the return of his guarantees and was told "Well, it wasn't a very big order." As he'd just spent £10,000, he wasn't very happy. And £98 seems like a lot of money for the rewind crank adapter: I'm hoping that the one off my M2 will go onto the MP. Years ago, there were third-party adapters like this one. I believe there will be again.

For the last few years - since they came out - I've been a huge fan of Voigtlanders. And just as I slowly integrated my Voigtlanders into my Leica outfit, until they all but displaced the Leicas, I can now see integrating an MP into the Voigtlander outfit. I can't see it displacing either my R2 or my wife's T, and quite frankly, I couldn't afford to replace all my Voigtlander lenses with Leica lenses even if I wanted to. But for me, the MP is a photographer's Leica par excellence.

A Healthy Obsession

I used to think that I was obsessive about photography. I enjoy it immensely; I think about it all the time; to a considerable extent I earn my living from it. But the longer I stay in this business, the more true obsessives I meet, and the more I realize that next to them, I hardly care at all.

To begin with, there are the equipment nuts. Should they upgrade their current Nikon to a later model? Or trade it in on a Canon? Or sell the lot and buy a Leica MP? What about medium format? Would they be better off with a small, light Hasselblad, or might a 'baby' Linhof be more versatile, with its substantially bigger usable negative area and camera movements?

I can't see that these questions are hard to answer. If the new Nikon has some feature that they really, really wish their current camera had, then yes, they should trade up. Otherwise, why bother? If they're into low-light reportage, then yes, a Leica MP or possibly a Voigtlander Bessa-R2 would be a better camera than a reflex. And if they need camera movements, yes, the Linhof is a vastly more versatile camera than the Hasselblad, but it's also a lot bulkier and slower to use. How much brain-power does it take to work this out? But of course, many of them don't actally take pictures, which does make it hard to work out what you need.

Weirder still, some of them do take pictures: excellent pictures. Why do they want to change? Answers range from, "Oh, I dunno... " to "I can't help wondering if I'll get better pictures." Tell them that their pictures are excellent, and they say, "Thanks, yeah, but they might be even better." They rarely take it well if you tell them that the best way to get better is to keep taking pictures, and stop worrying about new kit.

This is quite apart from collectors. I used to collect old cameras; I know quite a lot about them; my 'History of the 35mm Still Camera' (Focal Press, 1984, long out of print) is very highly regarded. But I can't get excited about variations in engraving style, or different body covering textures, or all the other minutiae that spur Leica collectors to near-orgasm.

Then there are the darkroom fanatics, usually followers of the Zone System. They spend their whole lives photographing grey cards and refining development times and techniques. Why? Obviously it's better to have a good neg than a bad one. But good negs aren't hard to make -- and if you screw up, you can always re-shoot. In any case, it's better to work with a less-than-perfect neg of a good subject than to have a perfect neg of a grey card.

Many darkroom addicts are given to strange obsessions. I remember one who was convinced that the secret of greater success was a 'dream' thermometer: mercury-in-glass, for speed of response, but heavily armoured (against breakage) and Teflon-coated (for ease of cleaning). "Why does no-one make such a thing," he cried. He was quite miffed when it was pointed out that the armour-plating and the Teflon would be a very successful heat-sink, increasing the response time and decreasing the accuracy, so no thermometer manufacturer in their right mind would consider it.

A sub-set of darkroom obsessives is the 'alternative process' brigade. Calotypes, daguerrotypes, bromoils, salt prints, platinotypes, argentotypes, cyanotypes, you name it. There is no doubt that some of these old processes give marvellous results, quite unlike anything that modern materials can deliver; but there's no point in producing a technically exquisite print if the subject-matter isn't worth looking at. All too many of these people spend so much time coating water-colour paper with peculiar chemicals that they never actually make any decent negatives to print on them.

Yet other photographers put themselves through purgatory to be in the right place at the right time with the right equipment: sleeping on the beach for three days to get the perfect wave at dawn, or trekking miles with huge, heavy large format cameras on their backs, or risking arrest as spies because the viewpoint they want is on military land. You might think that these would be the ones who got the best pictures, and it's true that many of them do get great pictures; but it's also true that many other photographers get equally great pictures, equally often, without subjecting themselves to anything like the same privations.

Another kind of obsessive goes on courses and workshops -- all the time. Maybe there's something to be said for going on the occasional workshop, if it's run by someone you particularly admire and you think you might learn something worthwhile; but most of the workshop groupies I have met will admit that nine times out of ten, the workshops are a disappointment and they learn next to nothing. Why do they go? The camaraderie, say some; others like the way it gives them the chance to meet other photographers. Sounds like they need to get out more.

There are plenty more kinds of obsessives. There are the ones who hang out at the camera store, as if it's a second home. There are the ones who amass monster libraries, which they never read. There are the ones who waste hours in computer chat-rooms, when they could be out taking pictures (or at least working in the darkroom). There are the 'purists' or ritualists for whom the only possible choice is shooting with a Leica M3 and a 50/2 Summicron on Agfa ISO 25 film developed in Rodinal and printed on Ilford Galerie paper developed in Bromophen and then selenium toned for 30 seconds in Fotospeed toner diluted 1+33. Anything else, they explain, is so hopelessly inferior that non-one but an idiot would bother. When any single part of their chain is disrupted one iota, their world falls apart for months. No doubt you can think of more kinds of obsessives. In fact, why are you reading this column? And why did I write it?

Swans And Sunsets

Swans and sunsets: don't knock 'em. Long a by-word for cliched camera club pictures, they suddenly look very good indeed when you stand them next to the vast majority of modern 'Fine Art' photography. Better still, they don't come encumbered with acres of pseudo-intellectual self-justification. They stand or fall as pictures, not as a socio-economic commentary on the dialectic of modernity and tradition in art and society in the 21st century.

If I seem unusually dyspeptic, even by my own demanding standards, it is because I wrote these words shortly after returning from the Rencontres at Arles in the south of France. This is the biggest gathering of 'Fine Art' photography in the world. Oh, dear! Give me the choice of forty pictures of swans and sunsets, or forty pictures of an androgynous Chinese in the nude, where every picture contains an all too visible reminder that despite his otherwise feminine appearance he is fully equipped with the usual masculine appendages, and I'll take the swans and sunsets every time.

For that matter, I don't want to see endless self-portraits by a painter who always wears the same shirt and assumes the same expression each time he takes his picture in front of a finished painting. Possibly his mother might find these shots interesting, but it's hard to imagine that anyone else would.

Besides, swans and sunsets are normally exquisitely printed. Looking at well-made prints is a lot more agreeable than looking at dark, muddy prints or (worse still) at pictures of the sea taken at night, where you can just about make out a line of what might be seaweed one-sixth of the way up an otherwise all-black print. Several photographers at Arles might have been very good, but the prints were so bad that you couldn't really tell. Maybe the dark, muddy prints were meant to be a reflection of the dark, muddy times in which

130

we live, but I don't care. I can draw simple and indeed simplistic parallels for myself: I don't need them rammed down my throat at every opportunity. I'd rather see the same story told in well-made prints.

Now, the thing about Arles, and indeed about a great deal of modern art, is that the pictures are not supposed to reinforce bourgeois concepts of what is and is not pretty (or beautiful, or even attractive, or merely competent) but rather to challenge the onlooker and make him or her think.

Well, they succeeded. I've thought hard, and I've decided that I'd rather see a photograph that conforms to my bourgeois concepts of beauty and photographic quality than a photograph of an ugly or unpleasant subject, badly printed. I have nothing against androgynous Chinese, even in the nude, provided I don't have to look at them. Incidentally, someone said that he was a transvestite, though I'm not sure how you can tell that when someone doesn't have any clothes on. There may be those whose highest ambitions are to study pictures of Chinese persons of unusual sexual leanings, but most people, surely, would prefer swans and sunsets. Or almost anything conventionally beautiful.

This is where I start to get really cynical. The great thing about taking snaps of drugged Chinese transvestites -- sorry, I forgot to mention the drugs before, partly because he wasn't drugged in all the pictures -- is that it's not difficult. You have instant shock value, rather like the three-year-old who screams 'BUM!' at the top of his voice for the pleasure of upsetting his parents. But this is as far from the photography of (say) Bill Brandt or Aleksandr Rodchenko or Margaret Bourke-White as yelling 'BUM!' is from Shakespeare's sonnets or Durrell's Alexandria Quartet.

Swans and sunsets, on the other hand, are surprisingly difficult. That's why this article isn't illustrated with a swan-and-sunset shot: I haven't shot a good one yet. Other difficult subjects include portraits -- there were some stunning portraits at Arles, taken by a Chinese miner of his work-mates as they came off shift -- or still-lifes, or industrial scenes, or landscapes, or architectural shots. To do anything well is difficult, so the majority of photographers whose work was exhibited at Arles didn't even try.

What they produced, instead, was what might be called 'high concept' photography: the sort that illustrates, however badly, a particular idea. For example, how would people react to being photographed with a nude Chinese transvestite? Easy: put a chair next to his, and invite Joe Public (and indeed Joanna Public) onto the stage. And guess what? There was not a single surprise in any one of the miserable snapshots that documented this exercise. Some looked uncomfortable; some tried for shock value; some stripped off themselves (and looked rather more comfortable than he did). But absolutely none of them told you anything that you couldn't have guessed, given the premise. They were, in the strictest sense, a waste of film.

Finally, a disclaimer. I don't have a problem with 'modern art', whatever 'modern art' may be. Sometimes, it's true, it takes me quite a long time to appreciate things that are truly new. It took me years, for example, to appreciate Ligeti's music, or Jackson Pollock's 'pure paint' paintings -- though there have been others (such as Liechtenstein and Kodaly) to whom I took immediately. For that matter, I don't have a great problem with three-year-olds who scream 'BUM!' provided they don't keep doing it in a restaurant where I'm trying to enjoy a meal. But I do have a serious problem with people who take a feeble, stupid, predictable idea and then fail to execute it even half-way competently. As I say, give me the swans and sunsets every time.

Note: Originally there was an illustration with the original article, and you can get some idea of what it looked from by reading the following. But you don't need the illustration: the caption says more than enough, without a picture.

"I shot this at Arles. It symbolizes the dialectic between the deliberate intent of the Artist, symbolized by the tiny figure on the extreme left, and the aleatoriness of Art itself,

symbolized by the cracked and peeling walls in one of the exhibition spaces. Placing the figure on the left, rather than the right, draws attention to the way in which Art is devalued by capitalism -- and of course the faded, cracked red paint is a clear allusion to the parallel failure of socialist ideals. A hidden sub-text is that these are the former workshops of SNCF, the French railway system, referring back simultaneously to a quasi-utopian era of public transport for the masses and the exploitation of those masses".

This is pure twaddle, made up on the spur of the moment; and as the wall was in focus, and without camera shake, it would in any case be disqualified from many exhibitions at the Rencontres, no matter how much pretentious rubbish I had written about it.

Criminalise Flash Now !

When I am Lord Protector of the Commonwealth -- or possibly, since my move to France, First Consul -- several aspects of flash photography will be criminal offences.

The least serious charge will using flash when you don't need it, or when it can't do any good. Actually, this will probably just be a charge of culpable stupidity (something else that I plan to make a criminal offence). A modest fine -- twenty pounds, say -- will stock the exchequer handsomely. Just think of all those people at sports events and the like who fire off their feeble built-in flashes at things that are going on two hundred yards away, when even a 10,000 Watt-second studio pack wouldn't kick out enough light to make a difference to a variable-aperture zoom working at f/12, mounted on a point-and-shoot camera loaded with ISO 100 film.

A considerably more serious offence will be annoying people in a restaurant or other public place. There may be a little leeway: one picture per table, or perhaps two. But after that, the fine will start at twenty pounds, or an hour in the stocks, and then double for each subsequent flash. For a dozen pictures, after two 'grace' shots, that will mean a fine of rather over L20,000 or six weeks solidly in the stocks. David Blunkett and the Daily Mail may regard this as a little too lenient, but most people will agree with me that it should have an adequate deterrent effect.

The most serious offence of all, though, will be manufacturing or supplying cameras where the flash fires automatically with every shot. This will carry a minimum of a year in prison, and the destruction of all stocks of the offending apparatus. The prison sentence will be doubled if the flash cannot be turned off quickly and easily, or if it has to be turned off afresh every time the camera is switched on. The manufacturer may be allowed to resume camera production after release, but only if there is no likelihood that he will re-offend.

Levity aside (assuming for the purposes of argument that I am actually joking), why do people use flash? Perhaps more to the point, why do the rest of us put up with this plague? Countless superb 'available light' pictures were taken in the 1930s, when the equivalent of ISO 180 was a super-speed film. Lenses haven't got a lot faster: you could buy an f/1.5 for your Leica in the 1920s, even before interchangeable lenses were officially introduced, and the 50/0.95 Canon 'Dream', the fastest general-application production lens ever made for a 35mm camera, has been out of production for decades. Films today are however a great deal faster.

With a modern ISO 800 film and even an f/2 lens, anyone should be able to live without flash: instead of the 1/5 second and 1/10 second exposures that our photographic forebears used to have to rely upon, we can work at 1/30 wide open in all but the poorest light. And even then, what's wrong with trying 1/15 and 1/8? Or switching to seriously fast film? In colour print, 1600 is not out of the way, and in black and white, the sky is the limit. Films such as Ilford Delta 3200 deliver excellent quality at EI 3200, and are still remarkably good at 6400 and even 12,500. How much speed do you need?

It is true that it is a good deal easier to get an image with on-camera flash than with using available light, but this is only true if you don't care what sort of image you get. It is actually a lot harder to take a good flash photograph than it is to take a good photograph by available light. Burned-out faces and foregrounds, murky backgrounds, hideous shadows: these are the norm in flash photography, not the exception. Flash completely destroys the atmosphere of a place, though mercifully there are times when the atmosphere takes its revenge: in a smoky back room, flash brings up the smoke and flattens the contrast, for a really nasty effect.

For the press, where it's 'f/8 and be there', there may sometimes be some excuse for flash; but if you want a picture for its own sake, rather that the worst kind of record shot, available light is almost invariably a far better bet. In any case, even the press doesn't need flash anything like as often as it is used: look at the pictures that Erich Salomon was taking in the 1930s with an Ermanox and an f/1.8 lens, and you realize there's no need for flash. Most of us can never aspire to Salomon's heights of genius, but equally, with the bare minimum of practice we can take pictures that put flash to shame.

Also, it's next to impossible to take a flash shot without alerting your subject to the fact that you have just taken a picture -- or worse still, if your camera has one of those horrible anti-red-eye multiple flash modes, that you are about to take a picture. What hope is there of taking natural-looking pictures under such conditions, or at best, of taking more than one natural-looking picture?

Don't get me wrong. I have nothing against flash, when it is used properly. For me, this means in a studio, or between consenting adults in private. But flash in public is about as attractive as a public display of those bodily functions that are normally confined to the smallest room in the house. It is, in fact, an indecent way to make an exposure. It's a form of pollution. We already have laws against (for example) overly noisy motorcycles, or against trucks that spew filthy smoke into the atmosphere. We don't allow people to smoke on aircraft. Why can't we treat flash the same way?

Longer – Wider – Faster

There is no such thing as a lens that is too wide, too fast, too long, too specialized or too expensive; no such thing as a lens that 'nobody needs'.

To be sure, there may be lenses you have no use for, or I have no use for, or neither of us can afford. There may be situations where a particular lens can be a bad, expensive solution to a problem that could be solved cheaper and better another way; but whenever I see statements that 'no-one needs' a particular lens -- and such statements appear with monotonous regularity in the letters pages of AP -- my blood fairly boils.

Maybe you don't need ultrawides, ever, but when I was shooting a book on the American Civil War, with all kinds of period and reconstructed interiors, my 17mm Tamron and later my 14mm Sigma were among the most useful lenses I owned. If I could afford it, or if I were commissioned for similar project, I'd buy a 12mm Voigtlander tomorrow. Don't tell me it's too wide!

Likewise, when I'm shooting inside a pub or a club, where everyone is enjoying the music, I really appreciate the fastest lenses I have -- anything up to f/1.4. OK, you can argue that an f/1 is 'too fast' because it has negligible depth of field, but in low light I'd rather have a lens that's too fast, rather than one that's too slow, any day. Flash destroys the atmosphere, irritates people and draws attention to the photographer: the last thing you need when you are trying to be unobtrusive. Maybe you don't shoot under such conditions -- in which case, why not just shut up, because it's a subject you know nothing about.

Likewise, long, fast lenses are all but essential for many kinds of sports photography. I've had 300/2.8 lenses on test, and they're marvellous. But I don't need one. If I could have one for free, I'd take it like a shot, but I'd still want to keep my old 200/4 Nikkor or 200/3 Vivitar Series 1, because they are so much smaller and lighter. I travel a lot by motorcycle, and a 300/2.8 is a lot of bottle. A slower 200, and a 1.4x converter that turns it into an even slower 280mm, is more use to me.

When it comes to expense, the vast majority of people who say that a lens is 'too expensive' or 'not worth it' have no experience of the lens in question and no means of paying for it. The most expensive lens I possess, the 38/4.5 Zeiss Biogon on my Alpa, is terrifyingly expensive, but from the results it gives, I'd say it's worth it. So were the 35/1.4, 35/2.8 PC and 100/2.8 Zeiss lenses we were lent by Contax. If I could have afforded them, I'd have kept them. I couldn't afford them, but I can see why they cost what they do.

How about ultra-specialized lenses such as the Dreamagon soft-focus? I'd be surprised if one photographer in ten would really enjoy using a Dreamagon, and maybe one photographer in a hundred could begin to exploit it fully. So? If there's a big enough market for Dreamagons to stay in production, how on earth can you say that 'no one needs' such a lens? The arrogance and stupidity of such a comment defies belief.

The same argument applies to pinhole cameras, subject of some astonishingly vehement correspondence in AP earlier this year (around June and July, as I remember). You don't like pinholes? So? I'm not wild about them either. I've taken maybe two or three pinhole pictures that I really like, using a fairly expensive pinhole camera (a borrowed Rigby). I don't think I'd buy one, because I get more of a kick out of other kinds of photography. But I can see, very easily, that if I worked a bit harder at pinhole photography, at choosing the right subjects and the right kind of composition, I could make a lot more pictures to be proud of. Just because I don't want to do it, there's no reason for me to condemn those who do.

Sure, nine-tenths of pinhole pictures are rubbish. But remember the words of Theodore Sturgeon, the famous science fiction writer. When someone challenged him, saying that nine-tenths of science fiction was rubbish, he reputedly replied,"Sir, nine-tenths of anything is rubbish." Regardless of his exact words, this has since become known as Sturgeon's Law.

Similar arguments can be extended to cameras and may other things in photography. When I call something a waste of money, I mean it would be a waste of _my_ money, not someone else's. In particular, I can't imagine a bigger waste of my money than a digital camera.

Yes, a digital camera would save me a modest amount of time, and possibly money in the long run. But I'd be hard pressed to get the quality I want for under about £1500 or £2000. Anything less would be a complete and utter waste of money for the kind of shots I want to take. I don't want happy-snaps: I want sharp close-up technical shots, such as I currently get on transparency.

What puts me off is that a new digital Nikon would be worth a fraction of its new price in four or five years -- which with the other cameras I use (Alpa, Gandolfi, Leica, Linhof, Nikon, Voigtlander) is no time at all. Depreciation looks very like 'waste' to me, because I don't trade my cameras in very often (or at all, in many cases). On a cost-benefit analysis, supplemented by the fact that I simply prefer silver halide, I've decided not to bother with digital.

You may take an entirely different view. Fine. But one reason I've decided not to buy a digital camera is that I can't afford both that and a new Leica MP - and I don't have any difficulty at all in deciding where I'd rather 'waste' my money.

Barge Museum, Faversham

The weathered, the old, the obsolete: all have long fascinated me. What I love about the Barge Museum is the endless range of textures and shapes, all functional, almost all beautiful. I shot this as part of a developer test: Paterson Acupan 200 (still available as Fomapan 200) in Paterson FX50. The camera was a Voigtlander Bessa-R with a 50/1.5 Nokton and B+W yellow filter. Sulphide toned.

Bicycles, Paris

Bicycles are a subject I find hard to resist: I don't know why. Quite apart from liking the shapes in this shot, I find it amusing. It looks to me as if the somewhat louche gentleman's bicycle has just made a slightly improper suggestion to the small, upright, prim lady's bicycle and is being determinedly ignored. This is the one picture that did appear as an illustration in AP. The film was Ilford HP5 Plus; the lens, a 35/1.7 Voigtlander Ultron; and the body either a Leica M4-P or a Voigtlander Bessa-R or R2.

142

Candlestick

This was originally shot to show the brightness range you can hold in a contact print from a large format negative (5x7 inch Ilford FP4 Plus), but I thought I might as well try for an attractive still life as well. I think I succeeded. As far as I recall the camera was a Gandolfi Variant with a 210/5.6 Rodenstock Apo-Sironar.

Cross and grass

'Street photography' in the countryside. Ilford HP5 Plus and a weak yellow filter has always struck me as a wonderful combination for good tonality. The lens here was, I am pretty use, the 50/1.5 Voigtlander Nokton but I can't remember whether it was on a Leica (M4-P) or a Bessa-R2. I am still puzzling over the reaction to this picture that I got from one book editor: 'Of course, we couldn't use that picture after September 11th.'

145

Frances

Frances likes this picture because, as she says, "It's the way I see myself in dreams, any age, no age: I could by anything from my late 20s onwards." I think it's one of the best portraits I've ever taken of her. We disagree about which lens I used. She thinks it was the 90/2.2 Leitz Thambar kindly loaned by Senggye ar Born, but I'm reasonably sure it was the 90/4 Dreamagon. If it has the Thambar, the camera was a Leica M-series, probably MP, and if it was the Dreamagon it was a Nikon F. The film was Ilford HP5 Plus.

Freedom fighter

We have done a fair amount of work for the Tibetan Government in Exile and this was shot in 1999 at their request as part of a sort of National Portrait Gallery. It was taken in Dharamsala on Ilford XP2 Super using a Leica (probably M4-P but might have been M2) and a 90/2 Summicron. We were slightly handicapped in having only two modelling lamps for the three flash heads that were available to us...

147

Mah jongg players

In 2005 we went to China, which was visually fascinating but confirmed all my prejudices against the communist government. This is in Lijiang, arguably a province of Tibet rather than China proper, though the Chinese drew the border of the 'Tibet Autonomous Region' somewhat to the west. I shot this on Ilford HP5 Plus with my 35/1.4 Summilux and either my M4-P or my MP.

148

Mao in the hutongs of Beijing
The face of the old villain and mass murderer still appears all over China.
Very roughly, Hitler killed 16 million people; Stalin killed 32 million; and
Mao killed 64 million. Yet we still do business with China... Alpa 12 WA,
38/4.5 Zeiss Biogon, Ilford HP5 Plus.

Prayer flags, India
As mentioned elsewhere, we have taken many pictures of Tibet in exile.
This is Sherab Ling in the Himalayas, known to some in the Tibetan
community as "Battlestar Galactica" because of its somewhat overblown
construction, which was heavily funded by western Buddhists. Leica M4-P,
35mm 1.4 Summilux, Ilford HP5 Plus.

150

Sophie as Pretty Baby

Sophie is a brilliant young woman who is also a superb model, and has been since she was a little girl: she's about 14 or 15 here, but with an IQ of 160+ that makes her mental age at least 22. Several times we were lucky enough to bribe her to pose for us: normally she's fully booked by her mother, the photographer Marie Muscat-King who took the portrait of Roger that appears every week in AP. This is actually Sophie's First Communion dress; the contrast between the dress and the deshabille, along with the expression and the slightly droopy stockings, gives it the air of a decadent late 19th century picture. As far as I recall I used a 150/4.5 Apo Lanthar on my MPP Mk. VII for this, shooting on 4x5 inch Ilford FP4 Plus, but we shot on several cameras and formats that day from 35mm to 8x10 inch.

St. Martin

Old buildings are one of my favourite subjects, and a few miles from where we live, there is a 'church without a village'; or to be more accurate, a church a mile or so from its village. No-one is quite sure why, though there are legends. In the thousand years or so since it was built, there's room to forget. KowaSIX, 85/2.8 lens, Maco Cube 400.

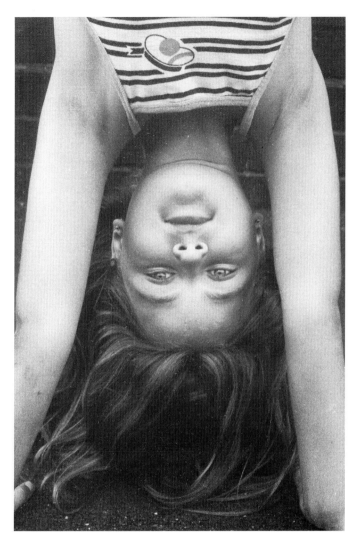

Upside-down girl

You wouldn't dare shoot this sort of picture any more in the UK, because you'd probably be arrested for paedophilia (assuming you weren't torn to pieces by a screaming mob). But which does it convey to you: perverted pornography, or a rather charming variety of childhood innocence? I shot it so long ago that I have no idea of what camera I used but it was probably either a Leica IIIa with 50/3.5 Elmar or a Nikon F with 58/1.4 Nikkor. The print is on Ilford Galerie.

Waterfall, Julian Alps, Slovenia
Moat of my best landscapes seem to be taken with longer-than-standard
lenses. One of my old Nikon Fs is more or less permanently fitted with a
200/3 Vivitar Series 1 and a weak (2.8x) Soviet-era orange filter. I shoot
exclusively Ilford HP5 Plus with this outfit: this is one of my favourites.

Xaghra Mill, Gozo

It's pronounced Shah-hrah (near enough): Maltese is an interesting language, as witness such words as dqiq (flour) or qaqocc (artichoke). Malta and its sister island Gozo are probably the most photogenic places on earth and we seriously considered moving there instead of France in 2001. Xaghra Mill was still a working mill when Roger lived in Malta in the 1950s. Leica M4-P, 12/5.6 Ultra-Wide-Heliar, Fuji Acros.

Yosemite

This works best as a lith print -- this is on Paterson Warmtone -- but unfortunately the budget for illustrations in this book wouldn't stretch to four-colour repro. Even so, it's one of the few pictures I've taken of Yosemite that I like: a useful reminder of the distinction between places that you like to photograph yourself, and places where others have taken pictures that you admire. I used a Leica (probably M2) with a Visoflex III and a 280/4.8 Telyt for this shot on Ilford XP1.

156

Standardisation

What would the world be like if we were all the same? A great deal easier, for a start. Few defend individuality more ruggedly than I; but standardization has its advantages.

Let's take a really easy example. What if the domestic electricity supply weren't standardized? What if we had to cope with AC and DC, at voltages from 80 to 250? That's how it used to be. But there are only two major systems today, both AC: 220-240v, as used in most of the civilized world, and 110-120v, as used in the United States and a few other countries.

How about film speeds? What if there were no ISO standard, and every manufacturer could make whatever claims he liked? Again, that's how it used to be: H&D, Scheiner, Weston, Ilford speed groups -- and they couldn't necessarily be related to one another, because they were often based on different criteria. In any case, because there was no standardized methodology, the marketing department often had more influence over a film's claimed speed than anyone who actually knew anything about sensitometry.

Now let's go a little further. What if 35mm film cassettes weren't standardized? Suppose we had to buy individual cassettes to suit each model of camera? Actually, you can see what happened there. The cameras that didn't take standard cassettes (introduced as a _de facto_ standard by Kodak) either adapted, as Robots eventually did, or died.

But 35mm raises an interesting point. Why 24x36mm? Most people find it too long and thin to be aesthetically pleasing, though apparently Oskar Barnack reckoned it the most attractive shape of all. He didn't invent the format, of course: several other cameras, contemporaries of the prototype Leica, used the same double-frame size (a single movie frame was already standardized at 18x24mm).

In fact both 24x32 and 24x34 mm have been tried, the former by Wray, Opema and Nikon in the late 40s and early

50s, and the latter very briefly by Nikon again: October 1949 to May 1951. Both are arguably superior, from an aesthetic point of view, but neither prospered. Probably the biggest reason for the demise of the 24x32mm format was automatic slide-cutting machines (think about it, and blanch). But even without those, it would be another slide mount size to stock, another negative carrier; this was probably what did for 24x34mm, too. The advantage wasn't big enough.

Changing examples again, to cable releases, the tapered PC (Prontor-Compur) thread may be fiddly, but you need to be pretty palsied before you can't make it work. Even my wife Frances Schultz, who has a fairly bad 'benign essential tremor' has no trouble with them except on a very bad day. We should all boycott cameras that use their own unique, expensive electric switch fitting which rarely works as well as a mechanical cable release anyway.

Likewise flash synch. There are at least two systems that are better than the PC nipple, the ASA bayonet and two-pin plugs, but the PC nipple is a dozen times better than a dedicated fitting that only allows the use of the manufacturers' own flash, and if it's a choice of a hot shoe or a PC nipple, PC wins every time. Both together are OK, of course.

How about standardized black and white processing, at least for 35mm? Feasible -- just. A good photographer -- one who takes pictures that people actually want to see, rather than a 'Fine Artist' given to disappearing up his own fundament -- should be able to survive on Ilford XP-2 alone, with its standardized C-41 processing; or possibly, if they prefer the tonality, with one of the Kodak chromogenics that is processed the same way. If we all standardized on C-41, there would be a lot more choice in chromogenic films, and a lot of mediocre photographers would be forced to concentrate on getting better pictures rather than pratting about with silly developers.

Last of all, if you really want to see the benefits of standardization, consider digital cameras and 'photo quality' printers -- or to use the technical term, 'land fill'. This month's memory medium or ink cartridge may be compatible with last month's, but quite possibly not with last year's, and certainly not with the next decade's. As the saying goes, the great thing about standards in computers is that there are so many to choose from.

Is each and every revision to digital photography a genuine improvements? Or does cynical marketing have a significantly larger part to pay? Or should we blame hyped-up young computer designers, playing with someone else's hardware at someone else's expense? To them, three years is forever, as it is to a child. No doubt all three factors have a part to play, but I cannot help harbouring deep suspicions as to the exact proportions.

Superstition and Substition

Terry Pratchett, as far as I know, coined the word 'substition'. It is the opposite of 'superstition'. Superstition, as everyone knows, means a popular belief in things that aren't there. Substition means believing in things that are there, but that hardly anyone else believes in: in short, seeing things as they really are.

There's a parallel in photography. A lot of photographers want to photograph what isn't there -- a pastoral dream, maybe from the 18th century, ornamented with a few elegant stone buildings -- while ignoring what is actually there: principally, the man-made debris (including a lot of the architecture) that has accumulated in the last 150 or so years. What they want to photograph could be called the 'Prince of Wales' vision of England.

Now don't get me wrong. First, I've nothing against Charlie-boy. In fact, I think he'll be an excellent king for the 21st century. As I am sure he does, I regret what has to happen first - the passing of his mother, our own dear Queen - but apart from that, I'm looking forward to it. If anyone asks why I'm a royalist, the answer is simple. President Wilson, President Thatcher, President Blair? No thanks. God Save The Queen!

Likewise, I've nothing against the kind of countryside (and towns, cities and villages) that HRH would like to see. In fact, one of the great pleasures of living in France is that much of the countryside really is like that. And when I get annoyed with the ugly clumps of wires that disfigure the corners of so many houses - and the French are geniuses at ugly clumps of wire - I reflect that the owners of those picturesque but disfigured houses really appreciate electricity. I know: I own one.

Third, I've seen too many photographs of ugliness to object to anyone's wanting to photograph beauty. To make matters worse, most of the photographs of ugliness have themselves been technically unpleasant: harsh, wonky and above all dull. Most of them have been cliches, repeated by every generation of Angry Young Photographers. Three out of four middle-aged photographers must have photographed bands in their youth, and often, the pictures set out to shock the oldies. That's part of the purpose of popular music, after all, and indeed of being young. Those same middle-aged photographers have all seen the same ideas trotted out again, every few years, as ever-younger photographers try to shock us. Got news for you, lads: we don't shock easy. The same goes for pictures of tramps/street people, graffiti, and urban wastelands generally. It also goes for deliberately shocking nude studies of your fellow students: you may not have seen all that many naked female art students when you're 18, but as you get older, you'll find that they're not exactly an unusual sight.

But there are two very powerful counter-arguments against pursuing arcadianism in photography. One is a short term benefit that can bring an immediate, or at least very rapid, improvement to your photography. It is that conflict can be a powerful stimulus to artistic vision. I'll come back to the other later.

When it comes to conflict, I'm not talking about hecatombs and great artists; I'm not talking Guernica. I'm talking about the way in which trying to find a picture in the ordinary, the everyday, even the ugly, can be more of a challenge than shooting a conventionally pretty-pretty subject. I'm also arguing that a challenge -- even if you don't want one every day -- is probably worth taking on from time to time so that your work doesn't become stale and uninteresting.

Should you look for beauty in ugliness, though? Isn't it more honest to show up ugliness for what it is? Should you not contribute, in short, to the Arcadian manifesto?

Yes and no. To be sure, there is a time to shock people, and it is often easier to shock them with ugliness than with beauty. But there are always two risks inherent in doing so:

banality, and lack of relevance. Show someone the same ugliness they see every day, and they will disregard it as banal. Show them ugliness they've never seen before, and they may well dismiss it as irrelevant to their lives.

For a surprisingly commonplace example of successful use of ugliness (and even with finding beauty in that ugliness), just look at the next crucifix you see. This is an image of a man being tortured to death in a peculiarly horrible way. Nothing could be much uglier. But strip away, if you can, the familiarity of the image of Jesus on the cross, and you can see the beauty and simplicity in the image, that makes the horror all the worse. If you can't begin to imagine it, pretend that you are trapped in a crashed car, dying in agony, and that instead of helping you, everyone has gathered around to watch and have a bit of a laugh.

I said, though, that there is a second advantage to photographing what is really there -- and somewhat to my amusement, a perfect example cropped up on the letters page of AP, just as I was getting around to writing this article. Eric Houlder (26 July 2003) described how he had regarded the strange denizens of the King's Road in the late 1960s as a nuisance, spoiling the timeless pictures he wanted to take. Now, of course, a street full of hippies (and Minis, and TRs, and city gents in bowler hats, and old advertising slogans, and all the rest) would be a much more valuable picture.

But I'll go further. It could have been a more valuable picture at the time, too. Show someone something that they have seen a hundred times, but show it to them in a new way: that is one way to create a great picture. And equally, show them something they have never seen before, but in a way that they can immediately relate to it. That is another way to create a great picture. But shoot the same old thing the same old way, pandering to the same old preconceptions, and who is going to bother to look at your pictures?

Three Myths

Countless photographers don't understand the theory that underlies their craft, especially in monochrome. In one sense this doesn't matter - if you get the results you want, who cares about theory? - but an awful lot of people waste an awful lot of time because they try to base their photography on erroneous theory. Three of my favourites are split-contrast printing; meters calibrated to an 18 per cent grey (a myth which I shamefacedly confess to propagating in print, before I knew better); and the belief that if you stop down more, your pictures will always be sharper.

Split-contrast printing is a popular technique for use with variable-contrast papers. It can mean two things, one valid and valuable, and the other with no theoretical basis whatsoever.

The valid and valuable version involves printing part of an image at one contrast grade, and printing (or burning) another part at a different contrast grade. The applications are obvious and require no further comment.

The other version involves using two filters instead of one, for the whole image. The 'theory' (if one can grace it with that word) is that one exposure gives you the shadow contrast, while the other gives you the highlight contrast. Unfortunately, that's complete codswallop. It sounds right; it feels right; and it's totally wrong. There is always a single filter value that will give you exactly the same contrast, in both the highlights and the shadows, as using two filters.

This doesn't mean that you shouldn't do it. If you are using discrete filters instead of a dial-in filter head, twin-filter printing is the only way to get intermediate values such as 2-3/4 or 3-1/8. And if you find it easier to do it this way, then that's fine too. But the 'theory' is wrong.

How about the 18 per cent grey? No-one even knows where this one came from. The original work (by Jones and Condit of the Kodak research labs in the late 1930s) found that the average overall reflectivity of an outdoor scene in the vicinity of Rochester, New York, was around 12 or 13 per cent. Not 18.

So why do we have 18 per cent grey cards? Well, 18 per cent is a visual mid-tone: Zone V, in Zonespeak. So? This is nothing to do with average reflectivity. Read the original instructions that come with Kodak 18 per cent grey (sorry, gray) cards and you will see that they are recommended only for studio work, only for colour (sorry, color) and that the card should be angled away from the subject-camera axis in order to take account of the fill light as well as the key. Angling it often means that the amount of light reflected back towards the camera is about 12 or 13 per cent of the light falling on the subject, from the camera's point of view...

A grey card gives you a consistent tone, which is handy if you don't have an incident light meter or a spot meter, but it is a poor substitute for either. With a spot meter and negative film, a grey card is a complete waste of time. Meter the darkest tone in which you want texture and detail and give about 3 stops less exposure: exactly how much less will depend on your film, developer, technique, camera and lens, but can be determined once for all time with a few frames of film. This will give you adequate shadow detail. Don't waste time looking for an 'equivalent mid tone', which is pure fantasy.

As for stopping down for sharpness, diffraction limits are the problem. At any aperture, there is an absolute theoretical limit to the maximum possible resolution of the image, the point at which contrast falls to zero. Throw in one fudge factor because zero contrast is not much use, a second because you are using the relative aperture rather than the numerical aperture, and a third for the various colours of light that make up 'white', and you can get a very good idea of the the diffraction limit (in line pairs per millimetre, lp/mm) by dividing the aperture into something between 1000 and 1500. Both numbers are defensible, representing realistic limits for the approximation. Diffraction limited resolutions are therefore as follows:

f/2 500-750 lp/mm
f/4 250-375 lp/mm
f/8 125-188 lp/mm
f/16 63-93 lp/mm
f/32 31-49 lp/mm
f/64 16-23 lp/mm

Few if any commercially available lenses are diffraction limited at f/2; the best will come in at around f/4, and by f/8, any top-flight lens should be diffraction limited. These are aerial figures: on-the-film figures will be lower, even with the finest-grained, sharpest films.

As soon as you stop down beyond the first diffraction limited aperture, resolution will begin to suffer. It almost certainly won't matter at f/11, and the effects will be modest (but detectable) at f/16. By f/22 the rot will clearly have set in, though. This is why 35mm lenses rarely stop down beyond f/22 (and often stop at f/16). Only large format lenses typically offer f/45 and smaller: 20 lp/mm looks very sharp indeed in a contact print, but you wouldn't want to start making enlargements.

How do these numbers translate into perceptible resolution? It's hard to say. For years, the figure I used was based on Lipinski: about 8 lp/mm. Since then, I have accepted two other on-the-print figures: 5 lp/mm and 30 lp/mm. The former is 'pretty damn sharp, at normal viewing distances'. The latter is the so-called 'vernier resolution', the smallest discontinuity in a straight line that the human eye is likely to be able to discern. The fact that these figures differ by a factor of six is a good indication of how vague the whole business is: be suspicious of anyone in photography who starts demanding accuracy of better than +/- 20 per cent, except perhaps in E6 processing.

And that's the bottom line. Beware of theory. Go for practice, every time. But if you insist on going for theory -- well, then at least get it right.

We'll Clean It Up In Photoshop...

Photoshop is deservedly one of Adobe's most successful products. On countless occasions, I have myself 'cleaned it up in Photoshop'. But a lot of very stupid photographers seem to use Photoshop to make life more difficult for themselves, not easier. And often, the results are far worse than they were in the days before Photoshop.

This is because it is normally a lot easier to take a few minutes more at the shooting stage (and indeed, at the processing and scanning stages, if you still originate your images on film) than to spend several times as long 'cleaning it up in Photoshop'. But people don't bother. It's almost as if they grudge every minute spent behind the camera, but don't count the time spent in front of the computer.

Some of the things that people leave undone are downright cretinous. Fingermarks and dust, for example. How long does it take to clean something before you photograph it? Or to clean a tranny before you scan it? A fraction as long as it takes to clone out all the marks in Photoshop, always supposing you are skilled enough to do so without making it obvious.

Then there is basic 'gardening'. Think of an electrical appliance with an inconveniently trailing flex, for example. Can you unplug it? If not, how can you drape it so that it is easiest to 'lose' in Photoshop? I have seen people spend ages trying to retouch a background, simply to remove an unnecessary shadow: unnecessary, because if they had thought about positioning the flex properly at the taking stage, it wouldn't have cast a shadow in the first place.

In fact, shadows are another thing that people are altogether too eager to 'take out in Photoshop'. Deep dark shadows under the subject can be ridiculously time-consuming to 'lose', but slightly more care with the lighting set-up would make the shadows softer and lighter and much easier to remove.

The same goes for reflections. In the days before Photoshop, when retouching was terrifyingly expensive -- the cost of an 11x14 inch dupe tranny was hair-raising, even before you started on the retoucher's time -- photographers took great care to 'lose' all unwanted reflections, especially brightly coloured ones. Nowadays: 'Oh, we'll take it out in Photoshop'.

The lazy and incompetent rely on Photoshop even when it comes to something as basic as lighting. Often, I have to photograph shiny silver cameras on a white background. It is very easy to lose (for example) the back of the top-plate against the background. For me, it's almost second nature to get out the Climpex and fix a little flag here, a little mirror here, to get the highlights and shadows where I need them. But more than once, I've heard people working on similar shots say, 'It's close enough -- we'll clean it up in Photoshop.'

In the same shots, I take considerable care to line the camera up nice and square, and often, I'll shoot with a roll-film back on a 4x5 inch camera so I can use the movements to avoid the converging verticals that you get if you point the camera downwards. If I shoot on 35mm, I use a nice, long macro lens -- at least 90mm -- so that the convergence is kept to a minimum. But I know of people who shoot with a wide-angle (because it focuses nice and close) and then, yes, 'True it up in Photoshop.'

Then there's 'comping', making composites from two or more pictures. Again, in the days of manual retouching, anything that was shot for 'comping' was photographed with immense care. Wherever possible, the different components were shot from the same distance, with the same focal length lens, and the same lighting. Today, any old junk is thrown down on the studio table, and the assistant takes a series of snapshots with the digital camera. The results is eyeball-aching inconsistencies in perspective and lighting -- and an absurdly long time spent nailing it all together in Photoshop.

I first learned the trade and craft of professional photography in a London advertising studio in the early-to-mid 1970s, under the incomparable tutelage of the late Colin Glanfield. In those days, there was probably more money (and booze) around in professional photography than any time before or since, but there is always a commercial pressure to do things as economically as possible. Part of that meant taking our pictures so that the ministrations of retouchers were either unnecessary, or at worst, kept to a minimum.

Today, like most photographers, I do my own retouching, electronically, in Photoshop. I've been using it for years now, and it still fascinates me. But precisely because I can do so much with it, I don't want to waste time doing things that I don't have to. As a rule of thumb, I reckon that a minute's foresight at the taking and scanning stages saves me five to ten minutes at the computer. That's not because my computer is particularly old and slow: it's because that's how long it takes me to do the necessary cloning, trueing-up, and so forth. Stop and think about that for a minute. Six minutes more in the studio (where I'd rather be) saves me half an hour to an hour in front of the computer (where I have to spend too much time anyway). How much do you love your computer?

Cameras as Jewellery...

Cameras as jewellery have always amused me. Inevitably, given what I do, I carry quite a range of cameras and I see quite a range of reactions to whatever I am carrying. What intrigues me is the way that different people are clearly thinking different things as they glance (or sometimes unashamedly stare) at the camera around my neck.

Recently, for example, I've been carrying a brand-new Leica MP with a 50mm f/1 Noctilux on it. The MP was on loan from Leica, while the Noctilux is the property of an extremely generous friend who thought I might like to try it. Recently I took it to Niort, which is about 50 miles from where I live: the 76th annual Niort fair had a Tibetan pavilion, and I'll do anything I can, however modest, to help support the Tibetan cause and end the genocidal Chinese occupation of Tibet. I shot a few pictures of the performers from TIPA (the Tibetan Institution for Performing Arts) and the making of a sand mandala.

In another pavilion was an exhibition of work by local professional photographers: some of it very good, much of it unbelievably abysmal. The photographers themselves took turns to man a stand at the head of the exhibition. One nobbled me and said, "We're running a photographic competition, are you interested?" I said that I wasn't. I didn't tell him that I've judged enough photographic competitions to know how much of it comes down to pure chance; or that I wouldn't trust the judgement of anyone who would hang half the pictures that were on display; or that I had no interest in the prize anyway.

As I turned to go, though, he was clearly thinking "Rich twerp, walking round with a flashy-looking camera, probably never takes a picture in his life." You could almost hear it.

At camera clubs, you don't want anything too exotic or most members won't know what to make of it, but something like the MP is guaranteed to polarize those present into the fondlers and enviers, who would buy one themselves if they could afford it, and the haters. The latter are usually of the sour grapes brigade: "Leicas aren't worth the money." Most people who say this have never used one.

In my extensive experience, there are very few cameras that aren't worth the money. The two big questions are whether they do what you want, and whether you can afford them. If they don't do what you want, they are no use at any price, and if you can't afford them, that's your problem. Not being able to afford them is my problem, too: I'd never have given those Contaxes back if I could have afforded to keep them.

Then there are camera stores. Once my wife and I wandered into one in Zurich wearing brand-new his'n'hers Alpa 12s, a few weeks after they were introduced. The shop assistant had to swallow several times before he could even say 'Good Morning'. You can't blame him. His reasoning must have been that anyone who could afford those could afford anything.

Occasionally I have to admit to malice aforethought. Years ago, I bought a field-grey Leica IIIc with 'Luftwaffen Eigentum' (Luftwaffe Property) all over it: body, lens and ever ready case. Whenever possible, I put at least one roll of film through any camera I own, so I shot a roll of happy-snap color and took it into a one-hour lab; it was in San Francisco. You could see the man behind the counter thinking "Does he know what he's got? Can I buy it off him? How much for?" To his credit, he didn't try. Then again, a friend of mine once covered photokina with a Leica 250.

To finish, there's the anti-snobbery. I have a high opinion of many top-of-the-line Sigma lenses, and indeed bought the 14/3.5 rectilinear and 15/2.8 fish-eye. I also like the original Vivitar Series 1 lenses from the 1970s and 80s, especially the 135/2.3, 200/3, 600/8 and 90-180/4.5 Flat Field macro.

About a dozen years ago, my wife Frances Schultz and I were using some of these in Gran Canaria: I forget exactly which ones. They were on a tripod-mounted Nikon F, itself out of production for almost 20 years at that time. Almost inevitably, another photographer strolled over. When he saw the equipment I was using, he became just faintly patronizing: he had a new Leica reflex around his neck. So I showed him our most recent book on photography, and pointed out in the captions the cameras and lenses that had been used.

He was grievously nonplussed. He wailed, "But I thought professionals always used the latest cameras, with the manufacturers' own lenses." And I told him that some do, and some don't, and he shook his head. He didn't know what to think.

To tell the truth, nor do I. One reason I value top-flight cameras is because they give top-flight results, but within reason, most of the serious cameras I own will turn in publishable pictures, even my 50-year-old Retina IIa. So the other reason I like top-flight cameras is that I get better treatment. People may never see my pictures or books, so they can't judge me by them, but they can see my cameras and judge me by those; and it's always easier to be treated with respect than with contempt, regardless of whether either is deserved. So maybe cameras as jewellery do have some use after all.

Growing Old Gracefully...

Look at an old, black-paint Leica. Brass shows through the paint at the corners: the paint itself is scuffed and dull, no longer shiny and bright. But it looks beautiful. It is worn in, not worn out. Much the same is true of a black-paint Nikon F. Strong men go dewy-eyed when they see mine, and say such things as 'Finest camera I ever owned' and 'Wish I'd never got rid of mine.'

Old, black, top-quality 35mm cameras are not the only ones that age gracefully. An elderly Gandolfi looks gorgeous, too, its lacquered brass yellowed and dulled, its lustrous wood dented and scraped in places, but still exuding quality from every pore. And a well-worn Rollei TLR has much of the same magic to it.

For that matter, there are other products than cameras that age well. Think of a Billingham bag. After a few years it acquires a patina that suits it perfectly. The leather straps curl; there are some dirty patches and stains that won't easily clean up; and the brass fasteners have that dull glow that comes only from the polishing of constant use.

Constant honest use is an important part of the story. Famously, some photographers can cover a war and bring the cameras home unscathed, as though they had merely taken a walk around the block, while others can take a walk around the block and bring the cameras back looking as if they had covered a war.

There's a level of normal use that falls between cossetting and macho posturing -- the kind of idiot who deliberately knocks his cameras about because he thinks that's what 'real pros' do. The simple truth is that a real pro takes the maximum possible care of his cameras that is consistent with getting good pictures: the wear that the cameras suffer is mainly from constant use, plus the occasional ding or scrape when it's inevitable and the shot takes precedence over the cameras. I've heard (though I find it hard to believe) that there are photographers who deliberately 'distress' their cameras with a mild abrasive such as toothpaste to give them what they believe to be the 'pro' look.

Ageing gracefully is by no means only a function of quality and honest use, however. Consider the lacquered chrome on some old Linhofs or 35mm Alpas (not the current roll-film models). Both are among the finest manufacturers of all time. The finish looked great when it was new, and for many years afterwards; but once it chips and rubs, it looks shabby, not comfortable. Another really awful finish was Leica's notorious 'black chrome' on the M4-P. Mine wore so badly and so fast that a Leica dealer friend advised sending it back under guarantee. I never did -- there seemed little point -- and I've still got the camera, and it looks worn but not attractive. I can certainly see why they went back to paint for the MP. As soon as I can afford one, I want one.

Then again, there's a difference between wear and damage. If the vulcanite is chipped off a Leica, it doesn't look attractively worn: it looks damaged. The same goes for a torn Billingham. But a dented prism on a Nikon F is somewhere in between. If it isn't too dented, it look like wear and tear: it's only when it's well pushed in that it looks like real damage.

It's also true that honest wear can distract attention from other cosmetic deficiencies. I have an Olympus Pen W, probably the rarest of the non-SLR Pen series, with the 25/2.8 lens (hence 'W' for 'Wide') and once again a black paint finish: as far as I know, the only non-SLR Pen to be finished in black. Like the Leicas and Nikons mentioned in the first paragraph, it has that lovely worn-through brass effect on the corners, but it has to be said that the paint itself is a bit scabby, even where it is otherwise unmarked: it has suffered from tiny blisters, big enough to feel as well as see. But I've had chrome cameras with a similar problem, and they look a good deal worse than the old W.

The question is, why are worn cameras (and bags, and even tripods) so attractive? I think there are two reasons. One is that it shows off the quality of the product: it shows, literally, that its beauty is more than skin deep. The other is that it reminds us that cameras are to be used, not fondled and worshipped or (worse still) left in their sealed boxes as "collectors' items" to "appreciate".

If we put the wear on the camera ourselves, it reminds us of all the pictures we have taken with it: this is pretty much the case with one of my Nikon Fs, which I used first as an assistant at Plough Photography and then bought for myself when I left the studio for the last time (at least as an assistant) in the mid-1970s. And if we buy the camera already worn, it is hard not to fantasize about what it must have seen, where it must have been. In short, it appeals to the romance in our souls; and if we have no romance, what sort of photographers are we?

Quality and Versatility...

Ansel Adams has a lot to answer for. He took one aspect of photography -- technical quality -- and blew it up out of all proportion to its actual importance. The result was almost identical to the old camera club ethos, which attached similar importance to the Rules of Composition. In either case, a picture can be ineffably tedious, but as long as it obeys the Rules, be they Zone placement and tonal management or the Rule of Thirds and diagonals for dynamism, it is a Good Picture and worshipped as such by lesser photographers.

Interestingly enough, though, the most successful cameras -- that is, the ones that have been used by the greatest number of photographers to create the greatest number of good pictures -- have not, in fact, pandered much to quality. Rather, they are both versatile and convenient.

It was versatility and convenience, after all, that accounted for the meteoric rise of high-end 35mm rangefinder cameras, epitomized in the 1930s by the Leica and Contax but later joined by Canon and Nikon. In those days, 'serious' photographers used at least half-plate cameras (4-3/4 x 6-1/2 inches) and preferably whole-plate (6-1/2 x 8-1/2 inches -- and you're right, half plate is bigger than half a whole plate). Alternatively they might use quarter-plate (3-1/4 x 4-1/4 inch) SLRs if they wanted to use fast or long lenses.

Bear in mind that 'fast' was f/3.5 or better, while 'ultra-long' for most photographers was rarely more than the equivalent of about 135mm in 35mm terms: a 16-inch lens, just over 400mm, on quarter-plate. Even a monster 40-inch 'Long Tom' is only a bit over 300mm in 35mm terms. Also remember that you couldn't use wide-angles with reflexes at all, because the mirror got in the way.

But with 35mm, as long as you could afford all the goodies, you could with a single camera body go from 28mm to 135mm (roughly 130mm to 630mm on half-plate, or

90mm to 420mm on quarter-plate), and you could shoot at f/1.5 with the 50mm lens (about 230mm on half-plate or 150mm on quarter-plate). Soon you could buy lenses as short as 21mm (call it 100mm on half-plate or 65mm on quarter-plate) and, with the reflex housings developed in the 1930s, there were 200mm, 400mm and still longer lenses.

To be sure, the technical quality was lousy. A half-plate enlargement off 35mm is a fraction under 5x, and even with today's films, you couldn't hope to approach contact-print quality with a 5x enlargement. With the films of the 30s, things were even worse. So? Technical quality wasn't everything. Look at the work of many of the great 35mm photographers of the 30s -- people like Drticol and Rodchenko -- and you can see how little it mattered. Weston shot his peppers on 5x7 inch and Ansel Adams was shooting Yosemite on 8x10 inch, and they were good pictures too; but they represented a tradition that was in decline, while 35mm was definitely in the ascendant.

After World War Two, the Hasselblad succeeded for the same reasons: the 1600F, 1000F and then the seemingly immortal 500-series. The square format is a technical compromise: without either a revolving back or a pentaprism, both of which add weight, bulk and expense, the only convenient way to build a reflex is with a square format, as Rolleiflex had proven with their TLRs in the 1930s. You couldn't get as much speed as with 35mm, and the range of focal lengths was more limited, but the 500C was (and remains to this day) an extremely versatile and convenient camera.

Also, given that a 10x8 inch print is only a fraction more than 4.5x off 6x6cm, and that 1950s films were a lot better than 1930s, you could get very impressive quality indeed. Arguably, at half-plate (under a 3x enlargement) you could get close enough to contact-print quality that the difference didn't matter.

For reasons of space I'll skip over the rise of the 35mm SLR, except to say that these are even more versatile and convenient than rangefinder cameras, and cut straight to the present day and digital SLRs.

By popular consent, 6 megapixel cameras deliver quality that is just barely acceptable as compared with the old 35mm paradigm. They are surprisingly good for ink-jet prints, but for high-quality photomechanical reproduction at whole-page size you need some pretty clever post-production work, including a good repro house. Newspapers, with their appalling print quality, can go much bigger off digital.

But digital SLRs are convenient. Well, fairly, though to anyone brought up on shutter speed dials and aperture rings, the idea of controlling all camera functions via buttons, LCD screens and knobs on the camera body seems a rather pointless and complicated way of doing things. And they are versatile. Again, fairly: as long as you can disable the autofocus and autoexposure when they aren't wanted, they can do anything that a 'real' camera can do.

In other words, most people don't care enough about ultimate quality to sacrifice versatility and convenience. If they did, we'd still be shooting half-plate and above, or at the very least, roll-film. The truth, however, is that a good photograph can survive bad technical quality, while first-class technical quality is very far from a guarantee of a good picture. The nearest thing to a royal road to better pictures is practice. This, if anything, is what digital photography should be about.

Not Wholly Die...

Non omnis moriar, said the immoral poet Horace: I shall not wholly die. In another context entirely, he said "Exegi monumentum aere perennius": I have erected a monument longer lasting than bronze.

Much the same can be said of any kind of photography. After all, there are still Daguerrotypists about (though not many), and I should be surprised if someone, somewhere, had not at least tried to make Lippmann colour pictures. By contrast with those two, Bromoils are positively flourishing. Perhaps more to the point, I would venture to suggest that there are almost certainly more people today who are shooting large formats (LF) for fun than ever before: 'large formats' being defined in the old Purchase Tax terms of 'bigger than quarter plate'. Quarter plate (3-1/4 x 4-1/4 inches) was the largest format that was regarded as 'amateur' under the old regulations.

Admittedly, professional usage of LF is grievously in decline, for a number of reasons. Perhaps the most pressing is that it is much less necessary than it was. Modern colour films, in particular, are so good that a 6x7cm transparency can now do the work that required a 4x5 inch shot when I was an assistant in the 70s, which in turn had required 10x8 inch in the 50s. Also, a lot of clients demand digital, not for quality but for speed: as the old, old joke among advertising photographers goes, "I want it yesterday. If I wanted it today I'd ask for it tomorrow."

Another point is (to put it delicately) that not all graduates from photographic courses are totally at home with LF: it depends on whether they are looking to take a course in photography, or one in free expression and youth unemployment reduction. I'm not saying that there are colleges that can't teach it, because I don't know; but I do know that at least some students successfully manage to avoid at least some of the rigours of LF work. I also know that for some young photographers, LF comes as a joyful revelation, and that some colleges teach it very well.

Even so, as I say, there must be more amateur photographers today doing LF for fun than ever before, because there are more photographers than ever before, and (hard though it may sometimes be to believe) they have more money than ever before, so more than ever before can afford to indulge themselves in a frankly off-beat and minority hobby.

Something on which I have firmer information -- from the USA, because paradoxically I have less information about the UK -- is that some photography colleges ripped out their traditional wet darkrooms and replaced them with 'digital editing suites', only to find that the students voted with their feet (and their dollars) and either studied something else or went elsewhere to study. I know of at least two American photography schools who have reinstated their wet darkrooms, at no little expense, and seen the students return afterwards. If anyone knows of similar stories about colleges, clubs, etc., who have done the same thing in the UK, I should be most obliged if they would let me know.

Do we see a trend here? I think we do. I would not condemn digital photography out of hand. I have been using a Nikon scanner, Paterson computer and Epson printer for several years, and I have just ordered my first serious digital SLR, a Nikon D70. There are many things that a digital camera can do very well. It may well yet be that I shall transfer my affections from silver halide to digital, though I can't imagine it happening quickly for a variety of reasons: I like the quality I get from my silver halide cameras, and I welcome the wet darkroom as deliverance from yet more hours in front of the computer. Just as photography did not kill painting, I do not expect digital to kill silver.

What I really expect to see, though, is for darkroom work -- especially black and white -- to become 'the ultimate alternative process.' I put that in quotes because I borrowed it from Robin Whetton of Nova, whom I thank for it. I think

179

he's right, too. 'Alternative' processes are already the entire foundation of a number of businesses, and very substantial contributors to the income of a number of others. Traditional silver halide photography has the potential to become a bigger 'alternative process' than all the others combined.

But only if we want it to. It may well be that it has to co-exist with digital. It may even be that more photographers than I reckon will be willing to abandon silver halide photography and switch purely to digital. It is without doubt that silver halide will never spawn another Kodak, or even Ilford: the market just ain't big enough. But the market is big enough, and (I firmly believe) can remain big enough, to provide a very comfortable niche market to keep film and paper available for many decades more, and with any luck, to keep film cameras operative well into the 21st century; by which time, barring remarkable medical breakthroughs, neither I nor anyone reading these words will need to worry very much.

Fantasies and Dreams...

How many of us base our photography on fantasies? I don't mean in the sense of deliberately constructing and shooting fantasies, as do a number of excellent photographers such as Marie Muscat-King. Nor do I mean daydreams, which revolve around the word 'If'. If I won the lottery... If I had a Leica... If I lived in the South of France.... To say nothing, of course, of dreams of fair young maids and matinee idols.

Rather, I mean unadmitted fantasies, and dreams that are not admitted to be fantasies. For most photographers, for example, publication is a dream that is never admitted to be a fantasy; but often it is a fantasy, for one or more of at least three reasons.

There are those who spend so much time worrying about equipment and technical perfection that they never devote enough time to taking real pictures. Their pictures may be of publishable quality, from a purely technical point of view, but they are also infinitely dull, so no sane editor is ever going to publish them.

Others never really understand what technical quality means. They snap happily away on colour print film and send it to the cheapest available processor, or worse still they shoot with low-end digicams and turn out tiny, garish prints where the colours make your eyes ache and the resolution is so low you can't make out the details anyway. But many of them still believe they have a chance of being published.

Yet others seem to regard publication as something that happens more or less magically. They seem to imagine that someone, someday, will see their pictures and be so utterly smitten than they will immediately propose a ten-spread magazine feature or a lucrative book project. The truth, of course, is that if you want your pictures published, you usually have to push and keep pushing, getting your pictures in front of as many people as possible until one of them agrees to publish.

But there are still deeper fantasies, ones that we may be unwilling to admit to ourselves. One of the most important, I would suggest, is the way in which traditionalists will often volunteer, if pushed, that they prefer the traditional 'wet' darkroom because they understand it better. They know how a mechanical camera works; they know the theory of the latent image; they know what developer does, and fixer, and how an enlarger works. A digital camera, by contrast, is merely a black box, which works or not according to the caprices of whatever deity is responsible for electronics -- possibly the Goddess of Hairdressers, in her spare time -- while computers and their associated software are are even blacker boxes and clearly under the domain of the Lord of Darkness himself, though this is a bit unfair to Bill Gates.

This is not, however, a totally convincing argument. Have you ever made up your own processing chemicals from basic ingredients? How about sensitizing your own materials? Building your own camera? Grinding your own lens? Knowing the theory, and actually doing it, are rather separate things. Besides which, do you go to the theatre, but shun television, because you know how a theatre works (or think you do) while you couldn't repair a television set? If you don't use digital, I'd suggest you should look a bit harder at your motives.

It's also true that a lot of people have a fantasy of comprehending. Film speeds are based on a lot of assumptions and approximations, and anyone who really wants to understand how to develop films and why you do things in certain ways needs to understand these. Alternatively, there's the Zone System, which reduces it all to a simple (if tedious) series of rote tests. Quite a few people who plough through these tests assume that they understand what they are doing, when in reality they are not much ahead of a well-trained parrot or a performing horse. Not all Zone aficionados are like this, and if you accept the limitations of the Zone System, it's a good way of establishing rules of thumb; but that's all it is, good rules of thumb, not real sensitometry.

Then there's the fantasy upon a fantasy, usually based on buying a new camera. The first fantasy is the admitted fantasy, the daydream, the 'If'. The second fantasy is that suddenly you would get better pictures. A large format camera would give you exquisite still lifes or landscapes; faster autofocus would give you better action shots; a digital SLR, by freeing you from the expense of film, would make you more experimental, creative, innovative.

Don't bet on it. Large format cameras are refractory beasts, and you are as likely to leave it at home because of the weight and bulk as to stride forth bearing it upon your shoulders. Faster autofocus might not be completely worthless, but you would still get better results by studying the game more, learning to anticipate, prefocusing and shooting at the right moment. And for the price of a digital SLR you can buy an awful lot of film.

The answer to the majority of photographic problems lies within the photographer. Some of the best boxing pictures ever made were taken with 4x5 inch press cameras. A lot of incredible landscapes have been shot on 35mm. And so forth. Repeat after me: "The reason I am not a better photographer has very little to do with equipment, and if I worked at it, I could become a very much better photographer with the equipment I already have."

Buggy Whips...

For most of history, durability and quality were the prime virtues of manufactured goods. Except perhaps for a few aristocrats, no-one bought style or novelty. A good pair of boots was more comfortable, more waterproof and more durable; a good knife took a better edge, was better balanced, and lasted longer.

As technology advanced, those who could afford it bought the new products: an iron sword is vastly superior to bronze, while glazed windows that admitted light but not cold air must have been a revelation.

But in real terms, everything was a lot more expensive than it is today. As recently as Victorian times you bought new clothes seldom unless you were well-to-do. You had a Best Suit, and when that became too shabby, it was relegated to Second Best or to Work -- and even when you reckoned it was worn out, it might well find another lease of life on someone else's back.

Well, OK, we still have charity shops that sell second-hand clothes, but these are mostly given away because people don't like them any more or because they have put on too much weight to wear them any more. In other words, we have entered upon Marx's period of material superabundance.

This brings us -- unexpectedly, perhaps -- to buggy whips and cameras. Buggy-whips are much favoured by a certain type of economist. Not for scourging the toiling masses, but as an illustration of what happens when A New Technology comes along. With the invention of the motor-car, say the economists, all demand for buggy-whips ceased, so the hapless buggy-whip manufacturers went out of business. Some are now making the same predictions about film in the light of digital photography.

But economists have to make wild assumptions and simplifications. Otherwise, their famously dismal science is completely impossible. Much of what they say makes absolute sense, until you put it in the context of real life. Cost-demand curves, marginal utility: it's all good stuff, if you like sweeping generalizations, truisms and platitudes.

If economists really understood what they were doing -- in other words, how specific cases work, rather than general theories -- far more of them would be rich from playing the stock market. Few are. One of the few that was noted for his business acumen was Keynes. This may tell you something.

Besides, there are still surprisingly many buggies in the world, and their drivers need whips. In relative terms, the market is tiny; but the population is so much greater than it was in the 1890s, and so many more people can afford a buggy if they want one, that someone somewhere is probably making a nice little living out of buggy whips.

So: how long should things last? 'Things' in two senses: technologies, such as buggies and silver halide film, and the tools used in those technologies, such as buggy-whips and cameras.

Any technology, surely, will last as long as people want it to, which is not a rational decision. Why would anyone bother with horses or horse-drawn vehicles, for example? From a utilitarian viewpoint, pretty much anything is better than a horse: a motor-car, a moped, a bicycle. But horses are seldom bought (at least in affluent societies) for utilitarian reasons.

Next, how long should a tool last? I'd suggest there are two components: how long before it wears out, and how long before it is superseded by something you both want and can afford.

The former is a question of time and use. The better the quality, the longer it lasts, and if it is little used, its life may be artificially prolonged. My late father-in-law's cavalry boots were bought in the early 1930s and worn occasionally for two or three years but then left in a closet for over 60 years. They are still superb boots today.

As for the latter -- when something is superseded -- many Leicas from the 1930s are still being used. Some people prefer them to modern Leicas because they are so small and light. Over half the classic 'series' Land Rovers built between 1948 and the 1970s are reputedly still on the road, as are the majority of Rolls Royces ever built.

Even so, there comes a point when something is so old that no matter how good it was when it was new, its continued use becomes a matter of habit, or nostalgia, or eccentricity -- or a mixture of all three. This seems to happen at between 25 and 50 years for most traditional top quality products, and only rarely does it exceed 75 years.

Of course there are exceptions. A digital camera may be hopelessly superseded in two years or less, while a violin may improve (or at least, not deteriorate) for centuries. But unless we have been completely taken in by the consumer society, I'd say that most of us expect at least a generation's use from the finest products available, and at least five or ten years' use from most everyday products except perhaps clothes: washing machines, fridges, and the like. Look around you (or look in your parents' houses, if you are under about 30) and see if you agree.

The Pernicious LCD...

Next time you see someone using a digital camera, just watch them for a little while. Watch how they hold the camera at arm's length, bobbing their heads like a pigeon walking, holding the camera with one hand, shading it with the other, narrowing their eyes, squinting, trying to see what's happening on that silly little screen on the back. And then, when they're satisfied and have taken the picture, watch as they lower the camera to chest level, frown, review the image, decide it's acceptable, and then get back to their lives.

That's the point: get back to their lives, back to reality. For anything from half a minute to a couple of minutes or more, they have been so engrossed in the camera and its technicalities that they wouldn't have noticed if Nicole Kidman had walked past in the nude or Osama bin Laden had been standing in front of them pulling funny faces.

Now, this is the way that a lot of snapshotters have always worked, even with a Box Brownie. You could see their brows furrowed in concentration, their tongues sticking out with the effort of thought, as they struggled with whether the subject was 'Portrait' or 'Distance'. But over the last thirty years or so, auto-everything compacts had made this approach ever less common. All they had to do was put the camera to their eye, and shoot.

Experienced photographers did much the same, except that they composed more carefully and took more pictures. Some relied on automation; others were sufficiently familiar with their cameras that they set everything manually, pretty much without thinking. But now, the horrible little screen on the back of the camera engages their attention for a totally disproportionate amount of time -- simply because it's there. Even experienced photographers start behaving like snapshotters.

Why? Because screens are very hard to ignore. Have you ever had a meal in a pub or cheap restaurant where there's a

TV screen? The programme may be garbage; the sound may be off or (worse still, unless you speak Hungarian) in Hungarian; but you still can't take your eyes off the wretched thing. Those little dancing images exercise a fascination out of all proportion to their actual worth.

Admittedly, there are times when the screen is invaluable, even for taking pictures. Recently, for example, I needed to take a picture at arm's length, to get past an obstruction between me and the subject. If I'd had a digital camera, I could have composed the picture at arm's length, but I didn't, so I had to guess. And there's no doubt that with non-reflexes, the absolute freedom from parallax that is guaranteed in close-ups is essential.

For the majority of shots, though, a plain, non-reflex viewfinder is a far better bet, because it engages you with the subject. This is why so many photographers like rangefinder cameras so much. The image is much more immediate. You aren't looking at an image on a screen, whether it's the ground-glass screen of an SLR or the LCD screen of a digicam. Rather, you're looking at the subject itself -- and it's worth noting that a lot of Leica users cultivate the habit of keeping both eyes open, one at the viewfinder, one scanning the scene. With practice, this is only a little more difficult than chewing gum and standing up at the same time.

This talk of 'engagement' may sound a bit mystical. Surely, if you're there, you're there, and it doesn't matter what sort of viewfinder you're using. Maybe that's true for some people. But it certainly isn't true for everyone. Ask anyone who rides a motorcycle and drives a car, and they'll tell you something very similar: a motorcycle is more immediate, more real, because the windscreen of a car is like a TV screen, a bell-jar cutting you off from reality, dividing the world into 'me' and 'them'.

What you have to do, therefore, is to find some way of ignoring the screen, and forcing yourself to use the viewfinder. At least, I do, and from all I've seen of other people using digicams, they do too. Use the screen for composition only when you have to, and use it for reviewing only when it doesn't get in the way of shooting.

It helps to think of the on-screen image as a Polaroid. In the studio, where you can re-shoot in an instant, take a break and check everything, Polaroids (and digital review) are invaluable. But in reportage photography, the subject would have changed utterly in the time between the Polaroid (screen image) and the final shot. This is as true of a child's birthday party as of a war. You have to shoot, shoot, and shoot some more. You never know if the shot you have just taken will be the last decent shot you get, or whether it will pale into insignificance against the vastly better shot you will get in ten minutes' time. And all the time you spend staring at a screen, you aren't shooting.

The Lord Giveth...

The Lord giveth, and the Lord taketh away; blessed be the name of the Lord. Less obviously, the same may be said of photography. It can give us a great deal, but it can also take something away.

It gives us, obviously, a greater knowledge of our world. From the most beautiful sunrise to the most horrific of war pictures, it shows us things we might never see otherwise.

It can also spur us to try to make beautiful pictures of our own. We may fail, but it's still better than sitting in front of a TV screen or computer monitor -- and people who get out and do things tend to be happier and healthier than those who merely accept everything passively.

Even when we aren't taking pictures, the habit of seeing that we get from photography can make us more aware of beauty. Have you ever had one of those days when everything is beautiful? When you are transfixed by the sight of a pebble and the shadow it casts, or the graceful arc of a single stem of grass? When you fully understand Blake, seeing a world in a grain of sand, and heaven in a wild flower? And hold infinity in your hand, and eternity in an hour?

The camera even helps to define (and refine) beauty. Valetta in Malta is a beautiful planned Renaissance city disfigured by a cat's-cradle of crudely strung power cables, telephone wires, and other pieces of electric string of indefinable purpose. In a perfect world, all this would be hidden underground or chased into walls. In the real world, there are financial and practical constraints: in a living, working city, a degree of 'necessary' ugliness must always exist.

When you are there, you can see the beauty behind the ugliness. But your camera cannot. The pictures you take home must be (in the telling phrase) 'picture perfect'. So must the pictures presented to the grant-making bodies, the governments, the potential tourists. And so the wires are gradually being tidied up, better hidden, integrated into the city. The camera is changing the world.

Photography can change the world in other ways, too. Blood, guts and spilled brains look much the same on any battlefield, but the painters who romanticized Waterloo conveniently omitted them. The more democratic medium of photography, with more people presenting more kinds of pictures, may shy away from the worst sights, or more likely, the media may refuse to publish them; but even sanitized shots of 'body bags' have a strong adverse effect on public support for a war.

If photography gives us so much, what does it take away? Well, 'take away' is something of an overstatement. 'Diminish' is a better word. There are two closely related ways, I suggest, in which photography can (if we let it) diminish our pleasure rather than augmenting it.

One is an awareness of beauty that is not visual. The other is the ability to enjoy to the full any beauty that cannot be photographed. In other words, photography may stop you grokking the fullness. If you are constantly looking for the perfect photograph, it can be all too easy to ignore or discount everything else: air like warm velvet, the faint smell of wood-smoke, the slightest stirrings of a breeze to twitch the prayer-flags and cat's-paw the water.

The second, at least as bad, is things that are visually beautiful but which we lack the talent, or equipment, or time, or understanding, to capture on film. This can be very frustrating indeed. For example, on my first visit to eastern Slovakia and the High Tatras in 2004 I could not believe what a beautiful country it is. It is endlessly stunning: mountain vistas, lakes, ruined castles perched on hills, houses painted in colours that once were intense but now are faded, patchy and cracked. I cannot begin to do justice to it.

But hold on a minute. Why should I feel the need to do justice to it? What is so important about me, about my photography, that I want to capture a whole country in a few days? Why am I not content to take what I can? And then go back, and take more? And then more again? This is what I have done in Malta: why not Slovakia? Besides, 'take' has connotations of exploitation which are not appropriate. I take only what is freely given in the realm of beauty, plus what I can afford in food and shelter.

Besides, if it were not for photography, I should probably never have gone to Slovakia anyway. If I had not gone there, I should have missed all the beauty I couldn't photograph, the kind of beauty I am slowly re-learning to appreciate. Photography giveth, and that which photography taketh away can be regained; blessed be the name of photography.

Health and Safety at Play

Health and safety at work is a serious issue. Throughout history, countless employers have exploited countless workers with little or no regard for their well-being. But health and safety at play -- for instance, in the darkroom -- is rather different, for a number of reasons.

Only the fiercest libertarian would argue that manufacturers should be allowed to sell dangerous products without warnings. But if (say) a particular developer is intensely poisonous, and the photographer is warned of this, he may still choose to use it with appropriate precautions. Pyrogallol is a good example.

But even pyro, which is quite probably the most poisonous chemical in reasonably popular use, is not necessarily all that dangerous. In the words of someone who has a pretty good grasp of the toxicology of photographic chemicals, "There are some things you worry about your children doing, and some things you worry about doing yourself." I wouldn't dream of handling pyro without gloves, let alone snorting it, but equally, I'm not going to worry greatly about very occasional skin contact with working-solution PMK.

There's also the point that when you're at play, instead of at work, you are usually reasonably wide-awake, alert and enjoying yourself. You may make mistakes, but they are rarely the same kind of mistakes that are made at work as a result of ignorance and over-familiarity (think Homer Simpson).

Let's take something less toxic than pyro or plutonium, for exammple: MQ developer. It won't do you any good if you drink half a pint of it, but stop and think. How long could you keep half a pint of developer down? For that matter, how likely are you to be able to drink that much of it? Why would you do so? Is it a real risk?

Sure, you don't want to store the stuff in lemonade bottles, especially in reach of children, because there's always the possibility that you might swig it from the bottle because you were thirsty or (worse still) that children might persevere with it, even though they didn't like the taste, because there are plenty of other grown-up drinks that taste pretty awful to a child. But the kind of precautions that you need to take are hardly taxing, and should be reasonably obvious to anyone who isn't actually mentally defective.

Now let's move out to something less toxic still: silver. I have seen it confidently asserted that silver 'like other heavy metals' is a cumulative poison. This is what I call arts-graduate science. Silver is a metal; it's heavy; some heavy metals are indeed cumulative poisons with very nasty effects; therefore silver is a dangerous cumulative poison. Except that it isn't.

If you don't believe me, check the website of the Center for Disease Control in Atlanta, www.cdc.gov. They will tell you exactly how deadly silver is, and the answer is, 'not very'. The CDC could never be accused of being overly relaxed about the risks posed by any toxin, but they certainly don't put silver in the same class as mercury or cadmium.

Even where there are genuinely nasty poisons in the darkroom, such as cadmium (which was a favourite ingredient of warm-tone papers in the past, and a true cumulative heavy metal poison), they are rarely banned because they pose a threat to the casual user: the concentrations are just too small. Rather, they are banned to protect workers in factories where they are made, or because of a danger of leaching into ground-water if they are present in large quantities in ground-fill -- as some heavy metals are, especially in batteries. It's an excellent idea to take your batteries to a recycling station, rather than just chucking them in the bin, but the risk that they pose to you when you are actually using them is very slender indeed.

Finally, let's move on to my favourite: that you should never eat or drink in the darkroom. There's certainly something to be said for not eating if you are going to dip your fingers in the developer and then eat cake with them, but the main reason I never eat in the darkroom is that I don't want crumbs and greasy fingerprints on my film. The risk to my health, provided I am not too stupid, is trivial; the risk to my pictures is what I worry about.

When it comes to not drinking, though, I am at a loss. I drink my beer out of a tall beer glass; my wine out of a stemmed wine-glass; and my whisky out of a cut-glass tumbler my brother gave me. In the unlikely event that I were to have a tot of vodka in the darkroom, I'd use a little shot-glass. I do not drink tea or coffee, but my wife does, usually (if she is just making it for herself) out of a mug.

None of these vessels is easily confused with a developing tray, or even a developing tank; and I am certainly not likely to remove the straw from my Pimms and stick it in the Nova tank. Likewise, I cannot readily imagine confusing a sip of ID-11 with a sip of Laphroaig, or a gulp of Corbieres with a gulp of selenium toner. In fact I suspect that I might notice the smell before I even put any into my mouth. Health and safety in the darkroom? Yes, fine: but be realistic.

Why I Can't Work In France

France is one of the most beautiful countries in the world. The French countryside -- the French themselves call it 'la France profonde' or 'deep France' -- boasts a stunning variety of scenery, dotted with gorgeous buildings, while French cities are (at least in their ancient hearts) miracles of adapting the past to the present. French villages are consistently lovely, though it must be said that part of this is down to what the French call 'desertification', the abandoning of the villages for the cities. There is simply not the money available to spoil them in the name of improvement.

Then there is French culture. Not just High Culture such as opera and theatre, though of course there's plenty of that. No: the everyday culture of bars and cafes and playing boules in the car-park and vide-greniers (the village-based equivalent of a British car boot sale, but infinitely more interesting). Then there are the regional festivals, fairs and events in which even the deep countryside abounds. There are food festivals, music festivals, folklore festivals, festivals that celebrate the ingenuity and craftsmanship of French artisans. Many are extremely photogenic.

But if you want to photograph them for publication, forget it. The vast majority of French people have absolutely no problem with being photographed, but a series of downright perverse lawsuits has made it extraordinarily risky for a photographer to publish the pictures. The concept of a 'right to privacy' has been extended so far -- largely by accident, it seems -- that it is an act of extreme rashness to publish a picture of virtually anyone. For that matter, there have even been examples of the owners of cafes and bistros suing (successfully) for recompense when their establishment appears on a postcard. You might think that the publicity would do them no harm whatsoever, and indeed, that they would welcome it. Most of the time you would be right. But the times that you are wrong could cost you dearly.

Of course you can publish if you have their written permission, but if you have to ask every person in a picture for written permission to use the picture, plus the owner of the building behind them, you are going to spend a lot more time seeking permissions than you are in taking pictures. This is hardly conducive to a rapid, fluid style of working. Besides, it would only need one refusal to put the kibosh on a whole picture.

Again, I should make myself clear. I'm talking about editorial use here, not advertising. In most countries, it is taken for granted that you cannot use someone's picture in a way that implies an endorsement of a particular project or lifestyle. I know one photographer who was sued for a lot of money by a surfer whose picture appeared on the cover of a music CD. Apparently the surfer in question was very well known, and accustomed to accepting large sums of money to endorse various products; and he took understandable exception to being shown to appear to endorse a collection of songs he had never even heard.

Editorial use is (or should be) another matter. A couple of weeks before I wrote these words, there was a festival in Oiron, a few miles from where I live. I was out of the country, so I missed it, but it was apparently excellent: jazz, rap, reggae, folk dances, just about anything you can imagine in the field of music and dance. All free, too. I've no doubt I should have enjoyed it, but as a working photographer, it would have been a complete waste of time because I'd have had to seek individual permissions for any pictures I'd wanted to use, and life ain't long enough. This would apply even if my photographs and captions were not merely factual, but flattering: if I'd said that Miss X stole the show with her beauty and her dancing, and produced pictures to show it, she could still sue me if she wanted.

Fortunately, I was in Eastern Hungary at the time, photographing a Transylvanian folk song and dance troupe another festival. A Miss X stole the show with her beauty and her dancing. But I can publish these pictures, which I could not if I had taken them in France. I had to spend a lot of time and money, and travel hundreds of miles, to get picture which I could probably have equaled a few miles away. I was in Hungary precisely because of the problem of French lawsuits. For a country which for so long dominated the world of candid photography, with masters like Cartier-Bresson and Brassai; for a country that today could be one of the premier photographic destinations in the word, France is certainly getting this one wrong.

Advice To Those Who Want Advice

Critiques, evaluations, portfolio readings, call them what you will: there is much to be said for having your pictures examined by someone experienced who will discuss them with you. But you have to be prepared, and you have to know what you want. Also, you have to be ready to listen.

At the July 2004 Rencontres at Arles Frances Schultz and I did print critiques on the Leica stand. The best portfolios were stunning: we learned more from them than ever they could learn from us. But some photographers weren't prepared: they didn't have the right prints, of the right quality, in the right order. Nor did they know what they wanted: they weren't clear on whether they were seeking advice about publication, exhibition, technical quality or their overall approach to photography. And at least one didn't want to hear what we had to say anyway.

Begin by putting yourself in the critic's place. What are your pictures about; what is the 'handle' by which the reviewer can grasp your work? It can be a genre such as landscape or portrait; a technique such as Polaroid transfer or pinhole; a theme such as Mexican wrestling or circuses; or an ambition to help a cause, be it the Tibetan freedom movement or a steam railway preservation society. You can even have two or three different themes, sets or ambitions. But show someone a diffuse, undifferentiated mass of pictures, indiscriminately mixing themes and techniques and genres, and there's a limit to what the critic can say: he or she just doesn't know where to begin.

Your theme must either be immediately visually obvious, or capable of explanation in a couple of sentences. If the critic still looks blank after the explanation, or says something like, "I'm sorry, I just don't see these as a unified set of pictures," you have two choices. Either accept that there is no point of contact, and thank them politely for their time and walk away, or stick around and listen to what they have to say on the grounds that you might learn something.

Either approach is entirely independent of whatever opinion you may have formed of the person giving the critique. You may think they are pompous ignoramuses who aren't fit to judge a camera club competition, or (worse still) that they are pompous ignoramuses who are fit only to judge camera club competitions. So? If you don't want to talk to them, don't. Otherwise, listen.

It's perfectly all right to try to elicit useful feedback with phrases such as "What I was trying to do was... " or "What I thought was... " but there's not much future for either party in arguing. Leave the critic to deal with those who want to listen to what they have to say; find someone else whose advice you find more helpful.

Probably the most useful advice we gave a number of photographers was on selecting picture sets and putting them in sequence. What we found at Arles was that often, two or more themes had been conflated, with the mixed pack then being bulked out further by pictures that were at best tangentially related to the theme. Often, too, there would be a number of strong pictures plus a couple of weak pictures. Dropping the weak pictures made the strong ones stronger.

The optimum number for a set to show someone is probably six to ten. Five or fewer pictures rarely say enough, and much after ten, visual fatigue sets in. By all means show someone three sets of six, but one set of 18 is likely to be a lot less successful. On the other hand, if you have only one set, then you don't want fewer than eight; ten is probably better; and you can get away with a dozen.

If there's a story, the pictures should be in the right order to tell it, while if the effect is purely visual, they should be in the most pleasing juxtapositions. The pictures should be stacked in order in the portfolio so that the photographer can lay them out quickly and apparently casually without having to read the backs, subtract pictures, hunt elsewhere, re-shuffle and generally waste time.

Because Arles is predominantly for 'Fine Art' photographers, technical quality was something of a vexed point. It is a truism that almost any 'fault' can be used creatively, and most were: soft focus, lack of focus, 'off' colours, camera shake, you name it. On the other hand, you have to present your pictures as closely as possible to the way you would like them to be seen: it is simply not good enough to say, "Well, they can true up the colours and make them more consistent when they print the book."

Ultimately you know -- even if the reviewer doesn't -- what you really want your pictures to look like. While you can try to fool both him and yourself, there comes a point when the pictures are rubbish, and both of you know it, but he's too polite to say so and you're too scared. Be prepared, and ready to listen, and everyone can get something out of it. Otherwise, why waste your time and theirs?

The Death of Black & White?

Think of a hundred million pounds. It's not exactly small change. At the most conservative estimate, that is the size of the world-wide market for black and white film and paper. Quite possibly, you could double that number. You might even be able to triple it. This is how accurate economic statistics often are.

Sure, this kind of money doesn't amount to much when you set it alongside the real mass markets such as motor-cars, make-up or pet food. But there has to be a very nice living, thank you all the same, for quite a few people who are willing to service that market.

This is why, even if I take a worst-case scenario, I find it impossible to believe that the collapse of Ilford -- whether it be complete and final, or (as I believe more likely) partial and temporary -- is actually the death-knell for monochrome. There are just too many people who love it too much. Reports of the death of black and white are, as Mark Twain said of the reports of his own death, greatly exaggerated.

But yet, we have already received numerous letters here at AP along the following lines: "Woe! Woe! Thrice Woe! This is The End! We shall all be forced to bow before the great god Digital!"

There are numerous earthy responses to such cries that spring to mind, none of them alas printable in a family magazine which (to borrow from the judge in the case of Lady Chatterley's Lover) your wife and your servants may read. Suffice it to say that this belief is codswallop -- a word which itself may have an even less elevated meaning than is immediately obvious.

A basic truth of capitalism is that wherever there is demand, supply is immediately forthcoming as long as the technical problems are not insurmountable. Many of these demand-supply pairings are illegal or undesirable or both, but this has relatively little effect on their flourishing: think of prostitution, drugs and child pornography. Once again, black and white photography is a real niche market next to any of these, but there is still enough money in it to make it reasonably attractive.

The question, therefore, is reduced to whether the technical problems are insurmountable. After all, running a film-coating line is significantly more difficult than leaving calling cards in London's telephone booths with such ambiguous messages as "For sale: Lovely chest with loose drawers," or even photographing a naked child with your digicam and putting up a web site. Unfortunately, too, there is a good deal less money in black and white photography than in cocaine refining or LSD synthesis, and although I have only an elementary grasp of either of these technologies, I have to say that coke and acid manufacture look an awful lot easier than coating film. The machinery is smaller and more affordable for a start.

There are, however, literally dozens of film-coating lines in the world, and they are not all going to go away overnight. Suppose for a moment not that only Ilford vanished, but also that Agfa, Fuji and Kodak decided to stop coating their own excellent black and white materials. This is deeply unlikely, but even if it happened, I'd still be perfectly happy to use the products of Foma in the Czech Republic, Forte in Hungary and Fotokemika in Croatia, and it wouldn't be impossible for Slavich in Russia and Hindustan Film in India to improve their quality control to the point where I'd use them too. Those are only the coating plants I know about; there are others all over the place, including (according to one rumour I heard recently) even Iraq. And anything that is true of film is even more true of paper, which is a good deal easier to coat.

In other words, even if Ilford is dead and gone -- and as I say, I should be very much surprised if it were -- then it isn't the end of the world. What I will do, though, is throw Ilford's failure back in the faces of many of those who are bemoaning their loss.

How much did you spend last year on film? And how much on cameras and lenses? Let's face it: if every camera manufacturer on earth stopped making film cameras tomorrow, there are still enough first-class cameras around to last for many decades, though the price of M-series Leicas and Nikon Fs would double overnight. But if all the film manufacturers stopped, we would be in trouble. If you want film to stay around, buy more of it, and stop wasting your money on illusory 'upgrades' to your equipment. As I said, the basic truth of capitalism is that supply springs up to meet demand, and if you don't create a realistic demand, you can't blame the manufacturers for failing to come forward with the supply.

Oversize Prints

Most people print too big. Look back to the jewel-like contact prints of 100 years ago. Very few are larger than whole-plate (6-1/2 x 8-1/2 inches, 165x216mm), and the largest size commonly encountered is half-plate (4-3/4 x 6-1/2 inches, 121x165mm). There are plenty of superb portraits even at quarter-plate (3-1/4 x 4-1/4 inches, 83x108mm.)

To a considerable extent, it is true, these limits were imposed by cost and weight: both equipment and materials was proportionally a lot more expensive than they are today, and even if you could afford the plates to fill them, a stack of loaded half-plate book-form holders weighed enough to daunt the stoutest soul.

Then came 'miniature' cameras: for in the early days, anything smaller than quarter-plate was regarded as a 'miniature' and Rolleiflex TLRs were lumped together with Leicas. The films available were truly awful. They were slow, grainy and unsharp, and until the widespread adoption of solvent fine-grain developers such as Kodak D-76 (which was invented in the late 1920s) the biggest picture you could really extract from your Leica while still retaining even half-decent print quality was around postcard size (3-1/2 x 5-1/2 inches, 89x140mm).

But the Leica owners couldn't resist showing off. They went to extraordinary lengths to get fine grain, including Odell's physical development process. This took an hour and a half; involved physically rubbing each exposure with a finger-tip to ensure even wetting; and wiped more than two stops off the already miserable film speed, which in the case of Kodak's original Panatomic was only about the equivalent of ISO 4 to begin with. Then they made lousy whole-plate prints from these negatives.

Of course, materials got better and better, and by the 1950s, if you weren't too allergic to grain, you could make an adequate 8x10 inch (20x25cm) print off a 35mm negative, and you could make a really superb post-card. So what did 35mm users do? They started making 12x16 (30x40cm) and even 20x16 inch (40x50cm) prints. And they do to this day.

Now, it's true that in colour you can make astonishingly good 10x enlargements, or even bigger, especially if you scan in the negative and make an ink-jet print; but in black and white, they always look like hell as soon as you examine them at anything closer than a (very long) arm's length.

There are several reasons for this, but a very important one is that they are not sharp. At that degree of enlargement, they can't be. To have 80 line pairs per millimetre (lp/mm) all across a 35mm negative would be very good indeed. Enlarge that almost 17x to a 16x20 inch (40x50cm) print and the maximum you can have, assuming a perfect enlarger lens (another reason for using a scanner), is about 5 lp/mm on the print: adequate from a metre or more away, but not much cop close up. But enlarge a 4x5 inch negative to 16x20 inches, and you are only going up 4x, so even a lousy (and easily attainable) 40 lp/mm on the negative is still 10 lp/mm on the print.

It is fair enough to say that you don't normally look at a big print from close up, but it is not fair to say that you shouldn't. Why shouldn't you, after all? The only real reason is because it will expose the shortcomings of the print: hardly a convincing argument, more a confession of failure.

A really great print, with detail that goes on forever, invites you to dive through the surface like Alice through the looking-glass, to enter the photographer's own magic miniature world. Somehow, this can be even more compelling in black and white than in colour, perhaps because black and white is more abstracted, more unreal, more like a dream; and a dream, as we all know, can seem more real than reality itself.

It's true that some prints 'want' to be big, and look better big, but an awful lot don't. All too often, the only reason to make a bigger print is because you can. Yes, it is more difficult to make a good big print than a good small one, but then, it isn't easy to make a really good small print, either. Besides, how much does size matter? With many pictures -- I'd say most -- a good print is a good print, big or small, and there is not much point in an empty display of bravado, which is all that many big prints are: a quick look at the average camera club competition or exhibition soon reveals that the people who make the biggest prints are far from always the ones who take the best pictures.

Increasingly, therefore, I favour quite small images, typically no more than 5x enlargements from 35mm, in the middle of a sheet of 8x10 inch paper. Although they cannot quite compete on pure quality with contact prints from bigger negatives (which we also shoot), they have much of the same charm and mystery; a charm and mystery that is lost when they go bigger.

Some may find it odd, or pretentious, to use a sheet of paper significantly larger than the image itself: after all, 5x off 35mm is 120x180mm, or about 4-3/4 inches by just over 7 inches, close to half-plate. But there is a good reason for doing so. A small piece of paper is often disregarded: it's a mini-lab cheapo, an amateur's throw-away, something printed that size to save money. By printing on 8x10 inch, you are drawing attention to the fact that you _want_ the print to be that size, that you think it looks best at that size. Try it. You might find the same.

Paedophile Paranoia

The first time I became aware of what I call 'paedophile paranoia' was in New York City some ten or fifteen years ago. There were some children playing baseball in a back alley, probably somewhere in the east thirties. It was as all-American a scene as one could wish for. But when I took a couple of pictures, a nearby adult came over and asked me to desist. I asked why. He said it was because people might take pictures of children for 'the wrong reasons', possibly with a view to kidnapping them.

I did not think much more about it for a few years, until I was living in Kent. Polaroid had given me quite a lot of slightly outdated sepia 4x5 inch film, and I was using it as fast as I could before it went off. One day, I stuck a box of it in my pocket and set off to the sea-shore at the end of the road to take a few hand-held pictures with my MPP Mk VII. As I recall, it was early autumn, so the sea-front wasn't crowded.

Even so, there were three or four teenage girls there, and there was the inevitable "Take me photo!" So I did, and (of course) I gave the girls some of the prints. Realizing that their parents might be a bit worried about a strange man giving their daughters what were, after all, quite expensive pictures, I wrote my name, address and phone number on the back of a scrap print and gave it to one of the girls with the words, "If your parents are worried, and want to know who I am, tell them to call me."

Half an hour later, the police were around at my house. Why was I taking pictures? What did I use them for? Why had I given the girls my address and 'phone number? I showed them some of the books I had written, and explained that this was what I do for a living: take pictures, and write books. As for the address, I explained that I realized that the girls' parents might be concerned, so I thought it best to give them my address and phone number to show that everything was above board.

The policewoman sniffed. "Huh. An opportunist photographer." I felt insulted and annoyed, but I also realized there was nothing I could say: this was the same attitude I had encountered in New York. If the parents had telephoned, that would be one thing: I was trying to be a decent human being. They treated me like a criminal.

Since then, I have heard of numerous examples of the same thing: of photographers on beaches being arrested and all their films confiscated, and of course of all the nativity plays and the like where photography has been banned. And I carefully refrained from pointing my camera at anyone below the age of about 18.

A while back, though, something happened which made me realize just how bad things have become in England. I was riding my motorcycle in rural France. A young mother was walking along with one child in a pushchair and a daughter of maybe six or eight beside her. The little girl saw the motorcycle, and smiled and waved. It was a beautiful smile. Her mother looked up and smiled too.

I suddenly realized that I could not remember the last time a child spontaneously smiled at me in England. I also realized that just as with George W's 'War on Terrorism', we are feeding the very fears and hatreds which cause the problems we seek to eliminate. Teach a child that every adult is a threat, a risk, a danger, and they will never trust anyone. If they don't trust anyone, they grow up in an atomized society in which no-one knows anyone else. And if no-one knows anyone else, it is a great deal easier for an unknown person to do something horrible to someone, child or adult, acting out some fantasy that might never have arisen if they had learned from experience that most other people are, in fact, much the same as themselves. Thus do we encourage our child abusers and our murderers.

Of course there has to be a balance. Precisely because we have built such an unpleasant society -- indeed, remember

Maggie Thatcher's famous dictum "There is no such thing as society" -- we have to be a lot more careful than we used to be. I do not know if it is possible to return to the state of relative innocence that exists in much of the world outside Britain and the United States. But I don't want to live in a country where children are afraid to smile.

What Is Truth ?

What is truth? I was a bit leery of using this quotation, given the person with whom it is most commonly associated (Pontius Pilate). But it is a fair question, legalistically, philosophically and -- to go from the sublime to the ridiculous -- in photography.

If we rely on a mini-lab or mail-order lab to do our printing for us, we know that truth is a flexible commodity. Too red? Too blue? Too green? Too light? Too dark? Overly cropped? "Nah, love, nobody else has complained." We can have it reprinted nearer to the heart's desire, but unless we stand over the printer with a whip and a revolver, we are unlikely ever to get very close to what we remember.

Even if we are doing the printing ourselves, we may not be able to get it right. My wife Frances Schultz once spent half a day trying to reprint a picture of herself holding a white cat belonging to her parents. She could not get the colour right. If her complexion was right, the cat was a pale pink; if the cat was a neutral white, her complexion was a very sickly green indeed.

A few months later, the next time we visited her parents -- we lived thousands of miles apart -- she looked harder at the cat and said, "The damn' thing IS pink!": it did indeed have the palest pink tinge to its fur. But everyone knows that you do not get pink cats, so she didn't print it that way. What we remember and what we can get printed are not necessarily the same thing.

Slides are better. To be sure, there are minor variations. When I was working as an assistant in London, we once had to change labs: I forget why. We shot half a dozen rolls of film of identical subjects under identical lighting, and sent them to the old lab and five others for processing.

These were top London advertising labs, remember, all with the highest reputations. And not one of the films matched. Colour variations ranged from +/- CC05 to CC10, and density variations were easily +/- 1/3 stop.

It didn't matter so much. Consistency is more important than a particular colour cast because you can correct consistent casts with CC filters. Besides, very few clients complain unless the colour is really bad, far worse than most photographers would accept -- though I remember a medical client who rejected several generations of Kodachromes until, in desperation, we resubmitted the original set. He accepted them with glad cries, asking us why we couldn't have got it right the first time.

In any case, what the origination house may do to colours is something that can barely be discussed in polite company. One of my pictures -- it's actually on the cover of Professional Travel Photography, Focal Press, 1998 -- has been reproduced half a dozen times, and each time the colour has been different. It's a picture of two women carrying water-pots in their heads on the banks of the Jumna, shot from the Taj Mahal. The sand is yellow; blue; brown; grey; red... No wonder I'm not too fussy about the precise density or colour cast of slides.

The real problem comes with digital images. With a scan from a slide you can make a reasonable fist at matching the screen, the tranny and the ink-jet print, though ideally you need colour-matched lights such as are provided by my estimable DW Viewtower. But with a digital picture, there is no 'original'. There is the image on the back of the camera, and the image on your monitor, and the image on the ink-jet print, and (for repro) the final printed image.

What I do -- I don't see much alternative -- is to get a TIFF image that looks right on the monitor, with the minimum of manipulation from the original Nikon RAW file, then try to get an ink jet that is reasonably close to the screen, using the colour-controlled light of my Viewtower. Then it's a question of sending that in as a reference print, and trusting to whatever deities preside over printing-houses. If I see proofs, as I do for books, I'm in with a chance: I can say 'cut magenta' or 'increase yellow' or whatever, but I'm still essentially back to sending prints into a minilab.

This is not a question of colour management, but of colour opinion. Not just balance, but saturation and contrast too. With traditional silver halide you can affect all this within modest limits. With digital, there are hardly any limits.

This is the most insidious part of all. If it doesn't look quite natural, the easiest thing in most cases is not to make it look more natural, but to make it less natural and more striking. That is not so much a fault in digital photography. It is a fault in ourselves.

Amateur & Pro Cameras

Fifty years ago, there was a big distinction between amateur and professional cameras. Even quite serious amateurs commonly used cameras with fixed triplet or at most Tessar-type lenses, and regarded a whole-plate enlargement as a rare extravagance. Whole-plate, for those who do not remember it, is 6-1/2 x 8-1/2 inches, 165x216mm, just under a 7x enlargement off 35mm.

Professionals, on the other hand, might still have been using whole-plate cameras and making contact prints; or 5x4 inch with modest degrees of enlargement; or possibly roll-film, though this was right on the edge from a quality point of view except for low-resolution applications such as newspaper photography. When professionals did use 35mm, it was normally the best available: initially Leica or Contax, later maybe Nikon and Canon as well. But for the first few decades of its life 35mm was very much an amateur's format.

All this changed significantly in the late 1950s and the 1960s. The average quality of cameras and lenses rose steadily, and perhaps more importantly, so did the average quality of films. What is more, prices in real terms fell. Excellent interchangeable-lens cameras, mostly Japanese, were within the reach of more and more people. Even 'second-string' cameras such as the Nikkormat were built to unbelievably high standards.

By the late 1960s, many amateurs were shooting to exactly the same technical standards as most professionals. Admittedly, you could get some rather nasty lenses that put price and convenience ahead of image quality, especially among low-end zooms and cheap, non-marque wide-angles, but with (say) a 50/1.8 on your Canon FTb you could still produce results that were indistinguishable from the best that the pros could do. With all but the cheapest medium format cameras, professional image quality was taken for granted.

But today, thanks to digital, we are very much back in the same position as we were 50 years ago. There is an enormous quality gap between amateur and pro equipment. The bare minimum that a serious studio photographer can afford to consider is 12 megapixels, and 20 or 30 is a lot better. It's true that 6 megapixels is perfectly adequate for news photography -- why do you suppose that the Nikon D2H offers nothing more? -- and it's also true that at 200 dpi, the de facto standard for ink-jet printing, a 6 megapixel camera can deliver about a 10x15 inch (25x37.5cm) print. But for high-quality photomechanical reproduction at 300 dpi, you can't even get a full-page image off 6 megapixels.

For most amateurs, this probably does not matter at all. Their pictures can easily be run across a half-page and they'll look very good: you don't need to worry about how your digital images will look in AP's gallery pages. But suppose -- fantasy of fantasies -- that our esteemed editor was so impressed by your pictures that he said, "That's it! Never mind Frans Lanting! We want this across a double-page spread!"

Now, if you had been using (say) an old Nikkormat and a decent prime lens, there wouldn't be any problem. With a 50-year-old Hasselblad you would be even better placed. Sure, there would be a number of technical concerns such as correct focus; an appropriate aperture to avoid depth of field problems; and (unless you used a tripod) a high enough shutter speed to avoid camera shake. Remember, too, that the bigger the enlargement, the easier it is to see camera shake.

But with a 6 megapixel camera, even if you have focus and depth of field and camera shake fully under control, you're stuffed. The picture may not actually look awful at double-page, but it is very unlikely indeed to look anything like as good as a 35mm film image of equal technical competence, let alone roll-film.

You therefore have three choices. You can stick with film, in the (perhaps vain) hope that your best pictures will be great enough to warrant splash treatment. You can switch to digital, and give up any real chance of big, professional images unless the subject matter is so extraordinary that no-one cares about the quality: a flying saucer abducting Tony Blair, perhaps. Or you can mix the two, reserving the digital for pics you know that no-one is ever going to want to use big, and keeping film for the very best you can do, or for times when digital isn't convenient: when you don't want to worry about battery charging, or having enough memory cards for an extended trip, for example.

The last is what I'm planning on doing: it's the Nikon D70 that has persuaded me. It's a superb camera. The trouble is, there have been all too many times when I've taken my best shots on whatever I had with me, and there have been other times when picture editors have made a full-page picture of something I thought warranted a half page at most. How do I know what to shoot on digital, and what on film? It's making me nervous.

The Good Old Days

There is nothing quite like reading ancient photo magazines to remind us that we are living, right now, in the good old days. We have more and better cameras; greatly superior materials, especially in colour; far more choices in how we work; and (above all) everything is much cheaper.

For example, I was recently reading an AP from June 1950. How does L125 for a Contax III with f/2 Sonnar sound? That's not inflation-adjusted: that was the asking price for a second-hand camera of a design that was at the time some 14 years old. Adjust it for inflation -- call it 20x for a credible round number -- and you are looking at L2500. What is really strange to modern eyes is that in the motoring press of the same era, Speed Six Bentleys were regularly advertised for the same sort of money, and there is not much doubt which would have proved the better investment.

All right, British prices were heavily distorted by post-war austerity and the near-ban on the importation of new cameras, so let's look at the United States, the economy of which was booming. Again, I'll apply a reasonable-sounding 20x correction factor to some 1951 prices: I don't have any US magazines from 1950. A new Contax IIa with an f/1.5 Sonnar was $476 ($9,500); a new Leica IIIf with an f/2 Summitar was $385 ($7700); and a Nikon with f/1.4 Nikkor was $349 ($7000).

Another thing that jumps out from the pages of old magazines the austerity of everyday life. In January 1939, Miniature Camera Magazine bemoaned the lack of a good, battery-powered enlarger. Why would anyone need such a thing? The opening sentence of the piece gives a clue: "Five out of twelve homes in this country have no electric light."

For that matter, as I was writing this article, the water supply to my house died suddenly for a few hours, because someone further up the village was being connected. It wouldn't normally have mattered, but I had just re-wired the darkroom following the installation on a second Magnifax Multigrade head and Frances was planning on an afternoon's printing. If you have to rely on well-water (fortunately I have a well) instead of running water, you have a sudden glimpse of the conditions under which so many of our photographic forebears laboured.

Of course this austerity had its bright side. Because people had to be more self-reliant, they often understood better what they were doing and how it worked. It was taken for granted that the average enthusiastic amateur would at least be able to compound his own chemicals, and books and articles on how to make things were commonplace: even equipment such as enlargers was quite often made at home.

The great thing about the present day, however, is not so much that we have such remarkable digital cameras as the Nikon D70, but that we can take our choice from most of the best of more than 150 years of photographic evolution. Silver? Digital? Colour? Black and white? Large formats? Small formats? Enlargements? Contact prints? Take your pick: it's all there for the asking (and, it must be said, the paying for).

One thing has never changed, though: the capacity of all photographers for bitter argument, preferably in the correspondence columns of photographic journals. They almost always argue over exactly the same thing, to wit, new technology. There's always an Old Guard saying that no-one needs all these new-fangled and expensive ideas such as panchromatic film, miniature cameras, fast lenses (f/3.5 and faster!), fast films (what's wrong with 1/5 second at f/3.5 for a theatre performance, after all?), flash, exposure meters, colour and of course digital. Against them there are always the Young Turks, jeering and taunting their elders and swearing that the innovations that they so enthusiastically embrace will soon result in the utter destruction of the old order.

Both sides are completely wrong, of course. Very little disappears completely, until demand falls so low that it is

218

uneconomic to continue commercial production -- and even then, you can still coat your own wet plates or make your own printing-out paper if you are so inclined. It's true that fortunes rise and fall: the rangefinder renaissance of the last few years is an excellent illustration of this, as are the troubles at Ilford. But then again, Gandolfi is still in business, as they have been since shortly after AP was founded. It's all photography, all drawing-with-light, after all; and it does not seem unlikely that AP will still be reporting on it, perhaps with Martian and Lunar correspondents, in 120 years' time.

If I Could Only Have One Camera

If I could only have one camera, I think it would be a Leica MP. The MP is essentially the same as my much-loved M2, but with three big advantages. It is 40 years newer, and even the finest machinery does not last forever. It has through-lens metering. And it takes the utterly lovely Leicavit trigger-wind base. Leicavits may seem to offer little advantage over the traditional thumb-lever, but once you are used to them, they are very hard to live without.

This is not to say that the MP is the only camera I could live with as my sole picture-taker. The second choice would probably be the Voigtlander Bessa-R2, for much the same reasons as the MP (including a trigger-wind base). After that it would be a tough fight between my Alpa (with 38/4.5 Zeiss Biogon and 44x66cm back) and a 5x7 inch Gandolfi Precision on a whole-plate chassis. Either, obviously, would entail a completely different style of photography from 35mm and from each other; but I think I could live very happily with either.

But then, to be realistic, I could also live very happily with my Kodak Retina IIa, though I'd prefer to have it serviced first by Kevin at Camerex in Exeter. Or there are my Nikon Fs and Nikkormats. Or my Linhof Technikardan 9x12 or Super Technika V 13x18. Or...

This is the point. I don't have to live with one camera. Nor do most people nowadays. This is especially true at the moment, when a flight to digital means that there are incredible numbers of second-hand top-quality film cameras available at absurdly low prices. They can be expected to last half-way to forever, and run on film which, contrary to the doomsayers and digital boosters, will be around for a very long time yet. If you have L1000 to spend -- the entry level for a decent-quality digital SLR -- you could just about buy, from the classified ads in an average week's AP, a 35mm SLR and a medium format camera and a 4x5 inch camera. You could certainly buy a 35mm SLR outfit and either a medium format camera or large format.

Now let's extend it a bit further. As I write these words, I had been using a Nikon D70 for a couple of weeks. There were several jobs I had put off until it arrived: for example, a couple of step-by-step articles that would be a lot more hassle to shoot on film, and a couple of book proposals where I wanted to explore the ideas on digital before committing to a full film shoot, probably on 6x7cm.

This is where it gets interesting. I can't readily imagine living only with a D70, despite the fact that it's probably the best price-quality compromise currently available in affordable digital SLRs, but then, I couldn't imagine switching from my trusty typewriter to a computer in 1985, either. And what am I using to write these words today? A computer. Actually, my wife and I between us have four computers in use: her writing computer, my writing computer, an image manipulation computer and an e-mail computer. Over the last 20 years or so we have had, and junked or given away or in one case sold, six others.

This is the burden of my song. I don't have to live with one computer any more than I have to live with one camera. Both Frances and I use what are, by computer standards, incredibly ancient machines for writing: 386s. So? They're only jumped-up electric typewriters, and they are quite heavily customised to that end. I had mine built with a fine-pitch mono-only screen, which is all you need for word processing, and a 5-1/4 inch drive to allow backwards compatibility with disks from the older machines. The image manipulation computer (a reasonably powerful Pentium) is shared and the e-mail computer (a Pentium laptop) is kept separate from the other three to minimize the risk of viruses and worms.

There is however one last point. In addition to computers I also use pens, pencils, paper, pocket calculators and even my own brain from time to time: the computer has not made any of them obsolete. Likewise, I do not expect the D70 to make my film cameras obsolete, any more than an SLR makes a rangefinder camera obsolete (or vice versa). Too many photographers see the world in either/or terms, when they would be a lot better off seeing it in and/and terms.

Camera Obscura

When Alhazen wrote about the camera obscura in the first half of the 11th century, he seems to have assumed that the basics were well known to his readers, other Arab scholars of the period.

The phenomenon of the camera obscura would not have been difficult to discover by accident: it means, after all 'dark' (obscura) 'room' (camera). Darken a room completely, except for a small hole the size of a coin or thereabouts in an outside wall (or more realistically, a finger-hole in a shutter over the window). If it is bright and sunny outside; if you allow your eyes some time to accommodate to the low light levels inside the room; and if the wall opposite the hole is white; then you will see an image of the world outside, projected upside-down upon the wall.

Most photographic historians then press the fast-forward button to Schultze's discovery of the blackening of silver salts in 1725 and Wedgwood's unfixed silhouettes on white leather in 1800 or so, before getting on to 'real' photography. According to national prejudice this tends to emphasize either Daguerre or Talbot, with a passing mention of Niepce.

In practice, the cameras used by Talbot and Daguerre relied on a lot more prior art than this. A lens was fitted to the camera obscura by Gardano in 1550; Barbaro added a diaphragm in 1568; and Danti suggested using a concave mirror to reflect the image and make it upright in 1573. Indeed, such refinements may well go back a lot further: Jan van Eyck's portrait of Jean Arnolfini and his wife incorporates a mirror between the two, which in addition to its mystical significance may be something of an in-joke by the artist, who died in 1441. The 14th century, of course, saw the rise of modern styles of perspective. Many art historians who are also practising artists, including David Hockney and my old chum Senggye ar Born, believe that this is because of the use of the camera obscura.

In the 17th century, portable black boxes were invented (as artists' aids) by Sturm in 1676 and Zahn in 1685. What Talbot and Daguerre did -- and no-one should minimize their achievements -- was devise the chemistry to capture a permanent image. The stage was set for Delaroche's famous comment that "From today, painting is dead."

Of course, that was codswallop. Painting is no more dead today than it was 100 years ago, 500 years ago or 5000 years ago. But it was an even less useful statement than it seems, because a very large number of artists from the late 15th century onwards had already been using cameras obscura to create their paintings.

In other words, far from being a break with the artistic tradition of the preceding centuries, photography was (and is) perfectly integrated with it. The biggest formal difference between Jan van Delft Vermeer (1632-1675) and William Henry Fox Talbot (1800-1877) is the ground and media they used: oil on canvas versus silver salts soaked into paper. The primary tool of both was the camera obscura, with (in Vermeer's case) brushes as a secondary tool.

This is not the same as saying that painting and photography are the same thing. Far from it, despite the generous overlap between the two: while some of John Salt's photo-realistic paintings owe almost everything to photography, Man Ray's 'Rayographs' have more in common with Bridget Riley's Op Art or possibly Jackson Pollock's 'pure paint' paintings. But the mere fact that we cannot immediately tell painting and photography apart does not necessarily mean they are the same thing.

Nor is it the same as saying that Vermeer and Talbot produced the same sort of pictures: this is a matter of subject or content, not form. It is however very significant that anyone who wants to learn how to compose and light portraits in colour can learn more from Vermeer than from Talbot.

Now for the kicker. The camera is a fairly well understood black box, which has been in use in art in various forms for some 500 or 600 years. That same black box can be used to produce a very wide variety of different results, from paintings to still photography to cinematography to video -- and anyone who doubts that the last two are different should note that they are often taught in different schools, with different agendas, curricula and technical standards.

Perhaps it is time to recognize that because of differences in media (dyes versus metallic silver or silver compounds), black and white and colour photography are very nearly as different as black and white photography and painting, and rather more different than colour photography and painting. A concomitant of this, despite the possibility for hybridization (shooting on film, scanning and printing) is that digital photography is sufficiently different from either, because of the differences in ground and media, to be recognized as a separate, third category of photography, neither better nor worse, but clearly not the same.

The 'Prentice's Tale

A friend of mine -- a time-served electrician -- was once asked if he didn't feel bad about sending one of his apprentices down a tunnel in filthy, oily, knee-deep water to check a connection. "No," he said. "That's what apprentices are for."

Apprentices have always been given the tedious or unpleasant tasks that the master craftsman doesn't want to do and can safely entrust to them. When I was an assistant at Plough Studios in the 1970s -- definitely a form of apprenticeship, though far from a formal one -- I had to sweep the floors and paint out the cove and so forth so that my gaffer, the late Colin Glanfield, had the time to glad-hand the clients, chase new business, and supervise the photography. I also had to do endless slide copying: in those days, of course, slide shows were still the standard audio-visual technique. Slide mounting, in glass, in sealed Perrot mounts, was even more boring.

Most people who have served apprenticeships, formal or informal, will tell you similar stories. They will tell you that an awful lot of their time was wasted. Partly they were given time-consuming jobs that a trained (or even untrained) monkey could have done, and partly they wasted their own time: most young people are singularly inventive and diligent when it comes to inventing ways of doing so, perhaps because they do not realize how fast time will fly as they grow older.

They will also tell you, if they are honest, that a great deal of this 'wasted' time wasn't really wasted. While they were sweeping the floor, or drilling 500 precisely spaced holes in a plate, or mounting slides, or chatting with fellow apprentices, they had time to think.

Often, it's true, the questions they asked themselves and each other were things like "Why the hell am I doing this," and "Are you going out with Linda tonight," but equally, they had time to think about what they had just been shown; or about what they were going to do next day when they were entrusted with something that involved a bit of creativity; or about the mess they had made the day before ("It'll come oot yer wages, laddie"); or most importantly of all, about how they would do things differently when they were the gaffer.

Sometimes they ended up doing things the same old way, of course: they came to realize that the Old Man actually knew what he was doing, in a way that offered the best ratio of advantages against disadvantages. But other times, they thought of a genuinely better way of doing things. A great deal of progress has come from the boredom of apprentices, including probably the majority of the Industrial Revolution.

Another thing that apprenticeships did was show you how the gaffer ran things. You could see whether he made money or not, and tailor your own approach accordingly. You could see if he was happy or popular or overstressed or whatever, and make a good guess at how much of this was down to his personality, and how much to his skill at what he was doing.

By "sitting next to Nellie", you learned where you could and couldn't take short cuts and chances. Or at least, you did if your gaffer was any good. In short, you learned the business from the bottom up, and in many ways it was better than a university or college education. And to be honest, I enjoyed my time as an assistant/apprentice more than I enjoyed the time I spent getting an LL.B. at university.

If you are reading this, though, the chances are that you are well past that stage in life where an apprenticeship is a realistic option. So why am I extolling its virtues? There are two reasons, two things from apprenticeships that we can usefully incorporate into our everyday life.

One is creative boredom. I know quite a number of photographers who dismiss film processing -- worse still, E-6 or compatible processing -- as boring. They are right. They therefore farm it out to a lab: in effect, to an apprentice, as a simple task they can't be bothered to do. This frees them for more 'important' work. But too many people have too little time to be bored today, except at work, and they spend too much time being important. Forcing yourself to do something boring, but related to something you find interesting, can pay unexpected dividends. What are they? I can't tell you. That's what makes them unexpected. But try it, and you might be surprised.

The other is closely related: tolerance, and understanding what a job involves. When a lab makes a mess of processing one of our films, we understandably complain. When we make a mess of it, we're unhappy, but we make excuses: we were tired, we'd just had a row with someone, it was a stupid slip, we should have checked so-and-so. Yes. All true. But maybe the person at the lab was tired, had a row with someone, made a stupid mistake. Do we really have the right to hold them to a higher standard than we hold ourselves?

Arles 2004

Things being what they are, my previous column on Arles --
the 2003 Rencontres -- appeared just a couple of months
before the 2004 Rencontres. I have to say, though, that 2004
was infinitely superior to 2003. The Rencontres are reputedly
the biggest gathering of fine art photographers in the world,
and there were very nearly as many good exhibitions in 2004
as there were good pictures in 2003.

To a very large extent, this was down to the guest curator
for 2004, Martin Parr, who did a superb job. It has taken me
a while to grow to appreciate Martin's work, but then, I often
need a bit of a run-up to deal with new art movements. Even
now, I'm not sure I'd want to hang his pictures on the wall:
I'd rather look at them in a book, or at a public exhibition.
And I could cheerfully have lived without one of his choices,
which consisted (among other things) of local photographs
from the Arles bullfight club, catalogue shots from a
furniture manufacturer, portraits of the Queens of Arles (a
sort of up-market carnival queen), pictures of traffic
accidents and pictures of Red Indians from the collection of a
long-deceased eccentric aristocrat: this was long before the
days when Red Indians were (more correctly and
respectfully) called Native Americans.

As soon as I look back over the last paragraph, I realize
that I have fallen into the trap which always yawns open at
Arles: the trap of dwelling on the negative rather than the
positive. The trouble is, it's so easy. The words
"organization" and "Arles" are hard to fit into the same
sentence without a negative creeping in somewhere. There
are endless examples. The exhibitions at the old SNCF
workshops will do as well as any. Last year, the entrance was
in one place. This year, it was in another. It would not have
been difficult to put an arrow on the gate of the old entrance,
saying "Entrance this way" or something similar. Did they do
it? No. We walked a quarter of a mile on the advice of an old

man seated by the gate, only to find that we had reached the exit (no admission via the exit) and had to retrace our steps and walk a quarter of a mile along the other side of the complex to reach the door. We were not the only ones who could not find the place: some apparently gave up altogether.

This would have been a pity. There were so many good exhibitions in those halls alone that I lost count: at least four or five, maybe six or eight. There was some stunning Russian photography; a brilliant wall of close-up portraits of great apes, almost in the style of passport pictures; some superb reportage from industrial England; a chilling collection of Jewish photographs from the Lodz ghetto during World War Two; and more. Admittedly there was the usual collection of pretentious garbage -- but there I go again, dragged down by the negative, ignoring the positive.

Some of the exhibitions were utterly unexpected. One, in an old church, was dedicated to anti-personnel mines. These were superbly, almost lovingly photographed on 4x5 inch Fuji Velvia and then printed maybe 12x16 inches or 30x40cm. Many of the mines and their sub-munitions or bomblets were beautiful. There was even humour, hard though it is to imagine: one face of the American Claymore mine says something very like "This Side Towards Enemy".

This exhibition said a lot more to me than yet more grainy black-and-whites of children in hospital beds nursing blown-off hands and feet. I'd like some of those mines as pieces of sculpture, and I know what they are, and I wouldn't knowingly go near them unless they were deactivated. To a child they must look like the most beautiful toys. Think about it. It won't be the only exhibition that makes you think.

The Arles Rencontres 2005 will be in early July, as they always are. There is little point in going into more detail than this, because next to nothing has been finalized yet: it never is until the last minute. Even when you get there, some of the venues will have been moved as compared with the locations shown in the printed guides. Some may not even be open. But don't let this worry you. The weather will most likely be stinking hot (though 2004 was the coolest Rencontres I have ever attended) and accommodation will be hard to find. Don't let that worry you either. Just go.

At the end of it, you'll probably come away with exactly the same reaction as I have had to keep fighting throughout this article. It will have been a shambles; the screenings in the old Roman Theatre will have been unbearably pretentious; you'll have plenty to shudder about. You'll have seen at least as many bad exhibitions as good, but the good ones will have been very good indeed. You may have had a chance to show your portfolio to people who can do you some good, or at least give you good advice. Overall, unless you have been really unlucky, there will be something that keeps you going back, year after year.

Go Your Own Way

Anyone with a long white beard and a penchant for wearing red is likely to have a rough time at Christmas. Children aren't so bad: they just look at me and wonder, and if their parents are wise they whisper, "Well, it might be, so you'd better be good." And I smile, and the parents smile, and the children smile slightly nervously, wondering what I know about them. Rather more wearing are the young men who shout, "Hur, hur, 'Oo are you then, Father Christmas?" as though they were being blindingly witty and original instead of blindingly stupid.

So whenever I can, I stay away from crowds. And, of course, I take pictures. For me, this is the ultimate Christmas present: the opportunity to take more pictures.

Fortunately, most people don't think this way. They want more stuff. More clothes, more electrical gadgets, more scent and make-up, and of course more cameras and lenses and accessories. So they spend a lot of time and money in hideously overcrowded shops buying them, and then, come Christmas itself, they huddle around the fire and watch re-runs of old movies. As a result, all kinds of beautiful, photogenic places are deserted, near and far, for several weeks. It's just the time to go for long walks with a camera, ice crackling under heavy boots, unspoiled snow with no more than a few deer-tracks, frozen lakes: you can be alone in dead silence. If you have a proper four-wheel drive like my old Land Rover Series III, snow chains and a mobile phone (in case of problems), you can venture even further afield.

Better still, you may be able to go abroad. One of the best Christmases I ever had, probably the very best, was in Goa in the late 1990s. It was one of those silly-cheap last-minute deals, two weeks in Goa, flights and accommodation, flying home Boxing Day morning. One of the reasons it was so cheap was that the timing didn't fit most people's preconceptions. The day after we booked it, my wife and I happened to see, in the window of another travel agent, a three-day Christmas break in Bath: Christmas Eve, Christmas Day, Boxing Day. It cost exactly the same per person as our two weeks in India...

Goa was wonderful. We hired a 350cc Enfield Bullet motorcycle, which is always easy in Goa with a handful of used notes (20-rupee Indian notes are sometimes very used indeed) and we chugged around on it. On Christmas night we were the only non-Indian diners at a hotel restaurant that served only Indian food. It was one of the best Christmas dinners I ever had.

That morning we had been sitting by the side of a river drinking Indian champagne (Marquise de Pompadour -- surprisingly good, and about four quid a bottle) and eating locally grown raw cashews. We had photographed men ploughing with oxen; women washing clothes in the river; huge Portuguese-era churches; Indian Christmas decorations; and a succession of stunning landscapes. I don't remember how much film we shot in total on that trip. It was about 40 rolls, I think, all 35mm: on a cheap charter flight, there is a limit to how much equipment you can carry.

Travel in winter doesn't always work, of course. Southern Portugal in winter is pretty good, but Northern Portugal, believe me, is vile. Never go to a warm country in cold weather, unless you stay in very expensive hotels. Most cheaper hotels subscribe to a common delusion that warm countries don't need heating. They shiver and put up with it, knowing that it's only a few weeks until spring comes. At best, you get a feeble electric radiator. This has happened to me in Greece and Malta as well as Portugal. Go either to a warm country, where it really is warm, like India or Australia (it's midsummer in the latter, remember), or to a cold country where they have to have good heating or they die: Russia, Canada, somewhere like that. Or New York City, for that matter.

At the end of it all, of course, you won't have a new camera or a new coat or a new television or a new computer -- but how much do you need one? How much do you need more stuff? I already have more stuff than I can handle. It might easily take me an hour to find my Pentax spot meter, for example, which I have not used for a while. It's probably in my study somewhere, under a drift of paper. Or it might be in the studio. Or in the hall cupboard. Or...

What you will have is more memories, and more pictures. Which would you rather have? Stuff, or memories and pictures? For me, there's not much contest.

Ambition

The traditional ambition of small boys is to become a train driver. I have to admit that I never subscribed. My first ambition was to be an architect. This lasted until my teens, when I wanted to be a psychiatrist. Too late I learned that this was an ambition I should not have attempted to communicate to the admissions committees of medical schools in the 1960s.

So I read law, and ended up as a photographer and journalist, via various side-lines such as lifeguard on a beach and teaching such subjects as art, remedial mathematics, English and modern Russian history. Seldom all at the same time, I hasten to add. For that matter, I was briefly articled to a firm of chartered accountants, before I went to the chief training partner and suggested (somewhat to his relief) that I was not cut out to be an accountant.

But all of these things, even teaching and accountancy, are the subject of legitimate ambition. I say 'even teaching' because I know how bad it was 30 years ago and I am told it is even worse today. When it is good, it is wonderful, and when it is bad, it is purgatory, but I understand that the ratio of paradise to purgatory has steadily been falling. And while lifeguarding is good when you are in your 'teens and twenties, it ill becomes middle-aged spread.

But how many careers today decently can inspire dedication and ambition? Does any small boy or girl really have a burning desire to be an assistant deputy manager of anything at all? Or to work on a supermarket checkout, or as a market analyst or spin doctor? Or to sell mobile telephones or advertising space? Or even for that matter to be an advertising account executive or merchant banker? These are things that we do because of historical accident, or because there is nothing else available, or because they pay well and we are too craven to trade them for something more exciting such as chartered deep-sea diver or chartered lion tamer. I'd like to thank Mike Solosy ACA for the latter suggestions.

Perhaps it is time, therefore, to try to inspire in our children ambitions which ignore mere paid work, and stretch instead to what they can do in their spare time. Could they be dancers? Musicians? Poets? Bareback riders? Belly dancers? Or of course photographers?

Here is where we -- the entire community of photographers -- can step in. We can show people that what you do for fun can be just as important, in many ways, as what you do for a living. But there is a catch.

Spare time today is artificially and disgracefully limited. When I was a boy, many pundits predicted that by the early 21st century we'd be working a four-day or three-day week. They were right -- on average. Most people do indeed work three-fifths as long as they used to. But instead of taking it easy throughout their working lives, they now work even longer hours, but for fewer years. The working life is curtailed at the one end by youth unemployment programs disguised as education, and at the other by enforced early retirement as employers hire new 'graduates' whose principal qualification is that they are are prepared to work for less money and with inferior conditions of employment.

By way of example, my chum John is in his early 50s. He is a self-employed builder. He left school when he was 15 and expects to work until he is 65: 50 years. His counterpart today will start work three to five years later, spending this time as an unpaid college student instead of being paid as a apprentice or sprog hand. At the other end of his working life, today's recruit can realistically expect to be on the scrap-heap well before he is 60. That's a 30 to 40 year working life as against 50. That's like working a 3- or 4-day week for 50 years. In a twisted sort of way, the 1960s prophecies have come true.

In other words, I have just has answered the very question I had hoped to raise. The reason we don't stretch our children's ambitions beyond work is that it makes them stroppy. Most people like to work, provided they don't have to work too hard, but the trouble with educating anyone beyond the barely utilitarian is that they tend to start to think. Once they start to think, they ask questions about what they are working for; what they really want out of life; and whether they might not cultivate ambitions beyond getting and spending, getting and spending.

I'm not sure, but I have a sneaking suspicion that this might spell the death of modern Anglo-American capitalism. This might or might not be a good thing: it is quite possible that the alternative to a world that is based on greed and stupidity would be even worse than the world we have today. But it's a debate worth pursuing, and one that is assiduously stifled by our political lords and masters.

Boredom Or Bust

David Hamilton is famous for his muzzy, sensuous studies of girls in their early teens. His pictures are both romantic and erotic, and his early books are now collectors' items.

Many, many years ago, the fourteen-year-old sister of a friend remarked that she really liked his work. I was surprised: few girls in their early teens take much of an interest in photography, and fewer still could name even one photographer whose work they like.

When I said that I had a couple of Hamilton books, she asked if she could borrow them. I readily acceded. She was a pretty girl, and both of us idly entertained the possibility of my shooting some Hamiltonesque shots of her.

Well, the shoot never happened, and it's so long ago I've forgotten both her name and the name of her older sister, whom I seem to recall I rather fancied; but I've never forgotten what she said when she handed the books back. She said, "You look at the first picture, and you think, wow, that's beautiful. And then you look at the second and third and think, hey, they're good too. By the time you're looking at the tenth or twentieth, you think, ok, what else can he do?"

At countless exhibitions since then I have asked myself exactly the same question. Without doubt, an exhibition or book must have a theme: a collection of unrelated pictures just won't do. But equally, it can be all too easy for a theme to shade into monotony on the one hand, or overload on the other. It's boredom or bust.

Monotony is what set in with my young friend. From liking those few pictures she had seen -- maybe even just one picture, I don't know -- she ended up liking none.

Overload, by contrast, doesn't stop you liking the pictures: it just stops you liking the exhibition. A recent exhibition of steam train photography was a perfect example. Many shots were superb, atmospheric, romantic, reminiscent of Night Mail. But the exhibition space was too big, and the photographer had more or less been forced to pad it out. The 'padding' pictures were still technically excellent, but you had to be a railway nerd to appreciate them. Much as I love steam railways, there's a limit to how much I can take, and this exhibition went well over that limit.

Both monotony and overload are central to appreciating and understanding exhibitions and books of photographs -- and there are essentially two ways of grouping together pictures, one of which is more appropriate for exhibitions, the other for books.

The first approach presents each picture as essentially separate, an image in its own right. This is what I would regard as the 'exhibition' approach, though it is also widely used in books: most of Henri Cartier-Bresson's books are like this, and so are David Hamilton's. Any one image could (and should, in the case of an exhibition) stand on its own: you could buy it, take it home, and hang it on the wall, and it would actually look better in isolation than it does with ten or twenty or fifty of its brethren. You could mix it with other pictures, which could be quite different: I'd be perfectly happy to hang a Cartier-Bresson and a Hamilton in the same room. But you don't want more of the same. Still less do you want inferior imitations of the same thing in the same room: Ansel Adams's acolytes' work alongside the work of the Master himself, for example.

In the other approach, each picture depends on some or all of the others. In a sense, it's a big picture essay. Sebastiao Salgado's work is a good example. Fairly obviously, this approach is better suited to books, though it's also true that one could buy an original and hang it on the wall. Better still, one could buy several originals and hang them together as a themed group.

With either approach, the onlooker has to exercise a degree of selectivity. As a child, one is taught to stand reverently in front of every single picture at an exhibition, trying to appreciate each one to the full. Well, this may work for a child (though I never found that it did -- I suspect it was

239

an adult trick to stop children going around the exhibition too fast) but I certainly can't see it working for an adult.

Usually, a long glance is enough to tell me whether I want to look more closely at a picture, and often, glancing at half a dozen photographs will tell me whether I want to spend any more time at the exhibition. You may consider this superficial. Tough. I don't care. I'm there for my pleasure and for what I can learn, not to show off my aesthetic sensibility and intellectual superiority. So why do you go to exhibitions or look at 'coffee table' books, and what do you get out of them?

Public and Private Art

The difference between public art and private art is easier to recognize than to describe. Essentially, private art is something you want to have in your house, to live with, while public art is something you are quite happy to see in a gallery or bank but wouldn't actually want to see every day at home.

Sometimes it's a question of scale: you would need a very big house to hang (say) an Alma-Tadema, and for most original purchasers, buying such paintings was as much a matter of displaying wealth as anything else. They bought what was fashionable, not what they liked.

It's not just scale, though: it's also content. I recently saw a collection of photographs called "The Book of the Dead" as part of an exhibition by The Moscow's House of Photography. They were stunning: big, but not too big to hang in a big room, and with the impact of a Hieronymus Bosch painting -- someone else whose work I love, but wouldn't necessarily want to live with. I don't know how they were done, but they were crowded family scenes in a somewhat Rembrandtesque style, except that all the people in them were presented as corpses who had apparently been the subject of autopsies. Fascinating work, but definitely not something I would want to see first thing in the morning. Public, not private.

So who decides what public art is? What criteria do they use? What criteria should they use? We all pay for public art, after all, whether it comes out of our pockets as taxes or as corporate profits.

A large and unsophisticated body, the artistic equivalent of the lumpenproletariat, takes one of two views. Either there should be no public art, which is the extremist utilitarian view, or public art should be the same as popular art, which is pretty much the National Socialist view: remember the famous Nazi exhibition of 'Degenerate Art'. These are the people who dismiss Robert Mapplethorpe out of hand as a pornographer, or describe Martin Parr's work as no more than snapshots. When faced with Serrano's famous (or infamous) 'Piss Christ', apoplexy sets in.

There is however much to be said for unpopular public art: the sort of stuff that you wouldn't necessarily want in the house. If the public galleries get in quick, they can acquire significant works for far less money than if they wait for the artist to become famous. Once an artist is famous, the price of his work will usually increase between tenfold and a hundredfold, and a thousandfold is far from impossible. In other words, the public galleries are well advised to take a punt on new work that they consider significant, because even if they get it wrong half the time, they will still build bigger, better collections than if they wait for public taste to catch up with their acquisitions policy.

At this point, we are getting into the famously dangerous territory of what art is for. At one extreme, there's the swans-and-sunsets and (dare one say it) Ansel Adams tradition of essentially decorative art, while at the other there are any of the 'movements' of the 19th and 20th centuries, such as the Fauves, the Cubists, the Modernists and Op and Pop Art, as well as individual artists such as Modigliani or Jackson Pollock. One extreme is uncontroversial and familiar; the other is (or can be) exciting and challenging.

But what is familiar today may well have been exciting and challenging when it was new: think of Roy Lichtenstein's comic-strip pop art, or Whistler's 'Nocturne in Black and Gold -- The Falling Rocket.' Or look at some of the truly awful mud-prints from the Linked Ring and the Photo-Secession, and remember that these were once an exciting, challenging reaction to the excessive literalism of 19th century photography. Then remember the f/64 group and Ansel Adams were an exciting, challenging reaction to the Linked Ring and the Photographic Brotherhood...

All art movements are as much reaction as innovation, and it's true that there is a lot of back-scratching, log-rolling and downright corruption in the art establishment. The last is the equivalent of insider trading on the stock market, where a stock is hyped so that the general public buy it and the value of the insiders' holdings rises. Even so, in the final analysis, it seems to me that while public art can never hope to please all of the people all of the time, it has a duty to present us with the new, even if it sometimes does so at the expense of the old or with a dash of dishonesty.

This may not be popular with the lumpenproletariat, who are quite happy to see the same old stuff and are outraged when their money is spent on something that they don't immediately like and can't immediately understand. But surely if you call yourself a creative photographer, you have to accept that the price you pay for aesthetic awareness is wading through (and funding) quite a bit of photography that you don't like, in return for the photography that you do.

On The Command "ONE"

There are famously three ways to do anything: the right way, the wrong way, and the army way. The latter is often laid out in some detail in Queen's Regulations. If it's not in Q.R. then it's almost certainly part of drill.

Now, it is easy to belittle Queen's Regulations and drill alike. But then you think what they are for. Think of a young man; tired to the point of exhaustion; in serious danger; scared for his life; responsible, quite possibly, for the safety of others as well as himself; and more than likely with an adrenalin hangover.

Which is better? Trying to work out how to do something? Or doing it by the book? In this situation, almost certainly, the latter. By way of example, doing things by the book saved the life of a friend of a friend. Twice. He was a US Marine during the Korean War.

The first time, he was on patrol when he felt a violent push in his back; he was nearly knocked over. He had been bayoneted by a Chinese soldier. Fortunately he had his mess-traps in his back-pack, as per instructions, and this stopped the bayonet. He grabbed his assailant's rifle and clubbed him to death with it.

The second time, his position was overrun. He was the only man wearing a helmet. He was also the only survivor, though he was admittedly in a coma for two weeks.

Now, most of us (thank God) will never find ourselves in anything like these situations. In fact it is bathos to make the comparison. Except that drill, and the equivalent of Queen's Regulations, can still make the photographer's life an awful lot easier. Drill is supposed to ensure that even if you can't think, you can still act, and still get the result you want. So it is worth designing your own drills, and practising them until they become automatic.

The most basic drill is knowing how to use your camera. You're dog-tired and 5000 miles from home. You are suffering from Delhi Belly and you're shivering with cold because you didn't realize how cold the mountains can be at this time of year. It's not a matter of life or death: just a traditional Tibetan wedding. But you know that if you want the pictures, it's now or never.

Fortunately, you are so familiar with your camera that you can operate it very nearly in your sleep. Which is close to what you are doing. This, I strongly suspect, is one reason why M-series Leicas are so popular with photojournalists. You can't accidentally select the wrong mode, or leave it on continuous instead of single-shot, or press the wrong two buttons at the same time and delete everything. There are so few controls that you can't mistake one for another, or dial in exposure compensation or a different ISO setting when you are looking for autobracketing.

Then there's making sure your camera bag doesn't get stolen. Of course you keep an eye open. But a useful piece of drill -- which I cheerfully admit to stealing from Indian railway porters -- is repeatedly counting your bags. I even do this in a sing-song Peter Sellers Indian accent: vun, two, t'ree piece.

This brings to mind the old Army procedure of doing things by numbers: "On the command ONE... " It's the butt of numerous old jokes, usually obscene. But there are a lot of things that are much easier if done by numbers. ONE, close shutter, TWO, set aperture, THREE, check shutter speed, FOUR, insert film holder, FIVE, remove dark slide... You have a much better chance of not missing out a step if you do it this way.

If you're working with an assistant or another photographer, there are other drills. One that's very useful -- and this is borrowed from Q.R. & A.I., Queen's Regulations and Admiralty Instructions, plus any normal Standing Orders -- is to repeat instructions back to one another: "Are you ready?" "Ready" or "Film loaded?" "Film loaded." Not "Yes" or "No", because there are too many circumstances when this can get you in trouble, especially when combined with sloppy framing of the question or mis-hearing.

Don't get me wrong. I'm the last person to advocate mindless adherence to Procedure -- except when you are effectively rendered mindless by being exhausted or bored, or when you're doing something you've done a thousand times and you're on autopilot. Then: well, on the command ONE...

If...

One man can change the world, with a bullet in the right place. I don't know whether that statement was lifted from somewhere else, or if it was original to Lindsay Anderson's film "If...."

On a considerably more cheerful note, one man has changed the world, initially with a single lens in the right place. The man was Hirofumi Kobayashi; the lens was the 15/4.5 Ultra-Wide-Heliar.

This one lens gave rangefinder users a tremendous fillip: you could stick it on the front of any interchangeable-lens Leica made since late 1931, or for that matter on the front of a Zorkii, and have unbelievably good performance for remarkably little money. Or if you wanted something a bit less dramatic for even less money, still with superb performance, there was the 25/4 'Snapshot' Skopar.

The original Bessa-L, of course, was very basic, with no rangefinder or viewfinder but with remarkably good through-lens metering. It made sense only if you didn't already have an old camera that could take these lenses; or didn't fancy buying a second-hand one; or couldn't afford a new Leica.

But the world, it seemed, had been waiting for something very like all this. The subsequent history of the Bessa marque is well known. Seven more bodies, the R, T, R2, R2C, R2S, R3 and R3A. Fourteen more lenses, for a total of 16: 12/5.6, 18/4, 21/4, 28/3.5, 28/1.9, 35/2.5, 35/1.7, 35/1.2, 40/1.4, 50/3.5, 50/2.5, 50/1.5, 75/2.5 and 90/3.5. Several were also mounted for Nikon S/Bessa R2S.

This alone would have been impressive. But the Bessa begat the Rollei, and then, in cooperation with Zeiss, the new Zeiss Ikon system, initially one body and seven lenses, 15/2.8, 21/2.8, 25/2.8, 28/2.8, 35/2, 50/2 and 85/2. At photokina a Zeiss spokesman indicated that there might well be faster lenses later: it is not too much to dream of 35/1.4

and 50/1.4 lenses, and a 50/1 and an 85/1.4 or even 85/1.2 should not be out of the way. All in Leica M-fit.

What are the lessons here? First, a vastly increased differentiation of the kinds of cameras available. A decade ago, almost every serious amateur used a high-end 35mm SLR or possibly a medium format SLR. Today, more and more photographers are making and/and choices rather than either/or: a Nikon D70 AND a Voigtlander Bessa instead of a Canon 35mm SLR OR a Nikon 35mm SLR, or a digital bridge camera AND a second-hand Hasselblad instead of a Mamiya RB67 OR a Hasselblad, or an old Nikon F AND a Gandolfi instead of a Wisner OR a Canham.

Second, we are seeing a paean to standardization. Sure, you can fault the D70 for not providing even stop-down metering with 'real' (non-autofocus) Nikkors, but the simple truth is that I can do an awful lot with the D70 and my old lenses: I've got fast lenses, macro lenses, long lenses, ultra-wides, all sorts of things I couldn't afford if I had to re-equip completely. Likewise the Voigtlander R2 and Voigtlander lenses integrate seamlessly into my Leica system, prompting in turn the acquisition of further Leica equipment and possibly, in due course, some Zeiss lenses as well. The four-claw Leica M bayonet has become the de facto modern rangefinder standard, just as the old Leica screw mount was before it.

Third, we are seeing the value of passion. Anyone who has met Hirofumi Kobayashi knows that the man is an enthusiast. As our estimable editor put it, "He's on our side." Of course he wants to sell cameras and make money, because if he didn't, he couldn't indulge his passion for rangefinders. But introducing the current Voigtlander rangefinder line wasn't the kind of safe decision that might have been made by an accountant who was focused myopically on the bottom line. It took passion.

The most cheering thing is that exactly the same passion is to be found at Zeiss. "We wanted to show what we could do." "I have a lot of old Contax lenses from the 1950s and I wanted to design something even better." "I keep different lenses of the same focal length for different purposes -- landscapes, portraits, whatever." For once, when someone trots out the old cliche "We are very excited," it sounds as if they actually mean it. And after a somewhat flat spot a decade or so back at Leica, the passion is aflame there again. I don't think there's been a better market in 'real' cameras since I took up photography in the 1960s.

Cameras As Pets

A camera is a tool, right? Well, yes, but it's more than that, or at least, it can be. Several of mine are pets.

What is a pet, after all? Something familiar, calming, more or less dependent. Oft-quoted research -- don't ask me who carried it out -- apparently indicates that people with pets live longer. The arithmetic is bizarre. One cat equals five years, or some such. If you have enough cats you could live forever.

My suspicion is that it's not the cat, it's the person. The kind of person who keeps pets lives longer. Or at least, the kind of person who keeps a certain kind of pet is likely to live longer. With Mike Tyson and his tiger I wouldn't be sure: allowing dangerous creatures like that to keep tigers is another matter. And there are people who, at the first sign of infirmity in their cat or dog, have it put down: "For its own good," of course.

Pet cameras are rather safer ground. Some of my Nikon Fs would have died of malnutrition by now, if they were alive. So would the later of my two Leica M2s: it has a severe vision problem, brought about by maladjustment of the frame selector. But they aren't alive; well, not in the usual sense, so I don't have to feed them. I can just take them out of their kennel from time to time -- a humidity-controlled cabinet that they share with the cameras I do use -- and stroke them, and talk to them, and reminisce to myself about them, and put them back. I feel better for it, and I hope they do too.

So why don't I get rid of them? Well, at least a couple of reasons. One of the most fundamental is that sometimes I like to go for a walk with them, as much for old time's sake as anything else. The walk is the thing; good pictures (and many of them will still deliver good pictures) are a bonus.

Of all of them, my Retina IIa is most like an elderly dog: I have to treat it gently, and not try to rush it, and allow for the fact that when it's cold its frame counter doesn't work. But as I might with an old dog, I can remember when it was younger: if not exactly a puppy, then at least in its prime. I had good times with that camera, saw good things, got good pictures. I still get good pictures now, though its rangefinder is a bit slow and sticky. I keep wondering about sending it to the vet (Kevin at Camerex in Exeter) but it's a lot of upheaval for a camera that's nearly as old as I am. Besides, I can always use something else if I'm that worried.

The other thing is -- and this is far less rational -- I feel I owe these old cameras something. They have helped me earn a living; now that they are too old and feeble to do so, or simply so old-fashioned that something else can do the job better, it just doesn't seem fair to throw them out or take them to a camera fair or consign them to the tender mercies of e-bay. The only way I'll sell them, usually, is to a fellow enthusiast who loves old cameras as much as I do and wants to use them. While I was writing this piece I agreed to sell my old 121/8 Super Angulon to a friend: I have a 110/5.6 Super-Symmar, and he can't afford anything new, so the SA is his at a friends' price of about half what it is worth on the open market.

As I said, it's irrational. But then, let's be honest: so is most photography. And, I'd suggest, so is most of what makes us human. Art? Compassion? Friendship? Humour? Love? You don't find these in robots, which is one of the things that makes me deeply suspicious of so-called 'artificial intelligence'. The famous Turing test requires that a computer be able to hold a two-way conversation with a human being, in such a way that the human being is unable to tell that he (or she) is conversing with a computer. Then again, I increasingly often find myself talking to human beings that I can't tell from computers...

Risk Avoidance

How much do you pamper your camera? I mean, how much risk do you expose it to? More and more, I find myself coming across examples of risk avoidance that I can hardly credit.

The first group deals with the risk of having your camera stolen or smashed. Well, I'll admit that I've been known to advocate caution. For example, I don't think I'd go into Amsterdam's red light district at night to take pictures with my Leica MP or Alpa 12: I'd be more inclined to carry my old Konica III or something else that cost a lot less than the insurance premium alone on either of those cameras.

But with the camera under my coat or even in a never-ready case, I don't I'd worry too much about even an expensive camera: as long as you're not actually taking pictures, or posing as the Fearless Photojournalist, most people will leave you alone. Sometimes, for that matter, you can make friends with the most unlikely people, and get pictures that the Fearless Photojournalist wouldn't get in a million years.

Now, I regard myself as a bit of a wimp for worrying about the pimps and whores in Amsterdam. But next to several people I have heard about, I'm Rambo. One was worried about taking his camera to Bombay (all right, Mumbai). Another asked -- quite seriously -- whether English pubs were safe. Not as places to take pictures: as places where you might be beaten up and robbed.

Where do you begin with these people? The last time I was in Bombay it didn't even begin to occur to me to worry. The same goes for my wife Frances Schultz, who is five foot two and not exactly aggressive. We wandered the back-streets of Mulund, shooting markets and religious fairs and all kinds of good things, quite apart from downtown Bombay, which is where the wimp was apparently going. As for the pub, words fail me.

The other group is more concerned with natural hazards. One fellow dropped his Leica MP in the sand; carefully blew off all the grit; and then (of course) went on the Internet for advice. As far as I am aware the camera was closed at the time, so it wasn't a question of sand in the interior: it was just what might have worked its way in.

At least half a dozen people must have advised him to have the camera professionally cleaned. One told him how his Nikon F had been written off by sand; another chided him for taking a Leica on the beach at all, and advised him to buy something cheap, even a disposable camera, if he wanted to go to the beach and take pictures.

Hold on a minute. This is a new or almost-new Leica, famously one of the toughest cameras ever built. If I thought my MP was so flimsy, fragile and poorly sealed that I couldn't use it on the beach, I'd chuck it in the bin. The same goes for just about any other professional-quality 35mm camera I've ever used.

On the beach, I've used countless Leicas (A, I, II, III, IIIa, IIIb, IIIc, IIIf, M2, M3, M4-P, MP) but I started out with Pentaxes (SV -- and I've also used a Z1 in heavy salt spray) before moving on to Leicas via Nikon Fs and Nikkormats. I've even, for crying out loud, used MPP Mk. VII and Toho FC45 4x5 inch cameras. It never even occurred to me not to.

Never mind beaches. Someone else was worried about long walks in the country: the damp, the mist, the risk of falling over. Why? I expect my cameras to be able to cope with any half-way normal environment: snow, any degree of heat that I can stand, cold down to freezing or a few degrees below (or quite a lot of degrees below in the case of some cameras, such as Leicas once again). Sure, I'll keep my cameras from getting soaked whenever I can; I won't leave them in full sunlight in the tropics; and I'll put them in a bag if I'm walking across difficult terrain where I might trip. In the monsoons I've even been known to tape over the joins on my Nikon Fs.

Basically, though, if I have to take any more than the most obvious and undemanding precautions, the camera isn't worthy of serious consideration. But at this point, I start wondering if some photographers are worthy of serious consideration...

Giving Up ?

Sometimes, when I get depressed, I think of giving up photography because it's no fun any more. Increasingly it's a branch of the computer business, and if there is one thing common to all big computer companies it is that they treat their customers with an indifference that borders upon contempt. If something doesn't work, it's your fault. Persist, and the software people will tell you it's a hardware problem, while the hardware people will tell you it's a software problem. And they will both sneer at you if you are using a computer that is more than 18 months old or any version of the software other than the latest.

But then I take heart, at least a little, from comparing computer companies with some of the camera clubs I have been to. You really don't need to change your definitions very much to see the parallels. What is wrong with your photography? Ask the club experts. They'll tell you. You need a new camera or lens or flash or possibly scanner or computer (hardware) or you need new film or developer or paper or possibly a new image manipulation program (software). Whatever it is, it's your fault, and they can't be bothered to give constructive advice because you are such a witless ignoramus as to be beneath their notice.

There is however a big difference. If you don't like a camera club, you can just leave. If it makes you feel better, you can be rude to a few people first: I've always liked the old definition of a gentleman as someone who is never unintentionally rude, though I once had to explain (to an American computer nerd on a photographic forum, naturally) that yes, I really did mean that a gentleman would go to great lengths to avoid giving unintentional offence, but would be quite willing to be deliberately rude if the occasion demanded it.

But by the time you are dealing with vast companies such as Microsoft or the telecoms giants, you can't just leave.

Well, you can, but at that point the choice is between giving up on computers and the internet entirely, or leaping from the frying-pan into the fire. What is more, you can't even relieve your feelings by being rude, because they are so vast they can simply afford to ignore you.

By way of illustration, a friend and I both subscribed to broadband internet access at the same time: I in France, she in England. Mine refused to work at all, and in the process stopped me logging on via my old pre-broadband account, but at least I could still make and receive phone calls. Her broadband worked OK but stopped her making any outward telephone calls. As I wrote these words, both situations had persisted for close to a month.

Now, it's perfectly possible to survive without computers at all -- if you don't want to make a living at anything related to photography or journalism. But today, if you can't e-mail your articles and preferably your pictures as well, you start out at an enormous disadvantage. The same is true of digital photography. When I pulled my Nikon D70 out of my camera bag to shoot the new 18/4 Voigtlander lens, Hirofumi Kobayashi of Cosina pointed at my Voigtlander R2S (with 21/4.5 Zeiss Biogon, of course) and said smilingly, "Everyone is doing the same thing. They have one of those around their neck, or a Leica, or something, but for the pictures, they use digital."

He was right, of course. In order to file my articles on time, I had to use digital. And there are other uses where I'd hate to go back to silver: step-by-steps and small product shots in particular, but also (to a much more limited extent) local snapshots. A professional is making life difficult for himself if he doesn't have a digital camera.

But this is why I don't give up photography. Ultimately, I'm not a professional at heart: I'm an amateur. And so are most professionals. It's a choice I don't have to make, fortunately, but if I had only two cameras left, my Nikon F and my Nikon D70, and I had to choose between them, I think it would be the D70 that went. I can use the F for the rest of my life, and probably scrape a bare living with it: a bit of lecturing, some fine art print sales, books and even a few magazine articles. The D70 saves me a lot of time and effort, and possibly even money in the long run, and earns me more, and I'd be crazy to get rid of it; but I can't imagine I'll ever love it the way I love my old, mechanical, silver halide cameras.

The Decisive Moment...

In 1952, the late Henri Cartier-Bresson's book 'The Decisive Moment' popularized a catchy new phrase. His argument was that there is a single moment when everything comes together, and that this moment, and this moment only, is the moment to press the shutter release.

Well, all right as far as it goes -- which upon analysis, is not very far. When considering his thesis, remember two things. First, HCB was French, and the French frequently estimate logic above reason. Second, when he was a young man there were countless artistic Movements, with a capital M. It was not enough to create art: it was essential that it also be a Movement, such as Surrealism, Vorticism, Socialist Realism, Expressionism and so forth.

Essentially, the whole concept of The Decisive Moment can be split in two parts. One part is a statement of the blindingly obvious, and the other is complete twaddle.

The blindingly obvious part is, well, blindingly obvious: some moments are better than others. Composition takes place in time as well as space, and the spatial relationship of many compositional elements changes with time. This is especially true with street photography and reportage. We have all waited for a big, fat, ugly tourist to shamble out of shot, or for someone to stand in a doorway that otherwise is a black hole.

The twaddle aspect is slightly more complex. First, there are plenty of subjects where the decisive moment goes on for a very long time. If I set up a still life in my studio, for example, then the main limit to the decisive movement is how fast the dust settles on it. If I had a less dusty studio -- the walls are bare stone, centuries old -- then the limit would probably be set by when the film went out of date or the camera seized up from lack of use.

Second, there are very few subjects where there is only one decisive moment. Reverting to our door example, we might shoot first when an average-looking man comes through; then shoot again when a pretty girl walks through; then shoot again when a young mother walks through with her winsome child. In each case, the person or people may be a minor but essential part of the whole composition: it wouldn't work without them, and some are better than others, but equally, it doesn't matter all that much which we use.

Third -- and this is the real killer argument -- if there really were only one decisive moment, one would only ever take a single photograph of any subject. At this rate, one would expect every single one of HCB's films to consist of thirty-six completely different images, each perfectly exposed. This was far from invariably the case. In fact, takin the argument to its logical extreme, HCB would only have taken a single picture in his entire life, in which everything came together. As soon as you scale back the idea of the decisive moment to allow for a sequence of pictures of the same subject, the logic fails: it's like being slightly pregnant, or extremely perfect.

What I am saying, therefore, is that HCB was, in one sense, exactly like another great master of photography, Ansel Adams. Both were sublime in their chosen fields, but their legacies -- the Zone System from AA and the Decisive Moment from HCB -- have very little to do with their greatness. The Zone System was invented as a means of simplifying sensitometry for college students: the naming of Zones was a work of genius, but the rest of the testing is merely a roundabout paraphrase of basic sensitometric ideas that date back to the 1890s. The only stroke of genius about the Decisive Moment is that it is a catchy phrase.

Today, as practised by vast numbers of inferior photographers -- and let's face it, most of us are inferior to AA and HCB -- both the Zone System and the Decisive Moment are pretty much in the realm of sympathetic magic. People adopt them as totems, in the hope that some of the attributes of their demigods will rub off on them.

To be sure, both concepts are worth exploring, not least as an insight into the lives and ways of two great photographers, but as sole routes to photography, let alone precepts by which to live your life, they are pretty lightweight. If you want to understand sensitometry, read a decent book on the subject rather than AA's own Zone System trilogy or (worse still) any of the books by his acolytes, and if you want to take good street pictures, get out and take pictures instead of wallowing in Gallc pseudo-logic and false philosophy.

Drink Taken

One of the many things I find hard to believe about photography in these degenerate days is how little everyone drinks. When I started as an assistant some 30 years ago, an important part of my job was making sure that everyone who wanted a drink (which meant just about everyone) had a full glass whenever they wanted which meant just about the whole time).

The wine was delivered by the case, and the first bottle was opened at around eleven, half an hour after I started work. After that, they kept being opened until everyone left in the evening, some time after seven -- often, well after seven. Or eight. Or nine. Or on a bad day, midnight.

Of course, different people drank different amounts. The photographers mostly drank wine, but on a steady, intravenous-drip basis like old-fashioned journalists. Models sometimes preferred something sweet and fizzy (but still preferably alcoholic), but a lot of them joined in on the wine. Likewise the 'creatives' and account execs preferred spirits, sometimes real 1970s creations like bourbon and coke, but if wine was what was going, as it was in the studio, that was what they took.

The printer, like most of the printers I have known, took whatever was going. I was much amused, a while back, when someone chastised me for suggesting that alcohol and the darkroom might be compatible. I wouldn't be allowed to drink in a commercial darkroom, he said, so why should I be allowed to do it at home? Excuse me? How many commercial darkrooms has he worked in? I don't know about the 21st century, but certainly in the mid-to-late 20th I knew more than one printer who was not averse to a dram. Also, if the printer is a secret drinker -- or for that matter an open one -- who is going to stop him, and how?

Then there were the clients. My favourites were a car customizing magazine who hired the studio every month.

Their cars came, for the most part, from their readers: young men with no girlfriends, who lived at home with their parents and spent every available penny and minute on their cars. I kid you not: these were the guys who worried that the models' scantily clad bums would scratch or dent their precious kandy-kolor tangerine flake streamline paintwork.

Besides, most of them had never seen a naked girl before -- though admittedly a lot depended on the silver tongue of the art director because the magazine didn't like paying full nude rates -- so they had to be kept out of the studio. My job was to take them next door to the pub and pour beer into them, possibly with the occasional chaser if they showed any sign of going back into the studio. At the end of the day we poured them into taxis and sent them to their hotels: they must have driven back to Barnsley and Bootle next day with the most appalling hangovers.

In those days, of course, a gentleman was supposed to be able to hold his drink. We still adhered to Dr. Johnson's standard: 'A man who exposes himself when he is intoxicated, has not the art of getting drunk.' I should add that by 'exposes himself' the Great Cham meant 'reveals his condition'. Or maybe that doesn't help.

The intriguing thing was that all of this truly impressive alcohol intake appeared to have almost no effect on the level of creative enterprise. London in those days was the creative capital of the world, as it still is to a lesser extent today: Lomdon training was an open sesame to Paris, New York and Milan, and photographers from Paris, New York and Milan would come to London to prove themselves. Some of them stayed too drunk to find their way home for years, if ever.

Am I defending this? Perhaps, and partly. I don't deny the many and well documented ill effects of alcohol, but equally, I would echo Churchill in saying that I have taken more from alcohol than it has taken from me. I'd also point to the old Macedodian belief that no plan can be considered truly soundunless it looks good both drunk and sober. It's true that the hurdle tends to be at the sober stage, rather than the drunken: a lot of ideas that look good through the bottom of a bottle or two of wine are less practicable in the sober light of next day. But we should not neglect the ideas that seem good when we are sober but which, after a couple of stiffeners, we realize that we do not really want to pursue after all. And whether you think I'm wrong or right; well, buy me a drink, and we'll argue about it.

Faith In Yourself

Thirty and more years ago there was an American stand-up comedian called Brother Dave. His schtik, you should pardon the Yiddish, was that of an old-style Southern Baptist preacher. One line I particularly remember was, "You got to have faith, dearly beloved. Faith is what makes old men chase young girls and dogs chase cars. Ain't neither of them could do a thing if they caught 'em, but they think they can. That's where faith comes in to it."

I was reminded of this recently when looking at several rolls of slides I had shot in the last few months with the Leica MP: one lot before I got the Nikon D70, and one lot after. There is a lot more bracketing on the slides that I shot before I got the Nikon, but in the ones I shot afterwards there are no unacceptable exposures despite the fact that I bracketed only on a couple of occasions.

Well, you might say, you should hope not: the MP is, after all, the summa summarum of the M-series Leica, complete with through-lens meter. But I was shooting on a day with fast-moving clouds -- sunny sometimes, cloudy others -- with some shots taken under open sky and others under trees. Perhaps more importantly, the range of subjects varied widely. Sometimes there were large areas of white in the frame; at other times, large areas of deep shadow. Both are guaranteed to upset any through-lens metering system.

What I was doing, therefore, was interpreting the through-lens meter's readings, sometimes using the centre spot, sometimes the left arrow, sometimes the right arrow, biasing the exposure up to a stop under or over depending on my assessment of the subject. For the kind of photography I was doing -- essentially reportage -- I didn't have time to check my exposures with an incident-light meter, even if I had remembered to bring it with me, which I hadn't.

And, as I say, I got it right. In very large measure this was because the D70 had considerably restored my faith in myself to judge exposures accurately: that, as Brother Dave used to say, is where faith comes in to it.

You may find it odd that such a paragon of automation as the D70 has improved my skill at metering, but as well as the 18-70mm zoom that came with the camera I have also used quite a number of manual lenses on it: macro, soft-focus, high-speed and tele. With a manual lens, the D70 offers no metering whatsoever. You set the shutter speed with the thumb-wheel on the camera body, and the aperture with the ring on the lens, and where you set them is down to you.

Now, I have lots of meters, but one of the most convenient for this application is the tiny Voigtlander shoe-mount meter, so that's what I use most of the time. As with the through-lens meter on the MP, I have to interpret the readings to take account of the subject, but I also found myself slipping back into my old Leica habits of ten and twenty years ago of setting the shutter speed and aperture that I thought would be about right, then checking the meter to see if it agreed.

The big difference, of course, is the instant feedback on seeing the pictures. With my Leicas, before I got the D70, I was ever more inclined to bracket, especially when I was far from home, because it might be days or weeks before I saw the photographs. In mid-2004, for example, we made a major tour of several of the new countries of the EU, and a re-shoot would have been out of the question. So I bracketed. Going through the slides, I can see that I very rarely needed to do so: the vast majority of the time, my best guess at the exposure (which is not necessarily the same as the meter reading) was all that I needed.

As a result, I have cut back dramatically on my bracketing. All right, it helped that I was a mere 50 miles from home, not 1000 miles or more: I think I'd still bracket more on that sort of trip, simply because the extra expense of a few rolls of film is neither here nor there. But I'm also reasonably certain that I shall be bracketing a good deal less from now on, even on major trips. Not only will that save me money in film -- quite possibly ten to twenty per cent of the total film and processing bill for a trip -- but it also means that I will have more time to shoot, because I shall be spending less time reloading. And all because the D70 has helped to restore my faith in my ability to judge exposures. As Brother Dave said, you got to have faith, dearly beloved.

What Do You Care About ?

Bokeh, for those who have not previously encountered the term, is a word meaning 'the quality of the out of focus image.' Very economical language, Japanese. If a lens has 'good bokeh' it means that the out of focus image looks nice, and bad bokeh means that it looks nasty.

Well, fair enough. We've all seen lenses where the out of focus image is quite peculiarly nasty, but it really has to be very unpleasant indeed before I notice it: I am simply not very sensitive to bokeh. But there are others, if the internet forums are to be believed, for whom bokeh is paramount. I have even seen that loathesome American phrase 'to die for'. Well, chum, if you want to die for bokeh, hand me that axe and then stand still for a moment: I'll see what I can do. I'll be doing the English language a favour.

Now, what is paramount for me -- after content and composition, obviously -- is tonality. I can put up with almost anything else: coarse grain, poor sharpness, any bokeh except the worst, as long as I like the tonality. If I don't like the tonality, I probably won't like the picture, unless the content or composition or both can transcend almost anything. I hasten to add, though, that I have never seen tonality (or indeed anything else in a photograph) that I would die for; or even, to borrow some older phrases, give my eye-teeth or right arm for. A few eye-lashes, or at most a couple of beard-hairs, is my top offer.

But to return to tonality, I have had people stick tonally vile prints under my nose and ask me to admire them solely because they are extremely fine grained. Devotees of the late and (by most photographers) unlamented Kodak Technical Pan were particularly bad for this: I have seen very few Tech Pan shots that I considered tonally tolerable, and none that I would describe as tonally exquisite.

Presumably, the people who were so proud of these pictures were vastly more sensitive to grain than I am and far less sensitive to tonality, though I have to say that I do like pictures which are both tonally exquisite and completely grainless. I delight to produce such pictures myself, but I do it the easy way, either making large format contact prints or shooting on Linhof 6x7cm (56x72mm) and enlarging just 3x to get a whole-plate (6-1/2 x 8-1/2 inch, 168x216mm) print. Trying to do it by over-enlarging 35mm just does not work as far as I am concerned: you may get fine grain, at least with the right films, but you won't get the tonality.

The question is, where do we get these sensitivities? I suspect that there are two answers. One arrives very early in life, and lies in the way our brains are wired up. Every one of us lives in a different sensory space, not just philosophically but as a matter of verifiable fact. Language provides a good example. A baby can learn any language, but if it is not exposed to certain sounds it will lose the ability to distinguish between them. The Japanese r-l sensitivity is well-known (I remember being told, on admiring a picture, "Yes, was taken with rong rens on Hasserbrad") but try getting many Americans to say 'duke' instead of 'dooke'. I'm not suggesting that such specifically photographic qualities as grain, sharpness and tonality are part of the way our brains are wired, but they may well be by-products of it. There is not much we can do about this aspect of things.

The other sensitivity, I suspect, arrives much later in life, and comes from the photographers and photographs we admire. Here, I would suggest that we can and should regularly re-evaluate what matters to us. As a young man I loved reportage and big hairy grain. I still like grain -- I'd argue that David Bailey's 'Goodbye Baby and Amen' is his finest work -- but I've also come to appreciate the grainlessless of a large-format contact print and even (ugh!) colour.

The reason we need to re-evaluate is that if we don't, we find ourselves in the classic army situation of being perfecly prepared to fight the war that has just finished. The equipment, techniques and mind-sets that served us well in our photographic past are not necessarily best for the kind of pictures we want to take in future.

This brings us back to over-enlargements from 35mm, and such strange by-ways as bokeh, which is where I started. The aim of photography is to get the pictures you want, looking the way you want. The things that are important to other people may not be the things that are important to you, so ask youself what you care about; what you are doing to get it; and what (if anything) you need to change.

A Drip Under Pressure

Most of the speeches that are made on school speech days are forgettable even as you listen to them, but there is one part of one such speech that I remember from around 40 years ago. It is, "Never forget the etymology of the word 'expert'. It comes from 'ex', meaning 'a has been', and 'spurt', meaning 'a drip under pressure'".

Of course you can dismiss this as traditional public-school anti-intellectualism, but actually I think it's a good deal deeper and more perceptive.

I have nothing at all against experts, in the sense of 'people who know a lot about something'. I have on occasion been called an expert myself. What I don't like is the kind of expert who believes that experts automatically have the right to tell the rest of us what to do. To choose just a few examples at random, and to put them in alphabetical order, I have been called to task (sometimes repeatedly) by accountants, economists, grammarians, health-and-safety people, lawyers, marketing men, social 'scientists', teachers and Zone System adherents.

Now, there there is no doubt that it is possible to amass considerable expertise in any of these areas. But there is equally little doubt that there are many different opinions. To resolve such differences, there are three possibilities.

The first and best, and the only one that can actually be decisive, might be described as the scientific approach. Both sides describe the facts; marshal their arguments; and present their views. The best man (or woman) wins.

The second might be described as the religious approach. It is appropriate when the same facts can be interpreted in a number of different ways, all equally valid (or invalid, in some cases). Here, you explain why you do things your way; acknowledge that there are other ways; and explain why you like your way better. You may hope to persuade the other person of your superior wisdom and knowledge, or you may simply want to make it clear that your approach works best for you, even though something else may work better for someone else.

The third approach, and incomparably the worst, is the Way of the Expert. You simply say, "I know more about this than you, so shut up and go away; you have no right to speak about subjects on which you are ignorant."

Admittedly there are times when this is a perfectly accurate assessment of the situation, but even then, it is seldom a good way to win either arguments or friends. If the other person is hopelessly stupid, they go away both stupid and resentful, and if they are hopelessly ill-informed then you should try to enlighten them. If you don't have time for the latter, just ignore them.

Often, though, the opinion of the informed layman is an essential corrective to an overly doctrinaire expertise, and very often it is an essential corrective to overweening self-importance: the sort of world-picture that says "I am a great expert and therefore my views on everthing, not just my area of expertise, are automatically more important than yours." This is the sort of person who, when challenged, does not even attempt to explain his viewpoint but simply denies the validity of the challenge, usually with a haughty "If you knew more about the subject, you wouldn't ask such a stupid question/make such a stupid observation."

Well, chum, if the answer is so clear and simple, how come you can't explain it quickly and easily? And if it isn't clear and simple, have you ever considered the possibility that others, possibly brighter or better informed than you, may have come to different conclusions? And that I may have encountered their opinions before encountering yours? For that matter, what would a reasonable outsider say? Might he not say, "Well, one of you may be an expert, but the other fellow has a point, so what is your answer to it?"

The most vocal 'experts' are, indeed, the drips under pressure, the ones who feel threatened by any challenge to their authority. Over the decades I have met quite a number of people who are at the pinnacle of their various professions, true experts of the highest order. The vast majority are surprisingly humble. They don't care whether you believe them or not. They are more interested in whether you understand them or not. And that, I think, is rather a significant difference.

Over-reaction

There are some mistakes that almost all beginners make. In black and white, three of the most common are under-exposing; over-developing; and snatching prints from the developer before they are ready, because they don't want to waste materials. I certainly used to be guilty of all three, and so are the vast majority of other self-taught photographers.

Then there are compositional problems such as not getting close enough, so the subject is lost in its surroundings, or composing against confusing or inappropriate backgrounds. The classic example is of course the tree growing out of the head. Quite apart from all this, there is shooting happy-snaps in bright sunlight so that the unfortunate subjects are squinting against the glare.

But precisely because all these faults are so common, we are warned against them (and we warn others against them) too much. We over-react, and adopt other habits which may not be quite as bad but which are straitjackets to creativity in their own right.

The net result is that there are far too many photographers who routinely over-expose and under-develop, often because they don't actually understand how metering works. Others waste huge amounts of paper, despite the fact than no-one else can tell the 34th reprint from the 33rd, or indeed for that matter from the 3rd. Likewise there are those who always get so close to their subjects that they never show any context; those whose backgrounds are bland and predictable to the point of boredom; and those who react to sunlight almost like a vampire, though they don't seem to mind overcast weather.

There are, after all, precious few hard and fast rules in photography. Of course there are some, like "Don't put the film in the fixer before the developer" and "Don't open the back of the camera until you have wound the film back into the cassette," but most of these do not take long to master.

There are lots and lots of guidelines, to be sure. Some are quite strong. With negative films, for example, almost everyone agrees that under-exposure is a bad thing. But there are always a few photographers who can turn in brilliant results by deliberately under-exposing. Likewise, although most people prefer their pictures sharply focused and free from camera shake, there is always someone who can turn either defect (sometimes both) to good effect.

Other guidelines are weaker. The so-called Rules of Composition are a good example. If you can see, immediately and instinctively, how a particular picture should be composed, the Rules are a complete waste of time. But if you think there's a picture in there somewhere, and you can't quite see how to compose it, then you are as big a fool to ignore the Rules as you are to follow them slavishly; ignoring them is, of course, another form of over-reaction. At the very least, if you try all the tricks -- the Thirds, diagonals for dynamism, leading lines, whatever it takes -- you will be looking hard at the subject. You may end up composing it completely at variance with the Rules, and that's fine, but at least they will have helped you along the way.

Whenever you read any advice on photography or anything else, you therefore need to look at the person who is giving the advice and ask yourself (to borrow a fine old Californian phrase) where they are coming from. For example, I have a deep aversion to the Zone System. This is mainly because I wasted a lot of time on it before I knew enough about photography to benefit from it; and then, when I came back to it years later, I found it to be for the most part a convoluted, tedious and jargon-ridden restatement of basic sensitometry, which by that time I understood. But this does not mean that it will not work for you. Your experiences, your prejudices, your preferences, are unlikely to be identical with mine.

What it comes down to is this. Whenever you hit a problem, and someone appears to offer you a solution to it, think hard about what they are offering before you adopt it wholeheartedly. Ask yourself what advantages you could derive from continuing to do it your way; whether you would do better to follow some parts of their advice and not others; and whether there is another way altogether of trying to solve the same problem. Surpringly often, there is. Above all, remember that the sort of pictures you want to take may not be the same sort of pictures they want to take. An old Tibetan saying is "A thousand monks, a thousand religions." In photography, it is (or should be) "A thousand photographers, a thousand ways to take a picture".

Buying The Package

Thinking for yourself can be hard work, so a lot of people don't bother. They buy their world-picture straight off the shelf, as a package. There's the Jack-the-lad package, the Upright Citizen package, the Concerned Liberal package, and so forth. The packages are clearly defined: most of their adherents can buy newspapers or magazines tailored to their precise views. Think of the Telegraph package (hanging, flogging and Liz Hurley) or the Guardian package (the government is invariably wrong, and no-one who is black can ever be a lying, thieving layabout).

The people who buy the package are normally the most vociferous, too. They really want you to know their views on such subjects as heavy drinking, the death penalty and underage sex. Either they are always for it, or always against it. They can't handle the idea that getting drunk occasionally is not the road to ruin, or that there is more to life than getting wasted every week-end. They won't accept that while the death penalty is morally repugnant and should never be applied when there is a shadow of doubt, the world would be a better place if some people such as vicious, unrepentant self-confessed murderers were shot out of hand. And they refuse to believe that some girls are more grown up at 14 than others are at 20, so it may be morally worse to seduce a naive and innocent 19-year-old than it is to sleep with a worldly-wise 15-year-old (which would be legal in France anyway).

Photographers are no different. The most divisive issue at the moment is between digital and silver halide. Either digital is completely without merit, and those who succumb to its dubious lures are buffoons with more money than sense, or silver halide is outmoded and worthless and those who cling to its non-existent charms are witless dinosaurs. Of course there have been countless other examples in the past: autofocus versus manual, autoexposure versus manual, SLR versus rangefinder, 35mm versus rollfilm, colour versus mono, ortho versus pan, wet plate versus dry plate, and for that matter Calotypes versus Daguerrotypes.

But this is crazy. We aren't talking about Gin Lane here, or employing hangmen, or debauching virgins. There are moral judgements -- as I've said before, I feel morally superior to someone who relies on a point-and-shoot auto-everything camera -- but as long as we don't get too hysterical, there's room for all of us. If you want to shoot digital while I shoot film, fine. If you like reflexes and I like rangefinders, fine again. If you prefer Canons and I prefer Nikons, that's fine too. In each case I'll feel superior to you (sorry, but that's the way it is) but I will equally accept your right to feel superior to me, misguided and ill-informed though you may be.

The trouble comes when we start getting hysterical about it: when you start screaming that not only is film dying, but it can't happen too soon, or I say in deadly seriousness that only a fool would use Canon. Then the other side starts to get frightened, and fear is the most potent of all fuels for aggression. Instead of being good-natured banter, it turns nasty.

Worse, it affects the money markets. All finance is essentially hysterical: look at the roller-coaster rides of the stock and currency markets. Money men don't understand businesses, in the sense of people who make things and provide services. Instead they understand Business with a capital B, or they think they do. In other words, they are constantly trying to second-guess what will make the most money in the short term. If they simply concentrated on making a good product or providing a service that people want, they might not make as much money in the short term, but they would probably stay in business longer and they would be a lot more popular.

So next time you find yourself taking an extreme view, ask yourself two simple questions. Are you merely being contrarian, in an attempt to make people think for themselves? (That's my excuse). Or are you buying into a mass-market package, and contributing to hysteria, like the gutter press and paedophilia? Above all, consider the possibility that things might be quite complicated, so that sometimes the answer is one thing, and sometimes it's another. Thinking clearly, after all, determines what sort of world we live in.

The Digital Bubble

(One way that AP keeps ahead of the news is via a small, portable time machine. Normally this is set just 10 days in the future, but last week a new cleaner nudged the dials inadvertently and the following column was received from our oldest contributor, Roger Hicks, who was (will be) 100 years old on June 15th, 2050).

One of the most intriguing aspects of the late 20th and early 21st centuries was what photographic historians call the 'digital bubble'.

Nowadays, we use screen grabs a dozen times a day, from our televisions, telephones and personal organizers. But few people realize that for almost 20 years this pedestrian, low-quality means of imaging was seen as a serious rival to silver halide photography. The flimsies we throw into the kitchen recycler without a thought are the descendants of an almost forgotten technology.

Actually, there were several technologies: 'digital imaging' (the generic term for electronic 'photography' using electronic image sensors instead of silver halide), scanners (much like today's), primitive telecopiers ('fax machines') and a bewildering variety of printers. And instead of today's standardized molecular memory cards, there were half a dozen different shapes and sizes of 'flash' memory cards based on rewritable chips.

If they have been preserved under museum conditions in an inert atmosphere, the prints from these antique systems may still look nearly as good as a modern silver halide print. They were on really heavy paper, unlike today's flimsies, which helped: very similar to modern photographic paper. When you reflect that the oldest of these prints were made long before King Charles III came to the throne, they are pretty remarkable.

But yet, but yet... The black and white prints, which are my special interest, suffer appallingly from metamerism.

They look fine under tungsten light, but under daylight they are mostly a sickly green. And the vast majority of colour prints are so badly faded that you can't really make any judgement.

You may also notice a peculiar flatness or deadness to the colours of images that were captured digitally, as distinct from captured on film and then scanned. I've never quite understood why this should be: I didn't understand it fifty years ago, and I don't understand it now. It's not just a question of saturation. Often, saturation was turned up far beyond what we would consider normal today -- even with slow films such as Kodak E800VS, which some reviewers have called 'too saturated' -- and it still looked flat and dead.

What killed 'digital imaging'? Nothing, of course: as I say, we all use its descendants a dozen times a day. But why did it never, as its proponents claimed it would, replace 'real' photography?

Quite a lot of reasons. Permanence, obviously. The fact that the quality could never quite match up to silver halide was important too. Convenience was something else: yes, you could take your camera to Tesco or Auchan to have the images downloaded and printed, but then (as now) it was a lot easier to drop off a roll of film, or to mail it to a processing house. Another major problem was lack of standardized storage media, and the high cost of those media that were available: memory was so expensive in those days that it was often sold in fractions of a gigabyte. And, as with all electronic storage media, there was always the risk of trying to open your image file, only to find that it had turned into electronic gibberish -- if it opened at all.

There was also sensor sensitivity. Today, when ISO 800 is slow and hardly anyone bothers with lenses faster than f/4, it is easy to forget that in those days, ISO 400 was 'fast' and (more importantly still) that most electronic sensors were at their best at ISO 100 or 200. Positive hole trap doping was known even before the end of the 20th century, but the development of today's fast, ultra-fine-grained films was retarded because billions of euros were poured into the dead end of digital imaging research instead of into silver halide.

My own belief, though, was that something deeper prevented digital imaging from assuming the mantle of silver halide. Photography, as all AP readers know, is an art, a craft and a science. 'Digital imaging' wandered too far from those roots. Would you trust a bar-code reader to give you great pictures? Ultimately, that's what 'digital imaging' was.

Or maybe it's deeper still. Can a machine have a soul? Artificial intelligence makes this an even more pressing question today that it was when I was 50. But most people would agree with me if I say that if you want to make absolutely sure that something has no soul whatsoever, run it through an old-fashioned computer at some point.

Show, Don't Tell...

Years ago, a member of my fencing club revealed that he was a food technologist. After I had made the sign of the cross, a traditional means of warding off the devil, I asked him why food technology always meant making things cheaper and nastier.

To his credit, he didn't waste time pointing out that it sometimes makes things better: yeast technology would be an excellent example. Instead, he said, "It doesn't start out awful. It's usually possible to synthesize something so well that it's extremely difficult to tell it from the real thing, at maybe half or two-thirds of the price. The trouble is, this becomes the new standard. Then someone else makes something that is nearly as good as the first generation of imitation. They only save a few pennies, but if you're selling millions of something, that soon adds up. By the time you get to the third or fourth generation, yes, it's really nasty. But you can still sell it because a lot of people have never tried the real thing, only the third- and fourth-generation imitations."

I always remember these words when I read about how easy black and white photography is these days. You shoot on colour neg, or digital; desaturate it in Photoshop; and crank it out on the ink-jet printer.

Well, I suppose that if you have never seen a really good, original silver halide black and white print, you might think that an ink-jet print is pretty good. But as an example of just how low most people's standards are, I recently read (on an Internet forum, naturally) a query from some fellow who was knocked out by the quality of the black and whites printed in books, and wanted to know if there was any way to get similar quality via home processing.

Aaargh! Clearly, the man had never seen a decent print. Not necessarily a great print, even: merely the sort of thing that any competent camera-club black and white photographer should be able to turn out as a matter of course. Rich blacks; delicate highlights; subtle tones everywhere; all these, clearly, were utterly unknown to him.

The question is, where are people going to see these prints? There are lamentably few exhibitions, and the audiences they attract are usually miserably small anyway; and on top of that, those who go to exhibitions are usually knowledgeable enough that this is pretty much a matter of preaching to the converted.

So here's a suggestion. On your own, or with a friend or two, or with a whole club, if you like, put together an exhibition of ten or twenty pictures. Ideally, they should be silver halide prints, but if you are good enough, they can be scanned (please, from real black and white film -- Ilford XP2 is excellent and doesn't give the loathsome deadness of desaturated scanned colour negative, or the short tonal range of digital) and then printed using a narrow-gamut ink-jet printer.

Initially, don't frame them. Mount them, by all means (I favour window mounts, but dry mounting can be good too) and put them in a portfolio case. Then go around all the public spaces in your neighbourhood, trying to persuade them to let you hang your pictures for a few weeks.

If there are galleries, ignore them. Instead, try restaurants and banks and public libraries and doctors' waiting-rooms. The aim, remember, is getting good black-and-whites in front of people.

It will cost you money. There's not just the expense of making the pictures: there's mounting and (worst of all) framing. Even if you do it the way I do, and buy cheap but matching ready-made frames, framing alone is likely to cost you anything between a hundred and two hundred pounds. You are unlikely to sell anything, but if you do, that's a bonus -- and price them high, rather than low, so that the people who see the pictures get an idea that photographs can actually be worth something.

What do you get out of it? Far more than you might think. First of all, it's a wonderful ego trip: referring to 'My last exhibition... ' is always fun. Second, it gives your photography some direction: far too many amateurs are blown by the wind, trying a bit of this, a bit of that, as their mood and the local club competition takes them. Third, it's a powerful incentive to get better: you go to more and more exhibitions yourself, and learn to see and to print better. Fourth, if you have ambitions to sell or to turn pro, it gets your name known: only a little at first, but each new exhibition builds on the previous ones. And fifth, you will be doing your bit to keep black and white healthy and prominent, and you shouldn't underestimate the importance of that.

Drowning In Props

A *vide-grenier* (literally an 'attic-emptying') is a French car boot sale, organized on a village or city basis. Small villages have them annually, cities once a month or oftener. A grand (or pretentious) *vide-grenier* is a *brocante*. The whole village may be cordoned off and traffic diverted; residents move their cars for the duration, from early morning to mid evening. At a big *vide-grenier* or *brocante* there are often additional attractions: stalls selling the local wines and cheeses, a bar, sometimes rides for the children. On the morning of the day I wrote these words, I had been to one *vide-grenier* at St. Clair and another at Pas de Jeu.

Like car boot sales and charity shops, *vide-grenier* can be a great source for props, defined as 'things that make good pictures' or 'things you can't resist because you want to photograph them.'

The big difference between France and the UK, though, is the proportion of beautiful old props to plastic toys, used bathroom fittings and cheap Chinese tools; and although prices are all over the place, they are often gratifyingly low. The day I wrote this, for example, I spent a whole Euro (call it 70p) on a rusty old pitchfork head. I envisioned it against the ancient walls of the stable-yard behind my house, the bright sun of the northern Aquitaine casting shadows on the patchwork of stone and oak and stucco. It will join all the stuff that I have bought before: such things as four pairs of blacksmiths' tongs, a three-foot-long augur like a giant's corkscrew, and, because I couldn't resist the symbolism, both a hammer and a sickle.

I got quite a lot of 'props' with the house, too. In the attic (*grenier*) there were no fewer than five old doors stacked against the wall. Scattered around the rest of the house were five more, along with several pieces of the ornate and complex ironmongery that the French use to lock windows, plus a couple of railings removed when the previous owners put the new shutters in. There's a manger inside the stable, a village-pump type water pump outside it, and various inexplicable but highly picturesque pieces of rusty iron either driven into the walls or hanging from the bits driven in. There are literally dozens of glass preserving jars with wonderful names like Le Parfait and Triomphe.

The trouble is, I'm now drowning in props. Many I never photograph at all. Others I photograph maybe once or twice. But I don't throw them out. Why not? Because they're too good to float-test, but not worth the effort of trying to sell on at another *vide-grenier*. At least, not to me.

Most photographers I know have the sane problem, if their houses are big enough. Marie Muscat-King (who took the portrait that accompanies my articles in AP) is very nearly as bad. Some of the things she has in her admittedly very large basements are beyond belief: painted 'marble' columns like something from a theatre set, yards of assorted fabrics, a camel saddle...

To some extent, you can integrate your props into your lifestyle. As I write these words, I'm drinking a Campari-and-soda out of a glass I bought at a charity shop. It's beautiful. And I drink my beer out of an assortment of pewter tankards, some dating back to the reign of our dear late Queen Victoria. But there's a limit to how many glasses you can use, even if you have no aversion to truly spectacular mis-matches: when we lived in California, this used to drive my mother-in-law crazy. My wife and I now walk determinedly past all the glasses in charity shops and at *vide-greniers*. We just don't have room for any more.

Maybe what we need is a prop exchange: a car boot sale for photographers, with everything priced only for exchange. The unit of currency would be the 'P' (for 'props'). My pitchfork-head might be 2P; a 1950s glass decorated with playing-cards, 1P; a set of railings, no more than 1/2P; the deck-chairs that I gave away when I left England, maybe 2P each. Nothing would be priced over (say) 5P: at that point, real money would come into it. This would be a market for stuff that's too good (or at least, too photogenic) to throw away, but at least it would get it out of the house. If someone really fell in love with something, the owner might decide to give it to them -- or maybe, to swap it for a print, which would always have a fixed value of 1P. Now all I have to do is to figure out how to get this whole scheme onto the internet...

Too Many Camera Stores

There are far too many photographic shops in Britain. Many don't deserve to stay in business. Worse still, there isn't enough trade to support all of those that do.

Why, after all, does anyone go to a photographic shop instead of buying by mail order? Partly, of course, for speed and convenience. But there are three other requirements.

First, they must have what you need. A while back a friend wanted some 8x10 inch RC paper. Not only was her local camera shop out of stock: the proprietor said it would be a week or ten days before he built up a big enough order to send in. Mail order was 30 per cent cheaper, with next-day delivery.

Second, they must be knowledgeable. You want to do so-and-so? Try this. Can I do this? Not like that, try it this way. What do I need in order to do this? One of these. Oh: and have you seen this? And so forth. With knowledgeable and enthusiastic staff, no problem. With trained monkeys (or indeed, untrained ones) behind the counter, no chance. No-one expects a camera-store assistant to know everything -- but neither should they know nothing. If they don't know the answer, they should be able to fetch the boss, who does.

Third, you must enjoy going there: a little chat with the staff, poking around the second hand stock, that sort of thing. But if the second-hand stock is three digicams and a bent Taiwanese tripod, or if the proprietor is the kind of grouch that makes you feel you're wasting their time by coming in and buying things, never mind asking questions, why bother?

Fewer and fewer camera stores seem able to meet all these requirements, and plenty have difficulty in meeting even one. Why?

There are at least three reasons, all probably irreversible. The present plethora of camera shops grew up in a very different commercial climate, which is why so many are dead in the water. Sadly, it has often been the best, rather than the worst, that closed their doors: Frank's in the Saltmarket in Glasgow, Brunnings in High Holborn, Cheltenham Cameras in Cheltenham.

The root cause was the abolition of retail price maintenance (RPM). This allowed manufacturers to set retail prices, and penalized dealers who sold at a discount. In the best shops, generous profits paid for service and advice to standards that have never been equalled. In the worst shops -- and there were plenty of those -- lazy and inefficient dealers survived when by rights they should have gone under. Once RPM was gone, the stage was set for discount mail order operations.

To this was added the ever-increasing cost of stock: poorer returns on a bigger outlay is not a recipe for commercial success. And more and more people acquired the despicable habit of coming in 'just to look'; pumping the proprietor for advice; and then mail-ordering from a discounter. In the 1990s, one of my friends simply closed his business, sold the premises and stock, and retired on the interest. As his accountant pointed out, this paid about the same as running the shop, without having to work for it. For two years, he had resisted his accountant's advice, because he enjoyed running the shop, but after the third break-in in two years, he lost heart.

Finally, the second-hand trade has come under multiple attack. I was living in the United States when camera fairs really took off, in the late '80s and early '90s, but when I came back to the UK in '92 the transformation was all but complete. No longer did dealers have those wonderful and ever-replenished 'junk drawers' that had been one of their greatest attractions (at least to me) for decades. Nor were there the serried ranks of cameras ancient and modern that used to decorate their windows. No: the vast majority of 'weird stuff' now goes through the camera fairs, to the detriment of the stores, or via internet auction sites.

Fortunately, there are still plenty of exceptions. With the huge over-supply of camera stores in the UK, even if only 10 per cent are any good, that's still a lot of good shops. Possibly my favourite camera store in the UK is Camerex in Exeter. Then there's Bernard Hunter in Bristol, Canterbury Cameras in Canterbury, and more: have you ever been to Mr. Cad in Croydon, for example? That's before I start on the collectors' shops.

The remedy is in your hands. Use the good shops as much as you can -- and don't go to the bad ones, because they are taking away business from the good ones, who may therefore have to close. Support your local camera shop? Without question; but only if it's worth supporting.

What Would You Do For A Picture ?

Cameras change the rules, and alter the habits of a lifetime. For example, I've always had a fear of heights: as a boy, I wouldn't even go close to the edge of a railway platform. Partly, this is because of inner-ear problems which mean that I have very poor balance: if I close my eyes, I start swaying, even stone cold sober. But put a camera in my hands, and I'll stand on the edge of a cliff, never mind a tall building -- though I have to admit that I still get that strange sinking feeling, once perfectly described by a little girl of my acquaintance as a "dizzy bottom."

When I'm shooting, I don't notice pain, either. When I was photographing a demonstration, a protest against the Chinese invasion and continued occupation of Tibet, people were smashing those cheap Chinese porcelain soup-bowls with the grain-of-rice glazes. When porcelain shatters, some of the shards can be glass-sharp, and I was shooting from no more than two or three feet from where the bowls were being hurled to the ground. Only afterwards did I notice the blood streaks on the back of my hands from cuts made by porcelain shrapnel. I dug a couple of porcelain chips out of my face, too.

Or again: although I almost never take my old 88-inch Land Rover off the road, my definition of 'road' is pretty broad. Often I've needed 4-wheel-drive and low ratio to overcome rocks, pot-holes, wash-outs and mud on forest tracks. Sometimes I've had to dig myself out, or use an off-road jack to get out of a ditch, to say nothing of the memorable occasion in Hungary when I fitted snow-chains in half a foot of water to get out of some particularly boggy, muddy going. But I'll do it if I think there will be a good picture at the end of it. In the 4-wheel-drive comics, however, they say you should never attempt to cross difficult terrain except in convoy: by implication, solo vehicles invite immediate and horrible death. Maybe the green lanes of Hampshire (where I have never driven) really are more dangerous than the Balkans (where I have).

Or for yet another example, I am not one of nature's early risers. I can easily sleep until 9 am (mind you, I was writing these words at 10 pm). But if I have to get up at dawn (or before) I'll do it -- for a picture.

Admittedly, there are some things I won't do for a picture. Early in 2003 I was in the Pyrenees in winter, in the Land Rover. The snow wasn't all that deep, but it was thick enough to cover everything with a white blanket. I had four wheel drive, but no snow chains. On one road I turned back because I was frightened. Partly this was because in a Land Rover you sit high, so you can see all too clearly into the abyss below. More, it was because most of the other people on the road wanted to go a lot faster than I did. Most had neither four-wheel drive nor snow chains.

Later in the trip I drove on worse roads, with worse snow, without being anything like as frightened. By then, however, conditions were so bad that there were far fewer people on the road; they were driving a lot slower; and as well as the four wheel drive, I had by this time acquired snow chains, though only for the rear wheels -- next time I find someone that has them in stock, I'll buy a set for the front wheels too. But as long as there wasn't some idiot pushing me faster than I thought was safe, I was OK.

One thing I certainly wouldn't have done is signed the Israeli Army's waiver, announced in May 2003, which said that anyone venturing into the Gaza Strip should agree, in effect, that if the Israeli Army shot them, it was their own fault. This amounted to a license to kill, signed by the victim. What happened if you refuse to sign. Did they refrain from shooting you? Next to this, steep drop-offs, flying porcelain shards and bad or snowy roads pale into insignificance.

But all, surely, are aspects of the same thing: the quasi-invulnerability that we all feel behind the camera. I don't think I'd willingly go into the Gaza Strip to take pictures, and if I did, I don't think I'd want to sign my own death warrant; but I do stand on the edge of cliffs.

To come back to less deadly situations, what would you do for a picture? What have you done for pictures in the past? When have you chickened out? And (let's be honest) was it worth it?

Clouding Over

It was a bright cold day in April and the clocks were striking thirteen as Winston Smith went out to take pictures. The battery of his camera was fully charged; the buffer card was clean; and he had logged on to Ministry of Truth Central before he left.

He carefully kept the camera inside its case, with his hands behind his back, as he strolled past the David Blunkett Memorial Library. Since 2006, taking a picture of a government building had automatically incurred an eighteen-month stretch in a CREC, a Community Re-Education Centre.

He glanced superstitiously at the huge windowless CREC that towered above even the offices and apartments here in the old Plymouth docklands. But at least it was modern. You heard stories about some of the old CRECs that were still in use: Dartmoor, Wormwood Scrubs. He smiled mirthlessly. At least he might see some of his old friends there. With ten per cent of the British population in prison, many of them without trial or even charge, you never knew who might drop out of sight, or why, or for how long.

Suddenly he realized that a Truthwoman in a police uniform was staring icily at him. "Smiling, citizen?"

His face fell into the correctly neutral expression immediately, eyes lowered. He raised them to look at her. "No, madam friend. A cold day. My face was going stiff. I had to exercise it."

She nodded, clearly not believing him but unwilling to pull him in: too much paperwork, and besides, it was a beautiful, bright day. Even she, surely, could not fail to be moved by it. "Taking pictures, citizen? Where are you going?"

His breath formed a cloud in the cold air as he tried to think of a reply. He hadn't really thought about it. It was just a beautiful day. He was an old man. It was hard to break the habit of going out and just, well, taking a few pictures on a beautiful day. It was one of the things he had always promised himself he would do when he retired. The Royal William Victualling Yard building would have made a wonderful picture, reflected in the calm, clear water, but of course it was a government building.

"Show me your camera."

Automatically he handed it to her, in its case. "The combination is four-five-six." Not that there was much point in telling her: the number had probably appeared on her screen already.

As if to confirm his fears she glanced at her screen and pressed the buttons. The case opened. "Hmmm. Not a film camera, then."

He shook his head. "No." He knew the penalty for owning one of those, too: two years in a CREC. He'd handed over his Nikons when the Misuse of Cameras act was passed, seen them thrown over the policeman's shoulder into a skip. On television he'd seen the conveyor belts feeding the rollers, watched the Leicas and Canons and Hasselblads coming out in bright splinters and twisted metal the other side. His current 30-megapixel Nokia DCRE was fully rigged to Central: everything he shot was first registered there, and would download to home computer only after approval. He had often wondered how they did it. When he was a boy, there had been primitive anti-terrorist and anti-pornography software on telephones and the internet, picking up on certain words. They must have something similar for shape recognition or something.

The Truthwoman was flicking through the images on the screen. "Who is the little girl?"

He leaned over to look. "Oh. My great-niece. Amanda."

"How old is she?"

"Ummm... Six, I think."

"Taking a picture of a child under the age of 21, citizen?"

"Uhh... Yes. It's allowed." It must be allowed, he thought. Central had passed it. He'd run the bar-codes on both his ID card and Amanda's past the scanner on the camera to prove family links. Central had passed it.

But she was already ignoring him, checking Ministry of Truth Central. After an eternity the message seemed to come back on her screen. She looked at it, nodded. "Seems to be in order, citizen. But watch it, next time."

"Yes, madam friend. Do you mind closing my camera case again? Only, we're within 100 metres of a school." She nodded and deftly closed it again, fingers dancing over the buttons, automatically scrambling the code. His hands were shaking as he took the camera back. "Thank you. And -- I think I'll go home now. It's starting to cloud over."

As an epilogue, a note from the publisher...

There are two publications that are traditionally read back to front – in other words, you read the back pages first and then work your way forwards. One of those journals is The Stage & Telvision Today and you read the back pages of that *publication first because that's where the jobs are. The second is Amateur Photographer, and you go to the back page first because that's where you'll find the Roger Hicks column!*

I'd often thought of writing to AP's editor just to tell him that even if AP didn't print any photographs, articles or revues, the magazine would still be worth the cover price for the Roger Hicks articles alone...

Then I had a better idea and wrote to Roger Hicks himself, outlining the idea for this book, and much to my surprise he was both agreeable and enthusiastic about the project. You can see the result for yourself and I hope you're as happy with it as I am. And I am *happy with this book because Roger has the gift of being able to put into words what so many of us feel about photography and he certainly has the knack of ruffling a few feathers – but that's what I love about this advocate of brass and glass. His ability to cut through the crap never ceases to amaze and delight me.*

He really gets to the heart of the matter – and that, I think, would be a marvellous title for his next book for Mage Publishing.

James Christie - October 2006